Lecture Notes in Artificial Intelligence 12879

Subseries of Lecture Notes in Computer Science

Series Editors

Randy Goebel
University of Alberta, Edmonton, Canada
Yuzuru Tanaka
Hokkaido University, Sapporo, Japan
Wolfgang Wahlster
DFKI and Saarland University, Saarbrücken, Germany

Founding Editor

Jörg Siekmann
DFKI and Saarland University, Saarbrücken, Germany

More information about this subseries at http://www.springer.com/series/1244

Tanya Braun · Marcel Gehrke ·
Tom Hanika · Nathalie Hernandez (Eds.)

Graph-Based Representation and Reasoning

26th International Conference
on Conceptual Structures, ICCS 2021
Virtual Event, September 20–22, 2021
Proceedings

Editors
Tanya Braun (iD)
University of Lübeck
Lübeck, Germany

Marcel Gehrke (iD)
University of Lübeck
Lübeck, Germany

Tom Hanika (iD)
University of Kassel
Kassel, Germany

Nathalie Hernandez (iD)
University of Toulouse
Toulouse, France

ISSN 0302-9743 ISSN 1611-3349 (electronic)
Lecture Notes in Artificial Intelligence
ISBN 978-3-030-86981-6 ISBN 978-3-030-86982-3 (eBook)
https://doi.org/10.1007/978-3-030-86982-3

LNCS Sublibrary: SL7 – Artificial Intelligence

This Springer imprint is published by the registered company Springer Nature Switzerland AG
The registered company address is: Gewerbestrasse 11, 6330 Cham, Switzerland

Preface

The 26th edition of the International Conference on Conceptual Structures (ICCS 2021) took place during 20–22 September, 2021, under the title "Graph-based Representation and Reasoning." For the second time, it was part of the Bolzano Summer of Knowledge, BOSK 2021, with several conferences and workshops complementing each other on topics such as Philosophy, Knowledge Representation, Logic, Conceptual Modelling, Medicine, Cognitive Science, and Neuroscience. Originally, the conference was to be held on-site in Bolzano, Italy, but was moved to a virtual venue due to the ongoing global pandemic. Tutorials, keynotes, and research presentations took place online to provide a safe environment for participants from around the world.

Since its inception in 1993, ICCS has been an annual event for the discussion and publication of new research methods and their practical applications in the context of graph-based representation formalisms and reasoning, with a broad interpretation of its namesake conceptual structures. The topics of this year's conference include applications of, theory on and mining of conceptual structures. The call asked for regular papers reporting on novel technical contributions as well as short papers describing ongoing work or applications. Overall, ICCS 2021 received 33 submissions out of which 25 were accepted for reviewing. The committee decided to accept 11 papers, which corresponds to an acceptance rate of 44%. In addition, 5 papers were deemed mature enough to be discussed at the conference and were therefore included as short papers in this volume. Each submission received three to four reviews, with 3.54 reviews on average. In total, our Program Committee members, supported by three additional reviewers, delivered 89 reviews. The review process was double-blind. After implementing a bidding procedure at ICCS for the first time in 2020, which proved to be very successful, we applied this feature again to ensure that reviewers received papers that fit best with their respective expertise. Final decisions were made after a rebuttal phase during which the authors had a chance to reply to the initial reviews. Next to the regular contributions, we were delighted to host two tutorials, "Concepts and Reasoning: Alternative Approaches" by Iain Duncan Stalker (University of Bolton) and "Foundations of Knowledge Graphs" by Mehwish Alam (FIZ Karlsruhe) and Sebastian Rudolph (TU Dresden). Furthermore, We were honoured to receive three keynotes talks: "Reconciling Knowledge-Based and Data-Driven AI for Human-in-the-Loop Machine Learning" by Ute Schmid (University of Bamberg) and "Mapping Patterns for Virtual Knowledge Graphs" by Diego Calvanese (Free University of Bozen-Bolzano). Moreover, we had the pleasure to listen to John F. Sowa's closing keynote, which was titled "Diagrammatic Reasoning." This volume contains the titles of all and the extended abstracts of some tutorials and keynote talks.

As organizing chairs, we would like to thank our speakers for their interesting and inspirational talks. Our thanks also go out to the local organization of BOSK who provided support in terms of registration and setting up a virtual conference. Special thanks go out to Oliver Kutz and Nicolas Troquard, both from the Free University of

Bozen-Bolzano and an integral part of the BOSK organizing team. We would like to thank the Program Committee members and additional reviewers for their work. Without their substantial voluntary work, this conference would not have been possible. We would also like to thank EasyChair for their support in handling submissions and Springer for their support in making these proceedings possible. Our institutions, the University of Lübeck, Germany, the University of Kassel, Germany, and the University of Toulouse, France, also provided support for our participation, for which we are grateful. Last but not least, we thank the ICCS Steering Committee for their ongoing support and dedication to ICCS.

July 2021   Tanya Braun
                                                                  Marcel Gehrke
                                                                    Tom Hanika
                                                              Nathalie Hernandez

Organization

General Chair

Tanya Braun   University of Lübeck, Germany

Program Committee Chairs

Marcel Gehrke   University of Lübeck, Germany
Tom Hanika   University of Kassel, Germany
Nathalie Hernandez   University of Toulouse, France

Steering Committee

Madalina Croitoru   University of Montpellier, France
Dominik Endres   University of Marburg, Germany
Ollivier Haemmerlé   University of Toulouse-Mirail, France
Uta Priss   Ostfalia University, Germany
Sebastian Rudolph   TU Dresden, Germany

Program Committee

Bernd Amann	Sorbonne University, France
Leila Amgoud	IRIT – CNRS, France
Simon Andrews	Sheffield Hallam University, UK
Moulin Bernard	Laval University, Canada
Pierre Bisquert	INRA, France
Peggy Cellier	IRISA, INSA Rennes, France
Peter Chapman	Edinburgh Napier University, UK
Dan Corbett	Optimodal Technologies, LLC, USA
Olivier Corby	University Côte d'Azur, Inria, France
Diana Cristea	Babes-Bolyai University, Romania
Licong Cui	UT Health Science Center at Houston, USA
Florent Domenach	Akita International University, Japan
Dominik Endres	University of Marburg, Germany
Catherine Faron Zucker	Université Nice Sophia Antipolis, France
Raji Ghawi	TU Munich, Germany
Ollivier Haemmerlé	University of Toulouse-Mirail, France
Dmitry Ignatov	National Research University Higher School of Economics, Russia
Adil Kabbaj	INSEA, Morocco
Leonard Kwuida	Bern University of Applied Sciences, Switzerland

Jérôme Lang	Paris Dauphine University, France
Natalia Loukachevitch	Moscow State University, Russia
Philippe Martin	University of La Réunion, France
Franck Michel	University of Côte d'Azur, France
Amedeo Napoli	University of Lorraine, France
Sergei Obiedkov	National Research University Higher School of Economics, Russia
Nir Oren	University of Aberdeen, UK
Nathalie Pernelle	Université Sorbonne Paris Nord, France
Simon Polovina	Sheffield Hallam University, UK
Uta Priss	Ostfalia University, Germany
Sebastian Rudolph	TU Dresden, Germany
Christian Sacarea	Babes-Bolyai University, Romania
Eric Salvat	IMERIR, France
Fatiha Saïs	University of Paris-Saclay, France
Diana Sotropa	Babes-Bolyai University, Romania
Srdjan Vesic	Artois University, France
Guoqiang Zhang	Case Western Reserve University, USA

Additional Reviewers

Yan Huang	UT Health Science Center at Houston, USA
Xiaojin Li	UT Health Science Center at Houston, USA
Fengbo Zheng	University of Kentucky, USA

Reconciling Knowledge-Based and Data-Driven AI for Human-in-the-Loop Machine Learning (Abstract of Invited Talk)

Ute Schmid

Cognitive Systems, University of Bamberg, Germany
ute.schmid@uni-bamberg.de

For many practical applications of machine learning it is appropriate or even necessary to make use of human expertise to compensate a too small amount or low quality of data. Taking into account knowledge which is available in explicit form reduces the amount of data needed for learning. Furthermore, even if domain experts cannot formulate knowledge explicitly, they typically can recognize and correct erroneous decisions or actions. This type of implicit knowledge can be injected into the learning process to guide model adaptation. The recognition that an exclusive focus on data-intensive blackbox machine learning alone is not suitable for many – especially critical – applications, has given rise to the so-called third wave of AI with a focus on explainability (XAI) [1], but also to a growing interest in interactive, human-in-the loop machine learning [4], and in hybrid approaches combining machine learning and knowledge-based AI [7].

A machine learning approach which naturally integrates induction over examples and the use of background knowledge and background theories is inductive logic programming (ILP). ILP is a family of approaches for learning logic (Prolog) programs and which is specifically suited for learning in relational domains. Thus, ILP is in itself a hybrid approach to machine learning. In the following, ILP is discussed in relation to XAI and human-in-the-loop learning.

Initially, the majority of XAI approaches has focused on visual local post hoc explanations for blackbox classifiers, often for convolutional neural networks applied to image classification. A visual explanation typically is realized as highlighting that part in an input which had the highest impact on the model decision. A further approach to explanation generation for blackboxes is to provide surrogate rule-based models [2]. Recently, more and more, this type of post hoc explanations are critizised and it is proposed to use machine learning approaches which directly result in interpretable models [5, 8]. Mostly, interpretable machine learning is associated with linear regression and with classic symbolic approaches to machine learning such as decision trees. ILP also belongs to the interpretable machine learning approaches and exceeds the expressibility of the other approaches.

Machine learning applications for complex real world domains such as medical diagnostis or quality control in industrial production often might demand explanations which are more expressive than visual highlighting and also more expressive than simple rules. To communicate model decisions to a human domain expert, information about relations (e.g., spatial relations such as *the tumor tissue intrudes into muscle tissue*), feature values (e.g., *the edge of the liver spot is irregular*), negation (e.g., *there is no blowhole*) might be relevant [9]. Mostly, having an interpretable model at hand is considered as already fulfilling the demands on explainability. However, complex models, just like complex computer programs, are inspectable and thereby transparent in principle, but there might be the need of guidance to focus on the relevant aspects given a specific task and information need. For this aim, different kinds of explanations can be generated from ILP learned models, such as near misses [6] or verbal explanations at different levels of detail [3]. We could show that such type of relational explanations support performance and can inspire (justified) trust in a system [11]. Especially in domains where labeling of training data is expensive and difficult, models should be adaptable by human corrections. Interactive learning mostly focuses on correction of labels alone. Having expressive symbolic explanations at hand, interaction can be extended to corrections of explanations [10] thereby keeping human experts in the loop and exploiting their knowledge to more efficient model adaption.

References

1. Adadi, A., Berrada, M.: Peeking inside the black-box: a survey on explainable artificial intelligence (XAI). IEEE Access, **6**, 52138–52160 (2018)
2. Dai, W., Xu, Q., Yu, Y., Zhou, Z.: Bridging machine learning and logical reasoning by abductive learning. In: Advances in Neural Information Processing Systems 32 (NeurIPS 2019), pp. 2811–2822 (2019)
3. Finzel, B., Tafler, D., Scheele, S., Schmid, U.: Explanation as a process: user-centric construction of multi-level and multi-modal explanations. In: Edelkamp, S., Möller, R., Rückert, E. (eds.) KI 2021: Advances in Artificial Intelligence (KI2021). LNCS, Springer (2021)
4. Holzinger, A.: Interactive machine learning for health informatics: when do we need the human-in-the-loop? Brain Inf. **3**(2), 119–131 (2016)
5. Muggleton, S., Schmid, U., Zeller, C., Tamaddoni-Nezhad, A., Besold, T.: Ultrastrong machine learning: Comprehensibility of programs learned with ilp. Mach. Learn. **107**(7), 1119–1140 (2018). https://doi.org/10.1007/s40708-016-0042-6
6. Rabold, J., Siebers, M., Schmid, U.: Generating contrastive explanations for inductive logic programming based on a near miss approach. CoRR abs/2106.08064 (2021). https://arxiv.org/abs/2106.08064
7. von Rüden, L., Mayer, S., Garcke, J., Bauckhage, C., Schücker, J.: Informed machine learning - towards a taxonomy of explicit integration of knowledge into machine learning. CoRR abs/1903.12394 (2019)
8. Rudin, C.: Please stop explaining black box models for high stakes decisions. CoRR abs/1811.10154 (2018). http://arxiv.org/abs/1811.10154
9. Schmid, U.: Interactive learning with mutual explanations in relational domains. In: Muggleton, S., Charter, N. (eds.) Human-like Machine Intelligence, pp. 337–353. Oxford University Press (2021)

10. Schmid, U., Finzel, B.: Mutual explanations for cooperative decision making in medicine. KI – Künstliche Intelligenz, Special Issue Challenges in Interactive Machine Learning 34 (2020). https://doi.org/10.1007/s13218-020-00633-2
11. Thaler, A., Schmid, U.: Explaining machine learned relational concepts in visual domains effects of perceived accuracy on joint performance and trust. In: Proceedings of the 43rd Annual Meeting of the Cognitive Science Society (CogSys21), pp. 1705–1711. Cognitive Science Society (2021)

Abstract of Tutorials

Foundations of Knowledge Graphs

Mehwish Alam[1,2] and Sebastian Rudolph[3]

[1] FIZ Karlsruhe – Leibniz Institute for Information Infrastructure, Germany
[2] Karlsruhe Institute of Technology, Germany
mehwish.alam@kit.edu
[3] TU Dresden, Germany
sebastian.rudolph@tu-dresden.de

1 Introduction

Since the beginning of the 2000s, Knowledge Graphs have been widely used for modeling various domains ranging from linguistics [1] to biomedicine [5]. Recently, Knowledge Graphs have become even more crucial for improving diverse real-world applications at the intersection of Natural Language Processing (NLP) and Knowledge Management, such as question answering, named entity disambiguation, information extraction, etc. [6]. Raising awareness about Knowledge Graphs in other research communities will allow them to benefit from the versatile Knowledge Graph formalisms, methods, and tools. To this end, this tutorial focuses on the foundations of Knowledge Graphs [4]. Starting from basic notions and techniques of Knowledge Graphs, the tutorial will then move on to more advanced topics such as how logical reasoning over these Knowledge Graphs [3], where formally specified background knowledge is taken into account to enrich the explicitly stated information by facts that can be logically inferred. Furthermore, we will discuss how to express real-world aspects such as context, time, and uncertainty in the Knowledge Graph framework. As they are typically used in an open-world setting, Knowledge Graphs can almost never be assumed to be complete, i.e., some information will typically be missing. In order to address this problem, different Knowledge Graph embedding models have been proposed for automated Knowledge Graph completion. These models are mostly based on the tasks such as link prediction, triple classification, and entity classification/typing. This tutorial will also target the topic of Knowledge Graph embedding techniques. Finally, various applications of Knowledge Graphs and Knowledge Graph embeddings will be discussed.

2 Program of the Tutorial

The program of this tutorial will be in three parts, (i) basics of Knowledge Graphs, (ii) logical reasoning over Knowledge Graphs, and (iii) various Knowledge Graph embedding Techniques for Knowledge Graph Completion.

- Knowledge Graph formalisms (RDF, RDFS, OWL)
- Different ways to encode, store, and access Knowledge Graphs (graph DBs, triple stores, SPARQL)
- Logical reasoning over Knowledge Graphs (ontology-based data access...)
- Different types of Knowledge Graphs, such as multi-modal, temporal, or uncertain Knowledge Graphs
- Algorithms for generating distributed representation over Knowledge Graphs, TransE, TranH, etc. [7]
- Algorithms for generating distributed representations over multi-modal Knowledge Graphs
- Applications: Knowledge Aware Recommender Systems, Question Answering Systems, etc.

3 Conclusion

Lately, there have been very fast advancements in the field of Knowledge Graphs not only in academia but also in industry. Various domains are modeling domain ontologies as well as the experimental data such as in the field of Materials Science. Logical reasoning continues to be an important technology of Knowledge Graphs and comes particularly handy in settings where little data is available, where the underlying domain knowledge is complex, and where accuracy is essential. On the other hand, the distributed representations generated using subsymbolic methods, i.e., Knowledge Graph embedding techniques have also been widely developed and being used in many applications. Currently, many studies are being conducted in the area of Neurosymbolic Reasoning [2] which integrates knowledge representation and reasoning with deep learning techniques.

References

1. Gangemi, A., Alam, M., Asprino, L., Presutti, V., Recupero, D.R.: Framester: a wide coverage linguistic linked data hub. In: Proceedings of International Conference on Knowledge Engineering and Knowledge Management (2016)https://doi.org/10.1007/978-3-319-49004-5_16
2. d'Avila Garcez, A., Lamb, L.C.: Neurosymbolic AI: the 3rd wave. CoRR abs/2012.05876 (2020). https://arxiv.org/abs/2012.05876
3. Hitzler, P., Krötzsch, M., Rudolph, S.: Foundations of Semantic Web Technologies. Chapman and Hall/CRC Press (2010)
4. Hogan, A., et al.: Knowledge graphs. CoRR abs/2003.02320 (2021)
5. Hu, W., Qiu, H., Huang, J., Dumontier, M.: Biosearch: a semantic search engine for bio2rdf. Database J. Biol. Databases Curation 2017, bax059 (2017)
6. Wang, Q., Mao, Z., Wang, B., Guo, L.: Knowledge graph embedding: a survey of approaches and applications. IEEE Trans. Knowl. Data Eng. **29**(12), 2724–2743 (2017)
7. Wang, Q., Mao, Z., Wang, B., Guo, L.: Knowledge graph embedding: a survey of approaches and applications. TKDE **29**(12), 2724–2743 (2017)

Concepts and Reasoning: Alternative Approaches

Iain Duncan Stalker(iD)

Institute of Management, University of Bolton, Bolton,UK
IS4@bolton.ac.uk

Theories of mind inform a breadth of disciplines from psychology to linguistics, philosophy to computer science. Fundamental to these are 'concepts' and yet there is no consensus on what constitutes a concept nor indeed its ontological status [1]. A diversity of opinions is not surprising given the range of interested parties. Arguably the most successful—certainly the most dominant—perspective has been one that holds that a concept has a definitional structure and consists in a complex (mental) representation that is composed of simpler components and identifies conditions that are both necessary and sufficient for an item to fall within its extension; this is often referred to as the 'Classical' or 'Traditional Theory' [1, 2]. Strictly speaking, a number of approaches are subsumed under the term 'Classical Theory'; indeed, definitional structures give rise to many formal representations including (first-order) logic [3], conceptual graphs [4], lattices [5], (other) set-based approaches [6], and even geometric spaces [7].

The ascendancy of the Classical Theory was vigorously challenged during the latter half of the Twentieth Century. One key criticism is that it is usually not possible to capture the full intent of a concept in definitional terms: for example, Wittgenstein illustrates the impossibility of providing a suitable definition for the concept of 'game' [12]; Rosch and Mervis [9] show that while it may be possible to identify a set of sufficient conditions for an item to fall within the extent of a concept, isolating a set of necessary conditions is not. A related challenge is that many concepts have indeterminate membership and deciding whether an item embodies a given concept is not always straightforward, cf. [13].

Concepts are essential to all aspects of cognition and an important strength of formal, definitional approaches is the systematic reasoning that they afford; the Classical Theory being most often associated with systems of logical analysis [1]. However, this imputed benefit was critically undermined through the work of Quine [8]. Moreover, the view of 'cognition as computation' that grew from logical reasoning and increased in popularity following the proposal that thinking can be modelled as an information processing task, e.g., [14], has attracted criticism and can no longer claim the prevalence that it once enjoyed. Developments in cognitive linguistics have shown that people typically reason using metaphors [15] and that these metaphors often derive from basic schemata [16]. Yet, traditional approaches to reasoning with concepts fall short of providing a satisfactory account of how these basic schemata combine [10].

In this tutorial, we will explore traditional and contemporary approaches to concept representation and reasoning. Our treatment will be pragmatic and focus on practical application. Most theories can be seen as a response to the Classical Theory [1], thus, we will begin with classical approaches that model concepts as (complete) definitional structures; we will show how this has developed into less strict approaches often referred to as 'neo-classical', where concepts are modelled as partial structures with conditions of necessity. Contemporary approaches will include geometric approaches [7], conceptual blending [10], reasoning by analogy and metaphor [15], argumentation structures [11], and prototypes and family resemblance, where concepts are represented by similarity to so-called exemplars [9]. In each case, using examples to support, key notions will be outlined, benefits and limitations summarised, and how each addresses shortcomings and criticisms of the Classical Theory will be highlighted. We shall close the tutorial by examining the complementary aspects of the approaches reviewed, with an intention of exploring how these may be used in combination.

References

1. Laurence, S., Margolis, E.: Concepts: Core Readings. MIT Press, Cambridge (1999)
2. Goguen, J.: What is a concept? In: Dau, F., Mungier, M.L. (eds.) 13th International Conference on Conceptual Structures (ICCS 2005), LNAI, vol. 3596, pp. 52–77. Springer, Germany (2005). https://doi.org/10.1007/11524564_4
3. Smullyan, R.: First-order Logic. Dover Publications, London (1995)
4. Sowa, J.: Conceptual graphs. In: van Harmelen, F., Lifschitz, V., Porter, B. (eds.) Handbook of Knowledge Representation, pp. 213–237. Elsevier, Amsterdam (2008)
5. Ganter, B., Wille, R.: Formal Concept Analysis. Mathematical Foundations. Springer-Verlag, Heidelberg (1999)
6. Pawlak, Z.: Rough Sets, Theoretical Aspects of Reasoning about Data. Kluwer Academic Publishers, Dordrecht (1991)
7. Gardenfors, P: Conceptual Spaces: The Geometry of Thought. Bradford/MIT, Cambridge (2000)
8. Quine, W.: Two dogmas of empiricism. In: From a Logical Point of View: Nine Logico-Philosophical Essays, Harvard University Press, Cambridge (1951)
9. Rosch, E., Mervis, C.: Family resemblances: studies in the internal structures of categories. Cogn. Sci. 7, 573–605 (1975)
10. Fauconnier, G., Turner, M.: The Way We Think. Basic Books, New York (2002)
11. Toulmin, S.: The Uses of Argument. Updated Edition. Cambridge University Press, Cambridge (2005)
12. Wittgenstein, L.: Philosophical Investigations. Blackwell, Oxford (1953)
13. Zadeh, L.: Fuzzy Sets, Information and Control, 8, pp. 338–353 (1965)
14. Miller, G., Galanter, E., Pribram, K.: Plans and the Structure of Behavior. Holt, New York (1960)
15. Lakoff, G., Johnson, M.: Metaphors We Live By. University of Chicago Press, USA (1980)
16. Hiraga, M.: Metaphor and Iconicity: A Cognitive Approach to Analyzing Texts. Palgrave Macmillan, UK (2004)

Contents

Mining Conceptual Structures

Applications of Conceptual Structures

On the Use of FCA Models in Static Analysis Tools to Detect Common Errors in Programming

Diana Cristea$^{(\boxtimes)}$ ⓘ, Diana Şotropa ⓘ, Arthur-Jozsef Molnar ⓘ,
and Simona Motogna ⓘ

Babeş-Bolyai University, Cluj-Napoca, Romania
{diana.cristea,diana.halita,arthur.molnar,simona.motogna}@ubbcluj.ro

Abstract. Static code analysis is widely used to detect code quality issues before execution. Thus, it can provide information that is important for improving programming skills. Such tools have been successfully used in teaching programming courses. In this paper we present algorithms for combining Formal Concept Analysis (FCA) with Pylint, a static code analysis tool, in order to detect and assess behavioral patterns in students' programming styles. We design a generalized framework that can be subsequently used to analyze any category/subset of errors. We apply the approach for detecting common errors related to design by considering two scenarios that tackle object oriented design and increased code complexity. We argue how the results can be used to understand common mistakes and to improve the teaching content and methods.

Keywords: Formal concept analysis · Static code analysis · Computer science education

1 Introduction

One of the main challenges in Computer Science education is how to efficiently achieve learning outcomes and to be able to teach students the theoretical foundations of programming, and also to make them acquire the desired programming skills. Different forms of blended learning have been proposed for teaching programming courses, with the clear objectives of increased student engagement and problem solving strategies.

Still, this is not an easy task since it involves some key issues that need to be addressed, such as assessing several aspects related to programming language features, design and development good practices and code quality. The situation becomes even more complex in case of large students cohorts, where class management needs to be addressed.

Tools that might assist teaching staff in programming courses have been proved to be useful, and data collected from them can be then further processed to improve teaching and assessment activities.

© Springer Nature Switzerland AG 2021
T. Braun et al. (Eds.): ICCS 2021, LNAI 12879, pp. 3–18, 2021.
https://doi.org/10.1007/978-3-030-86982-3_1

The data collected over time by such tools, that can be classified according to several criteria may be exploited by Formal Concept Analysis (FCA) techniques to detect behavioral patterns in students' programming styles.

Static analysis tools are acknowledged for identifying programming errors, bugs, code smells or vulnerabilities, and for providing useful information about source code before execution. Using them in programming courses have been reported continuously by the research community [1, 6, 10, 23].

The purpose of this study is two-folded: Firstly, to describe algorithms for one-valued and multi-valued criterion analysis, where the criterion and the associated threshold are specified by user. Secondly, we apply these algorithms to Pylint results corresponding to student projects written in Python, representing assignments for a Fundamentals of Programming course. Thus, given the amount of data and criteria, we show how the results can be used for detecting programming behavior and propose a specific methodology that can be useful in improving teaching content and methods, by emphasizing issues that are not completely understood by student and were identified as common mistakes.

The rest of the paper is organized as follows: Sect. 2 describes in brief the theoretical background, followed by reported related work. In Sect. 4, we describe the algorithms for building concept lattices for selected criteria, followed in the next section by applications of these algorithms to Pylint results for students assignments. Considering the subset of design issue, we highlight how common errors can be detected and, in consequence, be used to adapt teaching strategies. We conclude with some final remarks and future directions.

2   Theoretical Background

2.1   FCA

In the following we briefly recall some basic definition. For more details please refer to the classic literature [7, 11].

FCA was introduced by R. Wille and B. Ganter in the dyadic setting, in the form of objects related to attributes [7]. The fundamental structures of FCA are the formal context, i.e. a data set that contains elements and a relation between them, and formal concepts, i.e. maximal clusters of data from the defined context. Hence, a *formal context* is a triple (G, M, I) consisting of two sets, a set of *objects*, G, and a set of attributes, M, and a binary relation $I \subseteq G \times M$, called the *incidence relation*.

While in some data sets attributes might describe a property that objects have, in most cases attributes might have multiple values that describe some objects. A *many-valued* context is a tuple (G, M, W, I), where G, M, W are sets of objects, attributes, respectively values, and $I \subseteq G \times M \times W$ is a ternary relation s.t. for all $g \in G$ and $m \in M$ if $(g, m, w) \in I$ and $(g, m, v) \in I$ then $w = v$, i.e. the value of the object g on the attribute m is uniquely determined [7]. Thus, we will handle the data using many-valued contexts by scaling them into normal one-valued formal contexts.

In subsequent work, F. Lehmann and R. Wille extended FCA to a triadic setting, by adding the third dimension represented by conditions and by extending the incidence relation such that objects are related to attributes under some conditions (B) [11]. A tricontext is a quadruple $\mathbb{K} := (G, M, B, Y)$ where G, M and B are sets of objects, attributes, respectively conditions, and Y is a ternary relation between them, i.e., $Y \subseteq G \times M \times B$.

In order to create dyadic and triadic contexts and to visualize the concepts we have used FCA Tools Bundle [9]. We have chosen this tool mainly because it offers elegant and expressive dyadic graphical representations and because it allows navigation between triadic concepts by locking certain elements from objects, attributes or conditions or by choosing required objects, attributes or conditions that should be part of an interesting concepts list.

2.2 Static Code Analysis with Pylint

Static code analysis represents a collection of techniques that apply different strategies in order to provide meaningful information about the source code. These techniques based on formal methods applied to abstract syntax tree representation of the source code are able to detect different issues such as: software defects, code smells or security vulnerabilities.

They are of extreme importance as the information is available prior to program execution, thus the use of such tools enhances early error detection and significantly improve the overall software quality. Studies [12] reported their use as being responsible for detecting around 55% - 60% of software defects. Their use enhances program comprehension, helps practitioners understand causes of issues and improve maintainability, efficiency, security and reliability of the applications. Based on this, they become ideal candidates to assist programming education.

Lately, such tools, sometimes referred as "linter", have been proposed for several programming languages, can be easily customized (useful in team project management) and integrated in development processes. Some of these tools are specific to one programming language such as Checkstyle or Findbugs for Java, NDepend for .NET or Pylint for Python, while others offer functionalities for several programming languages such as SonarQube, Coverity or PMD.

Our study is focusing on Pylint static code analyzer, that uses an extensive rule set to check the source code relatively to code smells, coding standards or bugs, generating messages that help programmers diagnose their issues. A Pylint message has the following structure:

location : *type*(*code, short description*) *detailed description*
where: *location* specifies the line of code where the issue appeared, *type* $\in$ $\{I,R,C,W,E,F\}$ describes types of errors, *code* has the form $R0003$ where "R" is the type followed by a number and the two forms of *descriptions* are providing information about the issue. A complete explanation of the types and descriptions is provided by Pylint documentation [18], while our study will use errors of type "R", namely those associated with code smells.

The Pylint messages can be classified according to their type or by the perspective they are referring. The Pylint documentation offers several defined checkers such as design, typechecking or exception checkers. Also, based on the detailed descriptions of the messages, users can create their own checker list to group messages, for example prevent errors as presented in [14].

3   Related Work

We consider combining FCA techniques with static code analysis as having a large potential of applications, especially for teaching programming in an adaptive way, that might respond to concept misunderstandings that student expose. We focus this section on three directions, namely existing approaches of using static analysis in programming education, respectively scientific contribution on the use of FCA to solve software engineering problems, and in the end contributions of the application of FCA in education.

Several papers present the advantages of using code review and static analysis tools to assist teaching and evaluation of programming courses. The use of Checkstyle, PMD, Findbugs, together with two approaches based on graph transformation in automated grading and assessment is investigated in [23], where the benefits of the proposed approaches are compared. A study [6] including a large collection of Java programs has identified that static analysis tools can be successfully used to identify coding flaws that might generate errors and to perform different analysis, such as that experienced students produce less errors.

Building automated grading for MOOCs can also benefit from static analysis results as shown in [1], by enhancing the classical approach based on dynamic analysis. A method to use Pylint to assist students progress in a programming course was proposed in [13]. The authors showed how static analysis results can be used for one student progress during semester, or for performance of all students for a certain assignment or for comparing students performance between themselves.

Compared to the results obtained so far, our approach brings the following two important contribution: an in depth analysis of the results from static analysis tools using FCA and use of this analysis to identify common programming errors that can help professors to adopt corrective teaching strategies or change focus of teaching.

Several applications of FCA strategies to software engineering problems have been published over the years, such as: software reuse [8], reverse engineering and code inspection [3], object oriented analysis and design [5] or concept and fault location [2,15]. A literature review published in 2005 [24] presents a classification of these approaches.

Software development processes are more and more assisted by a plethora of tools that collect data, thus giving the opportunity to investigate, analyze these data in order to improve the processes. Approaches that represent, manipulate and classify data, such as FCA, can be applied to software engineering processes in order to discover new dependencies and influences.

A first argument for using FCA in education was proposed in [4], where an example of how kindergarten children gather mathematical knowledge is investigating using lattice analysis. Significant contributions have been made by Uta

Priss, from which we mention the investigation based on FCA of the data collected from computer based assessment tools to detect conceptual difficulties [16]. Recent work [17] reports the use of Semiotic Conceptual Analysis to analyze the structures and generate the conceptual models for learning management systems, and exemplifies it of Moodle. Our contribution is targeting teaching programming skills, and is addressing the open question stated in [16]: "how can one identify conceptual difficulties students are having by analysing their code submission?".

4 Concept Lattice for the Selected Criterion

In every domain there are large multi-dimensional data sets that can be processed in order to infer knowledge. Our purpose is to use a dyadic and a triadic FCA approach in order to discover connections among the data.

In the following, we propose two generic algorithms that use a triadic multi-valued dataset as input (but which can be adapted on any multi-dimensional data set) and offer the user a framework to explore the data from different perspectives. The first algorithm is based on a one-valued analysis where quantity does

---

Algorithm 1. One-valued criterion analysis

---

  function CREATECONTEXTFORONEVALUEDCRITERIONANALYSIS(G, M, B, W, Y)

    Input: G - a set of objects

           M - a set of attributes

           B - a set of conditions

           W - a set of values

           Y - the incidence relation on $G \times M \times B \times W$

    Output Concept lattice of the dyadic context generated by projecting on the chosen dimension

    print "Choose a criterion corresponding to a subset of the conditions"

    read C

    print "Choose the minimum threshold for the values"

    read k

    Let $\mathbb{K} = (G, M, C, Y_1)$ be the tricontext with the introduced criterion $C \subseteq B$ and the relation Y_1: for $g \in G$, $m \in M$, $c \in C$, $w \in W$ we say that $(g, m, c) \in Y_1 \iff (g, m, c, w) \in Y$, where $w \geq k$ for the chosen threshold k

    Query concepts with interactive n-concept finding algorithm in FCA Tools Bundle

    while $\exists$ undefined membership constraints **do**

        read membership constraint

        Propagate membership constraint

    end while

    print the set of triconcepts corresponding to the chosen membership constraints

    Let user lock one of the perspectives

    read perspective to lock on

    return Concept lattice of the derived context $\mathbb{K}_1 = (G, M, Y_2)$ generated by projecting on the dimension chosen by the user

  end function

---

not play an important role, while the second algorithm includes a multi-valued analysis. In this highly configurable framework the user can choose parameters such as: the minimum threshold for the values, attributes of interest, etc.

Algorithm 1 focuses on two different outcomes: mining triconcepts with constraints of the user's choosing and exploring the lattice of a dyadic projection on a chosen dimension. Besides the initial input data set, the user first chooses a particular criterion, i.e. a subset of conditions that are of interest to him, and a minimum threshold for the values (if 0 is introduced, then all values will be taken into consideration).

In the following the data set is processed in order to exclude all data that does not respect the input given by the user and it is interpreted as a one-valued triadic context, where a triple (g, m, c) belongs to the relation if it's corresponding value respects the minimum threshold k.

Algorithm 2. Multi-valued criterion analysis

---

function CREATECONTEXTFORMULTIVALUEDCRITERIONANALYSIS(G, M, B, W, Y)

    Input: G - a set of objects

           M - a set of attributes

           B - a set of conditions

           W - a set of values

           Y - the incidence relation on $G \times M \times B \times W$

    Output: Concept lattice of the dyadic context corresponding to chosen input

    print "Choose a criterion corresponding to a subset of conditions"

    read C

    print "Choose the attribute of interest"

    read a

    print "Choose the minimum threshold for the values".

    read k

    Let $\mathbb{K} = (G, C, W, Y_1)$ be the multi-valued formal context with the chosen criterion C and the relation Y_1: for $g \in G$, $c \in C$, $w \in W$ we say that $(g, c, w) \in Y_1 \iff (g, a, c, w) \in Y$ for chosen attribute a and $w \geq k$ for chosen threshold

    Normalize the values in W with respect to the maximum number for each condition in order to obtain a value $\in (0, 1]$

    Define scale on C by splitting the values interval $(0, 1]$ in smaller disjoint intervals I_k s.t. $\bigcup_k I_k = (0, 1]$

    Create the derived one-valued context $\mathbb{K}_{derived} = (G, C_{derived}, Y_2)$, with $C_{scaled} = \bigcup_k \{c$ with value $w_{normalized} \in I_k | c \in C\}$, and the incidence relation Y_2: for $g \in G$, $m \in C_{derived}$, where m is of the form c with value $w_{normalized} \in I_k$, then $(g, m) \in Y_2 \iff \exists w \in W$ corresponding to $w_{normalized}$ s.t. $(g, a, c, w) \in Y$ for chosen attribute a

    return Concept lattice of $\mathbb{K}_{derived} = (G, C_{derived}, Y_2)$

    end function

In the next part the user can explore the triadic context using membership constraints by specifying required or forbidden elements for each component (as defined in [19]). After finding a triconcept of interest the user can choose to lock one of the components in order to explore dyadic concepts having the elements of that component in common (as described in [20]). Therefore, the dyadic lattice of the projections is returned by the algorithm for further explorations.

Algorithm 2 offers a more quantitative approach to the analysis. Starting from the same input as the previous algorithm the user is asked to choose a criterion and an attribute on which the following analysis will be focused on and, optional, a threshold for the values. Next the algorithm filters the data set accordingly and builds the multi-valued context $\mathbb{K} = (G, C, W, Y_1)$.

In the following steps the algorithm takes into account the values in W in the analysis. First the values that occur for each condition in the criterion get normalized in the interval $(0, 1]$. Next a scale is defined by dividing the normalized value for the conditions in the criterion in disjoint intervals (the actual intervals are chosen by the domain expert). Hence, a triple (g, c, w) is replaced with $(g, $ "c with value in I_k"$)$. The concept lattice of the derived context is returned for further exploration.

The given algorithms provide a step-by-step description of the data mining process. When integrated in a tool, the proposed methods can be used by users that are not familiar with FCA. In this way, the user focuses on the data analysis part while the FCA methods are automatically applied.

Our methodology follows the steps: 1) establish the set of attributes to be checked, namely the set of Pylint rules to be used in the lattice construction; 2) build and use FCA lattices to determine cases and dependencies between them; 3) based on them, report the cases based on the results returned by algorithms.

5   Applying FCA to Detect Common Programming Errors

In this section we apply the algorithms described above to detect and characterize some programming errors that commonly occur in student code.

We exemplify the methodology using common errors related to design applied to assignment source code handed in by students during introductory programming coursework, but the same process can be followed to detect security or reliability issues in code. Furthermore, Pylint can be replaced with a fully-fledged static analysis tool such as SonarQube or NDepend to enable code analysis for other languages. In this use case, FCA lattices are used to detect common cases and dependencies between them; this can help teaching staff uncover trends and common bad practices in large data sets, which can be especially useful when applied for large student classes with several teachers.

5.1   Data Collection

Our work targets the source code handed in by the 225 registered first-year computer science students that took the introductory *Fundamentals of Programming* course during the 2019–2020 academic year. Taking place during the

Table 1. Assignments included in our scenarios, ordered by deadline. Rightmost column is the number of student submitted solutions that passed the plagiarism check

Code	Description	Solutions
A1	First assignment of moderate complexity. Focused on writing clean code using the procedural and modular paradigms	183
T1	The first timed test: implement a working program having a set of well defined functionalities using the procedural paradigm	192
A2	First assignment requiring an object-oriented implementation, with a single entity in the problem domain	132
A3	Multi-week assignment focused on object-orientation, layered architecture and the single responsibility principle; bonuses available for creating a GUI, or using *.properties* files to store program settings	143
T2	Second timed test: implement a working program with a well-defined functionality set using principles from layered architecture and OOP	204
A4	Develop a human vs. computer board game; bonuses for creating a GUI or implementing minimax for the computer opponent	128
A5	At least two implementations of the backtracking technique required as part of the course's problem solving methods section	55
E1, E2	Practical exams during the regular and retake sessions, respectively. Implement a working program similar in requirements to A3 and A4	200

first semester, the course was completed before activities were adapted to the ongoing pandemic.

The course provides an introduction to many important aspects of programming and software development, and targets students who already have a foundational understanding of programming that was gained during high-school. The Python 3.x language is used to implement several procedural, modular and object-oriented solutions. Table 1 details the assignments and coding tests included in our scenarios. Student solutions were graded by instructor-driven system testing through the user interface, together with a manual examination of the source code. This was aimed to encourage good coding practices and the avoidance of well-known code smells such as code complexity issues, excessive number of parameters, God class problems as well as inter-class and inter-layer dependency management.

Student solutions were downloaded and checked against plagiarism using Stanford's MOSS system [22], which uses winnowing and is able to identify partial similarity in source code [21]. Manual verification was carried out to

Table 2. Pylint codes corresponding to Design Checker perspective [18]. Values over the threshold result in the creation of a corresponding Pylint issue

Code	Description	Threshold
$R0901$	Class has too many parent classes	7
$R0902$	Class has too many instance attributes	7
$R0903$	Class has too few public methods	2
$R0904$	Class has too many public methods	20
$R0911$	Function has too many return statements	6
$R0912$	Function has too many branches	12
$R0913$	Function has too many arguments	5
$R0914$	Function has too many local variables	15
$R0915$	Function has too many statements	50
$R0916$	Expression has too many boolean statements	5

ensure student solutions were assigned to the correct assignment and that they did not include instructor-supplied or library code.

Each submission was scanned using the default Pylint 2.6.0[1] configuration. Default threshold values used for issues addressed in our study are illustrated in Table 2. A number of 1237 solutions were included in our study. Note that submitting solutions for all assignments was not required to pass the course. For each assignment, some students failed to produce a working program and chose not to submit their solution.

5.2 Common Errors Related to Design

Our focus in this study is on the Design Checker subset, which includes the codes corresponding to code smells depicted in Table 2. They identify two important types of bad practices in programming:

- Bad object oriented design: codes from $R0901$ to $R0904$ identify situations in which the design of classes, their instance variables and their methods are not respecting corresponding good practices such as single responsibility, the open/closed principle or encapsulation;
- Issues increasing code complexity: codes from $R0911$ to $R0916$ detect cases in which the conditional logic is needlessly complicated and generates a high cyclomatic complexity of that module.

The last column in Table 2 represents the threshold value that triggers the corresponding Pylint issue. For example, if one class has more than 7 parent classes through the inheritance hierarchy code $R0901$ is generated.

---

[1] https://pypi.org/project/pylint/.

```
elif len(command_arguments) ==2:
    try:
        sign = command_arguments[0]
        average_score = float(command_arguments[1])
        if average_score >= 0 and (sign == '=' or sign == '<' or sign == '>'):
            if sign== '<':
                position=1
                for x in list_contestant:
                    if average(x[0], x[1], x[2])< average_score:
                        set_score(list_contestant, position,0,0)
                        set_score(list_contestant, position, 1, 0)
                        set_score(list_contestant, position, 2, 0)
                    position=position+1
            if sign== '>':
                position=1
                for x in list_contestant:
                    if average(x[0], x[1], x[2])> average_score:
                        set_score(list_contestant, position,0,0)
                        set_score(list_contestant, position, 1, 0)
                        set_score(list_contestant, position, 2, 0)
                    position=position+1
            if sign== '=':
                position=1
                for x in list_contestant:
                    if average(x[0], x[1], x[2])== average_score:
                        set_score(list_contestant, position,0,0)
                        set_score(list_contestant, position, 1, 0)
                        set_score(list_contestant, position, 2, 0)
                    position=position+1
        else:
            ui_invalid_command()
            return
```

Fig. 1. Code excerpt exposing high complexity

Detect Increased Code Complexity Error in Design. Our first scenario investigates common errors related to inadequate use of statements, especially conditional ones, or too many identifiers (either arguments or local variables).

Figure 1 illustrates a code snippet demonstrating the overuse of nested conditional statements together with code duplication within the *if* statement blocks.

For this scenario we use Algorithm 1 in order to identify patterns that can emphasize correlations between error codes or student assignments We first consider the one-valued analysis in order to focus on whether an error code occurs or not. For the algorithm input we choose the set of assignments as the *objects set*, the set of student usernames as the *attributes set*, the set of error codes generated by Pylint as the *conditions set*, while the values are represented by the number of occurrences for an error code in the student's implementation of an assignment. The chosen criterion is the subset of error codes from Design Checker and the threshold is 0.

Code complexity increases due to the definition of functions, i.e. the use of too many arguments, local variables, statements, return statements or branches. While querying the concepts, we focused on finding triconcepts that have in their modi error codes corresponding to increased code complexity, i.e. codes $R0911$ - $R0916$. We detect most common pairs and triplets of codes that increase code complexity and we emphasize two different cases:

1. Identifying large groups of students and their corresponding group of codes that are sharing only one assignment;
2. Identifying correlations between different assignments and the final practical test.

We found that more than 20% of all generated triconcepts contain in their modi at least the error codes $R0912$ and $R0915$, while 16% of them contain $R0912$ and $R0914$. While analyzing patterns generated by pairing error codes, we noticed that 7.5% of all generated triconcepts contained in their modi the triplet $R0912$, $R0914$ and $R0915$. Thus, for both cases we only analyzed the set of triconcepts containing the above mentioned pairs or triplet.

Finding 1: *Approximately 30% of students use too many branches inside a module, and a few also use too many statements or too many local variables.*

For the first case we continued the filtering by choosing only those concepts having exactly one assignment in their extent, and at least 2 elements in their intent and modus. We have obtained 30 concepts and 6 of them group at least 11 students having these common error codes in their submitted solutions.

Finding 2: *From a programming practice point of view, this scenario identified the fact that the previous common error can further increase complexity by the fact that the pair $R0912$ and $R0915$ can be associated also with other codes, codes $R0914$, respectively $R0913$ (introducing either too many local variable or arguments).*

For the second case we considered concepts that have at least 2 elements in their extent, intent and modus. This strategy allowed us to observe that there are concepts containing multiple assignments or exams in their extent, leading to an analysis of common errors or error propagation throughout the semester. Table 3 presents a part of the first outcome of Algorithm 1 containing correlations regarding code complexity between assignments A1 and A3, A3 and A4, A1 and exam E1, and, respectively A3 and exam E1. We have also looked for those 4 students that we found in both our analysis, and we have noticed that for 2 of them the code complexity problem persists over the entire semester.

Table 3. Increased code complexity of the source program, with focus on error codes $R0912$, $R0914$ and $R0915$, objects: assignments, attributes: students' usernames, conditions: error codes

Objects	Attributes	Conditions
$[A1, E1]$	$[S1, S2]$	$[R0912, R0914, R0915]$
$[A1, A3]$	$[S3, S4, S2]$	$[R0912, R0914, R0915]$
$[A3, A4]$	$[S5, S6]$	$[R0912, R0914, R0915]$
$[A3, E1]$	$[S7, S2]$	$[R0912, R0913, R0914, R0915]$
$[A3, E1]$	$[S8, S7]$	$[R0903, R0912, R0914, R0915]$
$[A2, E1]$	$[S9, S8, S7, S2]$	$[R0912, R0914, R0915]$

Finding 3: *There is a small number of students who did not manage to improve the quality of their code.*

Afterwards, we lock on the third dimension, i.e. on the error code subset $\{R0912, R0914, R0915\}$, and obtain the final output of the algorithm shown in Fig. 2. It highlights the significant number of appearances of the common errors

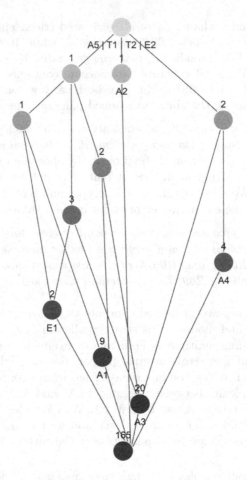

Fig. 2. Increased code complexity of the source program, with focus on error codes $R0912$, $R0914$ and $R0915$, objects: students usernames, attributes: assignments

(too many branches, too many local variables and too many statements) in the students' source code. Teaching staff can present these "bad examples" together with solutions, such as extracting the common code to another function and calling the function, thus decreasing complexity and improving code readability. As a consequence, teaching strategies can be adapted in order to focus on problem decomposition (in modular design), use of functions and the single responsibility principle at function and module levels.

Detect Object Oriented Programming Design Errors. In order to detect object oriented programming design issues we focus our analysis on assignment A3, the first complex assignment that evaluated OOP skills.

We first used a simplified version of Algorithm 1 for a dyadic context having student usernames as objects, Pylint error codes as attributes and their number of occurrences as values. The chosen criterion corresponds to the design checker and we perform one-valued analysis, i.e. each error code appears or not in the generated Pylint messages regardless of the number of occurrences. Using the interactive $n - concept$ finding algorithm we identified groups of students whose assignments generated the same groups of codes. We found an interesting pattern in 13 concepts where the triplet $\{R0902, R0903, R0904\}$ was included in the intent. An interesting fact of this pattern is that each concept has a minimum of 4 students in its extent and moreover, those 4 students are part of the corresponding extent for all 13 concepts.

Among the 30 concepts from the triadic perspective exposing codes $R0912$, $R0914$ and $R0915$ corresponding to the previous scenario, we found 13 concepts that also contained one of the codes $R0902$, $R0903$ or $R0904$.

Finding 4: *Students facing issues with object oriented design also faced issues when dealing with problem decomposition and keeping code complexity in check.*

Each error code might appear multiple times in the results generated for the same student and assignment. Thus, design problem patterns should be revealed by taking into consideration error code occurrences. Therefore, we next apply Algorithm 2 with the following input: student usernames as objects, assignments as attributes, Pylint error codes as conditions and the number of occurrences of the Pylint errors as values. The criterion corresponds to the design checker, the attribute of interest is assignment A3 and initially no threshold for the values is chosen ($k = 0$). For the scale used in Algorithm 2 we divide the normalized values for the number of error occurrences in the intervals $(0, 0.33)$, $[0.33, 0.66]$ and $(0.66, 1]$.

There are 44 concepts that correspond to student solutions for assignment A3 with less than 0.33 scaled occurrences of codes $R0903$ and $R0904$. Also there are 23 concepts which correspond to students handing the same assignment with less than 0.33 scaled occurrences of code $R0903$ and a number of occurrences between 0.33 and 0.66 for code $R0904$.

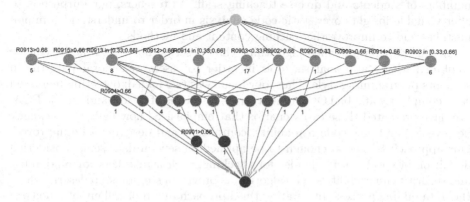

Fig. 3. Bad object oriented design for assignment A3. Objects: student usernames; attributes: pylint error codes; threshold: at least 4 occurrences of an error code

Due to the large number of concepts and in order to obtain relevant insights over object oriented design issues we selected $k = 4$ as threshold (i.e. the minimum number of occurrences of an error code), while keeping the rest of the input for Algorithm 2 the same as previously described. The output of the algorithm is depicted in Fig. 3.

We followed up with a manual examination to contextualise our findings. We observed that classes with too many ancestors ($R0901$) were generally linked with further extending GUI components from the TkInter or Qt frameworks; likewise, classes generated by GUI designers were responsible for many issues linked with too many instance attributes ($R0902$). In this regard, we've identified one such class that consisted of 116 instance attributes and 29 public methods ($R0904$); many of these methods were student written and responsible for the class having over 1,000 lines of code. On the other hand, classes with fewer than two public methods ($R0903$) were usually responsible for entity validation, consisting of a single validation method. We encountered a similar situation with classes responsible for management of program settings, with one such example consisting of 15 class attributes and a single public method.

Finding 5: *Static code analysis findings must be properly contextualized, as not all issues are immediately indicative of poor design and implementation.*

In addition to the proposals that can be used to address previous findings, we believe the introduction of suitable design patterns, and the practice of using them within the implementation of object-oriented assignments will provide students additional tools to address these issues over the long-term, and in many development contexts.

6   Conclusions and Future Work

Analyzing assignments in order to detect and emphasize code quality might be a really difficult task, which can be even more complicated in case of large numbers of students and diverse teaching staff. As teachers, our purpose is to offer valuable insights over static code analysis in order to understand common mistakes and to improve the teaching content and methods.

In this paper we defined algorithms that describe how FCA model can be combined with static analysis tools in order to assess behavioral patterns in students programming style. Thus, our focus was two folded: detecting increased code complexity and bad OOP design errors by means of dyadic and triadic FCA. We have presented these two scenarios that emphasized how bad practices may be revealed and how code readability, complexity and design can be improved. Our approach is general enough to be applied on several data sets, considering definition of specific sets of rules for checking, such as checkers for readability and security vulnerabilities. The algorithms provide a step-by-step description of the data mining process. Integrating this approach in a tool will enable choice of checkers based on course specificity. The methodology will assist teachers in their courses, giving the rules they want to check and providing them with common errors and behavioral patterns, without any requirement related to FCA, as this part will be automatically computed.

As future work we want to change the perspective over the data and analyse it from a n-adic perspective. Then, we would like to extend our framework as a recommendation system for a Python IDE in order to assist students in providing real time feedback while programming.

References

1. Bey, A., Jermann, P., Dillenbourg, P.: A comparison between two automatic assessment approaches for programming: an empirical study on MOOCs. J. Educ. Technol. Soc. **21**(2), 259–272 (2018)
2. Cellier, P., Ducassé, M., Ferré, S., Ridoux, O.: Formal concept analysis enhances fault localization in software. In: Medina, R., Obiedkov, S. (eds.) ICFCA 2008. LNCS (LNAI), vol. 4933, pp. 273–288. Springer, Heidelberg (2008). https://doi.org/10.1007/978-3-540-78137-0_20
3. Dekel, U.: Applications of concept lattices to code inspection and review, December 2002
4. Duquenne, V.: What can lattices do for teaching math. and education? vol. 331, January 2007
5. Düwel, S., Hesse, W.: Bridging the gap between use case analysis and class structure design by formal concept analysis (2001)
6. Edwards, S.H., Kandru, N., Rajagopal, M.B.: Investigating static analysis errors in student java programs. In: Proceedings of ICER 2017, pp. 65–73 (2017)
7. Ganter, B., Wille, R.: Formal Concept Analysis, Mathematical Foundation. Springer, Heidelberg (1999). https://doi.org/10.1007/978-3-642-59830-2
8. Godin, R., Mineau, G., Missaoui, R., St-Germain, M., Faraj, N.: Applying concept formation methods to software reuse. Int. J. Softw. Eng. Knowl. Eng. **5**, 119–142 (1995)
9. Kis, L., Sacarea, C., Troanca, D.: FCA tools bundle-a tool that enables dyadic and triadic conceptual navigation. In: Proceedings of FCA4AI@ ECAI 2016, pp. 42–50 (2016)
10. Lajis, A., Baharudin, S.: A review of techniques in automatic programming assessment for practical skill test. J. Telecommun. Electron. Comput. Eng. **10**(2), 109–113 (2018)
11. Lehmann, F., Wille, R.: A triadic approach to formal concept analysis. In: Ellis, G., Levinson, R., Rich, W., Sowa, J.F. (eds.) ICCS-ConceptStruct 1995. LNCS, vol. 954, pp. 32–43. Springer, Heidelberg (1995). https://doi.org/10.1007/3-540-60161-9_27
12. McConnell, S.: Code Complete, 2nd edn. Microsoft Press (2004)
13. Molnar, A., Motogna, S., Vlad, C.: Using static analysis tools to assist student project evaluation. In: Proceedings of EASEAI@ESEC/SIGSOFT FSE (2020)
14. Motogna, S., Cristea, D., Sotropa, D., Molnar, A.J.: Formal concept analysis model for static code analysis. Carpathian J. Math. **37**(3), 49–58 (2021). Special issue dedicated to the 60th anniversary of University of Baia Mare, Print Edition: ISSN 1584 - 2851. Online Edition: ISSN 1843 - 4401
15. Poshyvanyk, D., Marcus, A.: Combining formal concept analysis with information retrieval for concept location in source code. In: Proceedings of ICPC, pp. 37–48 (2007)

16. Priss, U.: Using FCA to analyse how students learn to program. In: Cellier, P., Distel, F., Ganter, B. (eds.) ICFCA 2013. LNCS (LNAI), vol. 7880, pp. 216–227. Springer, Heidelberg (2013). https://doi.org/10.1007/978-3-642-38317-5_14
17. Priss, U.: A preliminary semiotic-conceptual analysis of a learning management system. Proc. Comput. Sci. **176**, 3702–3709 (2020)
18. Pylint Documentation. http://pylint.pycqa.org/en/latest/user_guide/output.html. Accessed April 2021
19. Rudolph, S., Sacarea, C., Troanca, D.: Membership constraints in formal concept analysis. In: Proceedings of IJCAI 2015, pp. 3186–3192. AAAI Press (2015)
20. Rudolph, S., Săcărea, C., Troancă, D.: Towards a navigation paradigm for triadic concepts. In: Baixeries, J., Sacarea, C., Ojeda-Aciego, M. (eds.) ICFCA 2015. LNCS (LNAI), vol. 9113, pp. 252–267. Springer, Cham (2015). https://doi.org/10.1007/978-3-319-19545-2_16
21. Schleimer, S., Wilkerson, D.S., Aiken, A.: Winnowing: local algorithms for document fingerprinting. In: Proceedings of ACM SIGMOD, pp. 76–85 (2003)
22. Stanford MOSS Home. https://theory.stanford.edu/~aiken/moss/. Accessed April 2021
23. Striewe, M., Goedicke, M.: A review of static analysis approaches for programming exercises. In: Kalz, M., Ras, E. (eds.) CAA 2014. CCIS, vol. 439, pp. 100–113. Springer, Cham (2014). https://doi.org/10.1007/978-3-319-08657-6_10
24. Tilley, T., Cole, R., Becker, P., Eklund, P.: A survey of formal concept analysis support for software engineering activities. In: Ganter, B., Stumme, G., Wille, R. (eds.) Formal Concept Analysis. LNCS (LNAI), vol. 3626, pp. 250–271. Springer, Heidelberg (2005). https://doi.org/10.1007/11528784_13

Nested Conceptual Graphs
for Information Fusion Traceability

Claire Laudy[(✉)] and Charlotte Jacobé de Naurois

Thales, Palaiseau, France
{claire.laudy,charlotte.jacobedenaurois}@thalesgroup.com

Abstract. InSyTo is a toolbox of algorithms for information fusion and query relying on the conceptual graphs formalism and subgraph isomorphism search. InSyTo was used in order to develop many applications in different domains. Although the framework was used in several application domain and well received by end-users, they highlighted an urgent need for traceability within the information fusion process. We propose here an improvement of the toolbox, in order to embed traceability feature inside the fusion algorithm. The underlying conceptual graph representation of the information was extended from basic conceptual graph to Nested Typed Graphs. A lineage nested graph is added to each concept of the initial information graph, that contains it's processing history through the several processing steps. The lineage graph contains the information concerning the initial sources of each elementary information item (concept), as well as the fusion operations that were applied on them. The main advantage of this new development is the capacity of having a trustworthy framework aware of the current observed situation, as well as the interpretations that were used to build this situation from elementary observations coming from different sources. In this paper, after presenting the context of our work, we recall of the InSyTo toolbox approach and functionalities. We then define the new information representation and operations that we proposed for a matter of traceability handling.

Keywords: Conceptual graphs · Information fusion · Traceability

1 Introduction

With the aim of developing systems that use semantic information for decision support, we chose to use the InSyTo toolbox that provides functions for soft information fusion and management and was previously developed. Soft information is a term used in the information fusion scientific community to differentiate information provided by physical sensors (called "hard data" or "hard information") from information provided by humans (e.g., texts). It is called soft as it can embed subjectivity and needs complex tools in order to be transformed into information that can be further processed by fusion algorithms. InSyTo is

© Springer Nature Switzerland AG 2021
T. Braun et al. (Eds.): ICCS 2021, LNAI 12879, pp. 19–33, 2021.
https://doi.org/10.1007/978-3-030-86982-3_2

based on generic algorithms for semantic graphs fusion and comparison that may be adapted to a specific application domain through the use of an ontology. It was used in many projects in the past, as different as crisis management, [10], marketing content design [9] or oceanographic observation [10]. However, if the use of soft information was very much appreciated by these end-users, they also expressed the need to understand where the synthesized information comes from. They express the need for traceability capability within situation awareness and decision support systems provided. Indeed, traceability is highlighted in different guidelines and recommendations for a trustworthy AI [12,13].

In this paper, we propose an approach for traceability handling as an extension of InSyTo. InSyTo functions rely on the use of Conceptual Graph formalism for semantic information representation. Our approach to traceability is based on the use of nested conceptual graphs, in order to express, for each elementary component of the information, a lineage graph that expresses the whole 'history" of the information item throughout its evolutions regarding fusion and aggregation processes.

The paper is organised as follows. Section 2 provides the context and related works. It recalls the needs that we faced in previous and current projects regarding traceability and presents the basics of the InSyTo toolbox, emphasizing on the fusion approach that is used, regarding which traceability is an important issue. In Sect. 3, we describe the evolution we have performed in order to embed traceability capacity within the toolbox operations. After presenting the general approach, we define formally our proposition. Section 4 finally discusses and concludes our paper and presents future directions for our work.

2   Context

2.1   Conceptual Graphs as Formalism for Information Representation

Our aim is to develop systems for which the interaction with human operators is crucial in order to understand the results of the different processes. These results must be easily understandable, as well as should be the integrated analysis processes that lead to these results, such as information aggregation and fusion.

Therefore, the knowledge representation must easily be understood. Therefore, we propose to rely on the use of conceptual graphs. Conceptual graphs (CG) have been formalized by Mugnier and Chein [3] as finite bipartite labelled graphs where the building units of CG are types. Such graphs were proposed by J. Sowa in [14] as a graphical representation of logic. They allow representing knowledge in a easily readable manner for humans, experts of specific application domain, but non experts of knowledge representation formalism.

Several tools exist in order to create conceptual graphs knowledge bases and interact with them. Among them, Cogui [7] enables one to create a Conceptual graphs knowledge base and offers imports and exports capabilities to different semantic web formats. Cogitant [5] is a C++ platform that provides capacities to represent the different elements of the conceptual graphs model, as well as functions to reason over and manipulate the graphs. InSyTo is a JAVA tool-box of algorithms for information fusion and query relying on the conceptual graphs formalism and sub-graph isomorphism search proposed in [2]. It was fur-ther improved with uncertainty management capabilities [4] which enables us to manage some of the imperfection that may be found on reports provided by humans. For the information aggregation and fusion part of our work, we chose to use the functions provided by InSyTo for the possibility to add domain knowledge in order to tune the functions. We describe the toolbox hereafter.

2.2 InSyTo: A Toolbox for Information Fusion

InSyTo is a toolbox that contains several core functions. These functions can be combined in order to provide advanced semantic information management functions. InSyTo core functions are depicted in Fig. 1 and described hereafter.

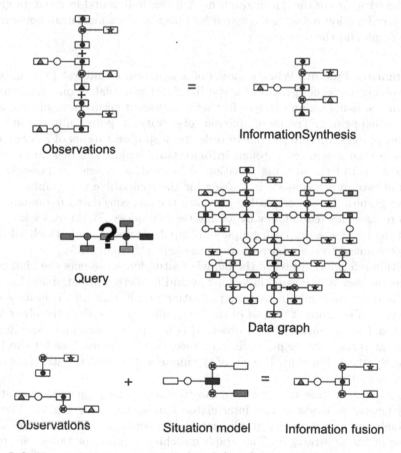

Fig. 1. InSyTo core functions. In this figure, each graph represent a conceptual graph. A rectangle represents a concept and a circle represents a relation. The InSyTo core have mainly 3 functions describe below.

Information Synthesis enables one to collect and organize information about a specific subject. Through information synthesis, all the gathered information items are organized into a network. The redundant part of the information items are detected and eliminated.

The fusion strategies are used within information synthesis, in order to enable the fusion of information items that are slightly different but describe the same situation of the real life. These discrepancies may appear when different sources of information with potentially different levels of precision for instance, are used to draw a picture of an on-going situation.

Information Query. All the instances of information corresponding to a specified graph pattern may be found within a network of information, through the **information query** function.

The specialization relationship between the query and the data graphs implies that the structure of the query graph must be entirely found in the data graph. The query function relies on the search for injective homomorphism between the query graph and the data graph.

Information Fusion. When a model of a situation of interest (e.g. an activity involving a specific person at a specific date) is available, one may want to monitor the situation and trigger further processes if an instance of such a situation is happening. Therefore, different observations, potentially coming from different sources, are filtered out in order to keep observations of interest only. They are then assembled through **information fusion** in order to provide a representation of the ongoing situation of interest, as precise as possible. The fusion of two graphs consists in looking for the compatible sub-graphs between the two graphs. These compatible parts are the one considered redundant. The fusion remove this redundancy by joining the two nodes. To do so, we keep only one of the two nodes for each couple of compatible nodes, and attach all nodes that were linked to the removed one to the kept ("fused") node.

Within information fusion, the model of situation represents the kind of situations the user is interested in looking at and be alerted about. Therefore, it is formalised as a partially instantiated situation graph, that may contain generic node types. Therefore, it is most of the times more generic than the observation graphs and is instantiated with observed concepts that are more specific and contain markers. Further more, fusion strategies may be used, as for the Information Synthesis function. The use of the model constraints the structure of the fused observation.

To implement these core function, InSyTo encompasses a generic graph-based fusion algorithm made of two interrelated components (see Fig. 2). The first component is a generic sub-graph matching algorithm, which itself relies on the use of fusion strategies. The graph matching component takes care of the overall structures of the initial and fused observations. It is in charge of the structural consistency of the fused information, regarding the structures of the initial observations, within the fusion process.

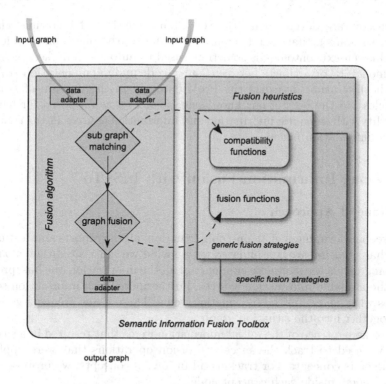

Fig. 2. InSyTo algorithm

The fusion strategy part is made of similarity, compatibility and functions over elements of the graphs to be fused. They enable the customization of the generic fusion algorithm according to the context in which it is used.

2.3 The Need for Traceability in Information Fusion

InSyTo is used in order to develop high level information managing functions such as alarm raising, event detection, inconsistency detection in reports. It was deployed on several projects ranging from crisis management to investigation and oceanography. In many of these application, if the management of information coming from soft information sources (social media, police reports...) was a new and interesting topic, the need for traceability of the information was raised.

Indeed, when multiple fusions occurs on graphs, it could be necessary to know where and how this information was constructed, to find and/or follow the history of the fusion process and to measure the ability of the fusion system to provide an accurate and unbroken historical record of its inputs and the chain of operations that led to its conclusions. Keeping trace of a all fusion processes in a way that is verifiable and reproducible is necessary for different use-cases.

This feature is called **traceability**. Traceability is known to be applicable to measurement, supply chain, software development, healthcare and security also. On software development, the traceability consists of following relations between software artifacts and requirements during the development life cycle [6]. In this context, ontology is sometimes used to automatically keep a trace of requirements [1], or artifacts between source code and documentation [16].

In the litterature, it exists the ProV ontology in the domain of trust [9]. Nonetheless, to the best of our knowledge, no work was proposed for handling traceability with semantic information and information sources in the context of semantic information fusion.

3   Tracing Information Fusion with InSyTo

3.1   General Approach

When keeping awareness of an on-going situation, all the reports and testimonies about that situation are consolidated within what we call a *situation graph*. This situation graph is the synthetic summary of all the information one has, provided by all the available information sources. Furthermore, each information sources provides what we call initial information items. These items are aggregated and fused together into the situation graph.

So, to keep a trace of the initial information items that resulted in a situation graph, we need to track the successive fusion operations that were applied to each one of its concepts. For tracking all fusions of concepts, we propose to add a *lineage graph* inside each concept node.

At the beginning, before the fusion process, the lineage graph of a specific concept node contains specific information about the source of this information.

3.2   Background: Simple, Nested and Typed Conceptual Graphs

Conceptual Graphs (CGs) [3] are a family of formalisms of knowledge representation, made of ontological and factual knowledge. They are bipartite graphs defined over ontological knowledge stored in the vocabulary.

The ontological part of a CG is a *vocabulary*, defined as a 5-tuple $V = (T_C, T_R, \sigma, I, \tau)$. T_C and T_R that respectively correspond to concept and relation types are two partially ordered disjoint finite sets, where ordering corresponds to generalisation. An example of T_C, used in the illustration below is given in Fig. 3. It contains a greatest element $\top$. T_R is partitioned into subsets $T_R^1 \ldots T_R^k$, $1 \ldots k$ ($k \geq 1$) respectively, meaning that each relation type has an associated fixed arity. σ is a mapping associating a signature to each relation. I is a set of individual markers. τ is a mapping from I to T_C.

The conceptual graphs themselves represent facts. In our work, they represent the situations that are observed. A CG is a 4-tuple $G = (C,R,E,label)$. G is a bipartite labeled multi-graph as illustrated on Fig. 4. A CG is made of concept and relation nodes. On Fig. 4, the rectangular boxes represent concept nodes and the ovals represent relation nodes. C and R correspond to concept and relation nodes, where elements of C are pairs from $T_C \times I$ and elements of R are elements

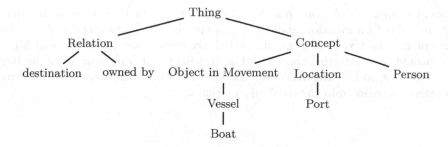

Fig. 3. A simplified vocabulary example

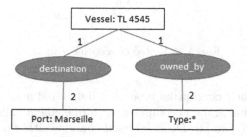

Fig. 4. An example of conceptual graph $G1$. The rectangular boxes represent concept nodes and the ovals represent relation nodes.

of T_C. E contains all the edges connecting elements of C and R and *label* is a labelling function.

Concept nodes are made of a conceptual type defined in T_C and an individual marker. The term **concept** is used to refer to a concept node. The concepts represent the "things" or entities that exist. A concept is labeled with two components: the conceptual type and the individual marker.

The **conceptual type** defines the category to which the entity belongs. For instance, in Fig. 4 the concept [Port: :Marseille] is an instance of the category Port, i.e., its conceptual type is Port.

The **individual marker** relates a concept to a specific object of the world. The object represented by [Port: :Marseille] has the name (or value) Marseille. The individual markers may also be undefined. An undefined or generic individual marker is either blank or noted with a star *, if the individual object referred to is unknown.

The term **relation** is used to refer to a relation node. The relation nodes of a conceptual graph indicate the relations that hold between the different entities of the situation that is represented. Each relation node is labeled with a relation type that points out the kind of relation that is represented.

Nested Conceptual Graphs are an extension of basic conceptual graphs. They are used in order to provide different levels of knowledge related to concepts of a graph. While concepts and relations linked to a concept provide external contextual information about the concept, internal information about the concept may be provided as graph, nested inside the concept. Chein and Mugnier provide the didactic example in Fig. 5, where a drawing, made by the boy Paul sits on a table (external contextual knowledge). Furthermore, this drawing represents a green train (internal information).

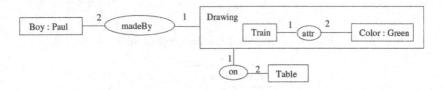

Fig. 5. A nested conceptual graph.

In addition to their conceptual types and individual markers, each concept c of a nested conceptual graph encompasses a third element called *description* of c and denoted $Descr(c)$ in [3]. $Descr(c)$ itself contains either a nested conceptual graph that describes the contents of the concept c or the value $**$ meaning that no further nested description is available.

Nested Typed Graphs are used when the universe of discourse is broken into independent parts. In our study, the situation graph and its set of lineage nested graphs define different parts of knowledge that may not be mixed. Thus, nested typed graphs appear to be naturally well suited in order to represent the tracked situation graphs, broken into the situation itself and the historical knowledge of the fusion operations over the situation concepts.

3.3   Nested Typed Graphs as Concepts' Lineage

As explained in the general approach, the traceability of each concept of a fused situation graph is a property of this concept containing internal information about its state and its so called *history* through the fusion operations. Thus, we add a *nested lineage graph* to each concept node of an information graph. For each concept c of a situation graph, this lineage graph is added to the concept, additionally to the type and marker that the basic conceptual graph already contains, as the value of $Descr(c)$.

The lineage graph of a concept is a nested typed graph, defined on a specific vocabulary and with a limited number of relations that we define hereafter. The situation graph is defined on a different vocabulary than the lineage graphs. The two sets of graphs, situation and lineage will never be mixed during the fusion of 2 situation graphs. However, the fusion of two situation graphs modifies the set of lineage graphs as defined hereafter. To emphasize on this distinction, we use typed graphs for situation and lineages graphs, each having a different type from the set *Situation, Lineage*. Figure 7 presents the tree of graph types for our tracked situation graphs.

At the beginning, before the fusion process, the lineage graph of a specific concept node contains specific information about the source of this information. Figure 6 depicts an example of lineage graphs before a fusion operation has occur.

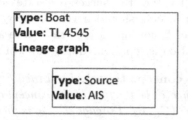

Fig. 6. Example of the definition a concept with type: Boat, Value: TL4545 and lineage graph. The Lineage graph is composed of type: Source, Value: AIS, that is to say the [*Boat* : *TL*4545] cames from AIS source.

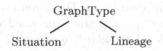

Fig. 7. Types of graphs used within InSyTo

In order to ease the understanding, in the following definitions we refer to elements of a situation graph such as concepts and relations using the adjective *situation* (*situation concept* and *situation relation* for instance), while we use the adjective *lineage* for the elements of the lineage graph.

Definition 1 (Tracked situation Graph). *A tracked situation graph S is a nested typed basic graph. The graph S is of type* Situation.

Definition 2 (Tracked situation concept). *Each concept node of a tracked situation graph is called a* tracked situation concept. *The field description of a tracked situation concept node c contains the lineage graph of c, denoted Lineage(c).*

Definition 3 (Lineage graph). *The* lineage graph *of a tracked situation con-cept c is a typed basic conceptual graph denoted Lineage(c). Lineage(c) is of type* Lineage. *It is defined on a vocabulary* $T_{lineage} = (C_L, R_L, Lineage, I)$, *where* C_L *and* R_L *are respectively the partially ordered set of concepts and relations of the lineage graph defined hereafter.*

It is to worth noting that as the lineage graph of a concept c describes the evolution of c through the sequence of fusion operations that were applied on different instances of this concept, the c and its lineage graph share multiple co-reference links. However, as each level of the lineage graph describes a different context of observation of c (i.e. the successive states of c and its successive values), the co-referent concepts should never be merged. The different levels represent the sequences of fusion operations that were applied on the concept nodes. Each fusion operation is represented as a level of nesting in the graphs.

Definition 4 (Lineage concept types). *Let Lineage(c) be the lineage graph of the concept c and let type(c) be the type of the concept c. Lineage(c) is defined on a vocabulary* $T_{lineage} = (C_L, R_L, Lineage, I)$ C_L *is theall concepts from situa-tion vocabulary, the uncomparable types* Source, FusionStrategy, FusionFunction *and* SimilarityMeasure *and their descendants.*

The root part of the tree of conceptual types C_L is depicted on Fig. 8. The *FusionStrategy, FusionFunction* and *SimilarityMeasure* types may have addi-tional sub-types, according to the fusion strategies defined and used within the InSyTo specific domain application. For a matter of readability, we noted *TrackedConceptTypeSubTree* the sub tree composed of the subsequent types: $type(c) \cup ancestor(type(c)) \cup descendant(type(c))$.

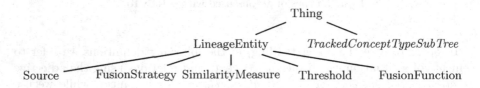

Fig. 8. Set of concept types for the lineage graphs

Definition 5 (Lineage relations). *The set of lineage relation types* R_L *is unordered and the set of lineage relations signatures is composed as follows.*

- *compatibility_function: FusionStrategy* $\mapsto$ *SimilarityMeasure * Threshold*
- *fusion_function: FusionStrategy* $\mapsto$ *FusionFunction*
- *produced_by: FusionStrategy* $\mapsto$ *TrackedConceptTypeeSubTree * TrackedCon-ceptTypeeSubTree*

3.4   Information Fusion

The fusion over situation graphs based on the jin operaton over the graphs, where
the join of concepts is replaced by a fusion function over the concepts, that,
among others, takes the two markers m1 and m2 and produce a new one. The
new marker of a fused concept is processed through the fusion strategies, applied
to the two initial concepts. This new marker can be m1 or m2, a combination of
the marker or the result of another computation over these markers. It depends
on the fusion function. A detailed definition is present in [8] and we briefly
introduce fusion strategies hereafter.

Fusion strategies are heuristics that are part of the merge operation of concepts between conceptual graphs. They are rules encoding domain knowledge
and fusion heuristics that are used to compute the fused value of two different
but compatible concept nodes. On the one hand, the fusion strategies extend the
notion of compatibility that is used in the maximal join operation. According to
some fusion strategy, two entities with two different values may be compatible
and thus fusable. On the other hand, the strategies encompass functions that
give the result of the fusion of two compatible values.

Fusion Strategies. The fusion functions available in the toolbox are are
expressed as the composition of two functions:

Let E be the set of concept nodes defined on a support S. Let G_1 and G_2 be
two conceptual graphs defined on S. A fusion strategy $strategy_{fusion}$ is defined
as follows:

$$strategy_{fusion} = f_{fusion} \circ f_{comp} : E \times E \rightarrow E \cup \{E \times E\}$$

where $f_{comp} : E \times E \rightarrow \{true, false\} \times E \times E$ is a function testing the compatibility of two concept nodes, and f_{fusion} is a fusion function upon the concepts
nodes of the graphs. The extended version of f_{fusion}, taking into account the
nested lineage graph, will be formally defined in the next section.

The compatibility function is defined by the similarity between the values
(markers) of two concept nodes. This similarity is defined by domain experts,
given the requirements of the application. The definition of the similarity function makes it possible to take account of context of the considered concepts.

The similarity measure is compared to a threshold defined by domain experts,
thus the compatibility function f_{comp} is then defined as follows:

$$f_{comp}(c_1, c_2) = sim(c_1, c_2) \geq threshold_{sim}$$

The fusion strategies applied on two concept nodes result either in a fused
concept node if the initial nodes are compatible, or in the initial nodes themselves
if they are incompatible.

The similarity function and fusion function are defined according to the end-
users' need and may be taking into account either neighbouring nodes or even
the whole initial graphs.

3.5   Tracked Fusion of Situation Graphs

As fusion strategies may not be a commutative operation, according to the specific fusion functions used, there is a need for traceability when applying several fusion operations on several situation graphs into a single situation graph. We define hereafter the tracked fusion operation over two situation graphs. The fusion strategies are not impacted by the tracking of fusion history into the lineage graph, however, their use must be memorized in the lineage graph.

f_{fusion} is a higher level function, taking into parameter three fusion functions, each one applying on one of the elements of the concept node:

- $fusion_{type}(c_1, c_2) = most\_general\_subtype(type(c_1), type(c_2)) = type(c)$
- $fusion_{marker}(c_1, c_2 = fusion(c_1, c_2)$ where $fusion : \{true, false\} \times E \times E \rightarrow E \cup \{E \times E\}$ is a fusion function upon the concepts nodes of the graphs that is application dependant.
- $fusion_{lineage}(c_1, c_2)$ is the fusion operator on lineages defined hereafter.

Definition 6 (Lineage graphs fusion operation). *Let G_1 and G_2 be two situation graphs defined on $V = (T_C, T_R, \sigma, I, \tau)$.*

Let $G_1 = (C_1, R_1, E_1, label_1)$ and $G_2 = (C_2, R_2, E_2, label_2)$.

Let c_1 and c_2 be two concepts defined of respectively G_1 and G_2. Let L_1 and L_2 be the lineage graphs of respectively c_1 and c_2.

The fusion operator over lineage graphs is defined as follows:

$$fusion_{lineage} : C_1 \times C_2 \rightarrow C_L,$$

with E_L the set of concepts of the fused lineage graph L.

The result of the fusion of the two lineage graphs is as follows:

$$
\begin{aligned}
fusion_{lineage}(c_1, c_2) = \quad\quad\quad\quad\quad\quad\quad\quad\quad\quad\quad\quad & L \\
= \quad produced\_by(FusionStrategy(f), c_1, c_2) & \\
\wedge compatibility\_function(FusionStrategy(f), & \\
SimilarityMeasure(sim(c_1, c_2)), & \\
Threshold(threshold_{sim})) & \\
\wedge fusion\_function(FusionStrategy(f), & \\
FusionFunction(fusion_{marker}(c_1, c_2))) &
\end{aligned}
$$

L is the nested typed graph depicted on the green part of the Fig. 9.

To rebuild the original sequence of operation, one needs to walk through the graph, starting for the deepest level of nested graph up to the first level and reconstruct the fusion operation that occurred at each change of level.

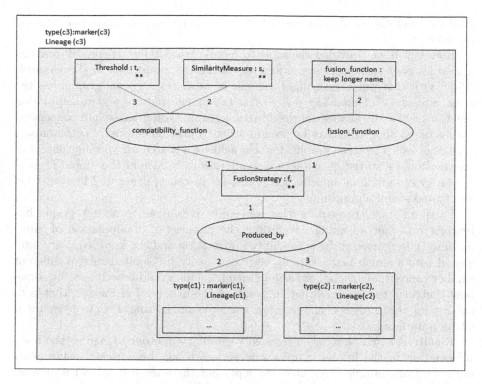

Fig. 9. Concept c_3 (fusion of (c_1 and c_2)) and its lineage graph resulting from the fusion of the two concepts c_1 and c_2 in the green part. The "..." can represent different sources of information or fusions that occurred prior to the one described on the picture. These sequences of fusions are each represented by a lineage graph nested in the upper concept.

4   Discussion and Conclusion

We proposed an improvement to the InSyTo toolbox which enables traceability capacity as the use of nested graph with a lineage graph in order to embed traceability feature inside the fusion algorithm. A lineage nested graph is added to each concept of the initial information graph, that contains it's processing history through the several processing steps. The lineage graph contains the information concerning the initial sources of each elementary information item (concept), as well as the fusion operations that were applied on them.

This improvement enables the end-users to understand where the synthetic information in the situation graph comes from. Thanks to the lineage graphs of each concepts of the situation graph, one may rebuild the whole aggregation and fusion process, even in cases where the fusion strategies are not commutative. We developed a first use case and were able to visualize the operations achieved on information items. Adding traceability to the applications developed with the framework improves the trust end-users have on the system through the availability of explainable elements over the underlying and aggregation fusion processes.

However, if we provided the tools to handle traceability, there still remains a need for easy visualisation and analysis of the trace information (for example [15]). With that purpose in mind, the use of nested conceptual graphs has the great advantage of enabling one to use the same analysis and manipulation functions as for the analysis of the situation graph. Graph based and conceptual graphs based algorithms can be used in order to provide end-users with analysis capacities over the trace graphs. On can achieve a search for specific sources of information, or statistics of the fusion operations used and the global level of similarity of individual information items, for instance, using well known, tried and tested graph algorithms.

Furthermore, representing the concept's lineage as a nested graph has brought an other advantage, regarding the easiness of manipulation of information. Indeed, even if the traceability information and the knowledge are integrated into a single nested graph, they can easily be isolated in two different smaller conceptual graphs [$situation, lineage$]. This would be achieved by somehow "cutting" the nested situation graph at the first level of lineage, that is to say cutting the lineages of the situation concepts and storing them in a separated graph data base.

Finally, if we chose to use a reduced vocabulary in order to express the trace information in the lineage graphs, our approach can be enriched using other ontology (for example [11]). One can represent the lineage graph with another vocabulary and relations if necessary. Identically, if one wants to improve the toolbox with other operations, their application to a concept node can also be represented in the $lineage$.

Acknowledgment. This work was partially performed under the 883347 H2020 project EFFECTOR, which has received funding from the European Union's Horizon 2020 Program. This paper reflects only the authors' view, and the European Commission is not liable to any use that may be made of the information contained therein.

References

1. Assawamekin, N., Sunetnanta, T., Pluempitiwiriyawej, C.: Ontology-based multi-perspective requirements traceability framework. Knowl. Inf. Syst. **25**(3), 493–522 (2010)
2. Laudy, C., Ganascia, J.G.: Using maximal join for information fusion. In: Graph Structures for Knowledge Representation and Reasoning (GKR 2009) Collocated with the Twenty-first International Joint Conference on Artificial Intelligence (IJCAI-09) (2009)
3. Chein, M., Mugnier, M.L.: Graph-Based Knowledge Representation: Computational Foundations of Conceptual Graphs. Springer, Heidelberg (2008). https://doi.org/10.1007/978-1-84800-286-9
4. Fossier, S., Laudy, C., Pichon, F.: Managing uncertainty in conceptual graph-based soft information fusion. In: Proceedings of the 16th International Conference on Information Fusion, pp. 930–937. IEEE (2013)

5. Genest, D., Salvat, E.: A platform allowing typed nested graphs: how CoGITo became CoGITaNT. In: Mugnier, M.-L., Chein, M. (eds.) ICCS-ConceptStruct 1998. LNCS, vol. 1453, pp. 154–161. Springer, Heidelberg (1998). https://doi.org/10.1007/BFb0054912
6. Gotel, O.C., Finkelstein, C.: An analysis of the requirements traceability problem. In: Proceedings of IEEE International Conference on Requirements Engineering, pp. 94–101. IEEE (1994)
7. Hamdan, W., Khazem, R., Rebdawi, G., Croitoru, M., Gutierrez, A., Buche, P.: On ontological expressivity and modelling argumentation schemes using COGUI. In: Bramer, M., Petridis, M. (eds.) Research and Development in Intelligent Systems XXXI, pp. 5–18. Springer, Cham (2014). https://doi.org/10.1007/978-3-319-12069-0_1
8. Laudy, C.: Semantic Knowledge Representations for Soft Data Fusion – Efficient Decision Support Systems - Practice and Challenges From Current to Future. Chiang Jao Publisher (2011)
9. Laudy, C., Mattioli, J., Mattioli, L.: Semantic information fusion algebraic framework applied to content marketing. In: Proceedings of the 21st International Conference on Information Fusion, FUSION 2013, Cambridge, UK, 10–13 July 2018, pp. 2338–2345 (2018). https://doi.org/10.23919/ICIF.2018.8455566
10. Laudy, C., Ruini, F., Zanasi, A., Przybyszewski, M., Stachowicz, A.: Using social media in crisis management: SOTERIA fusion center for managing information gaps. In: 20th International Conference on Information Fusion, FUSION 2017, Xi'an, China, 10–13 July 2017, pp. 1–8. IEEE (2017). 10.23919/ICIF.2017.8009880, https://doi.org/10.23919/ICIF.2017.8009880
11. Lebo, T., et al.: PROV-O: the PROV ontology (2013)
12. Sharma, S., Henderson, J., Ghosh, J.: CERTIFAI: counterfactual explanations for robustness, transparency, interpretability, and fairness of artificial intelligence models. arXiv preprint arXiv:1905.07857 (2019)
13. Smuha, N.A.: The EU approach to ethics guidelines for trustworthy artificial intelligence. Comput. Law Rev. Int. **20**(4), 97–106 (2019)
14. Sowa, J.F.: Conceptual Structures. Information Processing in Mind and Machine, Addison-Wesley, Reading (1984)
15. Ware, C.: Information Visualization: Perception for Design. Morgan Kaufmann (2019)
16. Zhang, Y., Witte, R., Rilling, J., Haarslev, V.: An ontology-based approach for traceability recovery. In: 3rd International Workshop on Metamodels, Schemas, Grammars, and Ontologies for Reverse Engineering (ATEM 2006), Genoa, pp. 36–43 (2006)

Generating Layered Enterprise Architectures with Conceptual Structures

Matt Baxter[1], Simon Polovina[1(✉)], Wim Laurier[2], and Mark von Rosing[3]

[1] Conceptual Structures Research Group, Sheffield Hallam University, Sheffield, UK
a7033771@my.shu.ac.uk, S.Polovina@shu.ac.uk
[2] Université Saint-Louis, Brussels, Belgium
wim.laurier@usaintlouis.be
[3] LEADing Practice, La Bruère-sur-Loir, France
mvr@leadingpractice.com

Abstract. Enterprise Architecture (EA) uses metamodels to document and align organisations' business, information, and technology domains. This structure then enables these domains to work in harmony. Layered Enterprise Architecture Development (LEAD) builds upon EA by introducing layered metaobjects connected by semantic relations that make up LEAD's layered metamodel. Previously, an algorithm was developed to elicit active semantic relations to achieve a view highlighting the metaobject dependencies. Subsequently, CG-FCA (Conceptual Graph and Formal Concept Analysis) and a LEAD case study were used to develop an enhanced algorithm that also generates the LEAD layers. The resulting layered FCA lattice shows a way to discover the hitherto hidden insights in LEAD, including the relationship between business and information technology.

Keywords: Business problem solving · Conceptual graphs and formal concept analysis · Layered enterprise architecture

1 Introduction

Enterprise Architecture (EA) promotes the alignment of business, information, and technology domains within organisations by a principled framework, method, and approach that draws on holistic thinking. The Layered Enterprise Architecture Development (LEAD) Ontology adds to this rigour by structuring that thinking according to 91 metaobjects arranged in business, information, and technology layers and categorised further via various sublayers [4,7]. These metaobjects are linked by semantic relations both within and across layers, thus describing how a metaobject views itself in relation to another. Consequently,

In Press: ICCS 2021 (https://iccs-conference.org/), Springer LNAI.

the interdependencies within organisations can be elucidated and used to the benefit of industry decision-makers.

Conceptual Graphs (CG) represent knowledge via the formalised ordering of concepts and their relations [6]. Formal Concept Analysis (FCA) uses a principled approach to ascertain the conceptual hierarchy of a set of objects and their attributes [3], meaning LEAD's metaobjects can be ordered using their shared attributes. Ergo, the CG-FCA application allows us to convert the ternary semantic relations of LEAD into binary relations, which are then mathematically validated as a conceptual hierarchy by the FCA element of the application [1]. By complementing CG-FCA with an algorithm that identifies the active semantic relations (defined as those relations whereby a metaobject directs another), we aim to create a Formal Concept Lattice (FCL) that is ordered according to LEAD's three business, information, and technology layers.

2   The Metamodel Diagram

Figure 1 is a metamodel created using the Enterprise Plus (E+) software (www. enterpriseplus.tools). LEADing Practice (www.leadingpractice.com) is a not-for-profit group of LEAD practitioners, and are the developers of E+. This software captures LEAD's comprehensive reference content, including its metaobjects, semantic relations, and supporting artefacts. Figure 1 reflects the warehouse pick pack process of a UK manufacturer, based on the LEAD Enterprise Ontology (LEAD ID#-ES20001ALL) [7]. Figure 1's semantic relations are two-way, revealing how a metaobject views itself in relation to another and vice versa. The metamodel in the figure includes 30 two-way semantic relations, with a modeller-imposed limit of one relation between each adjacent sublayer, and zero instances of relations that span more than one sublayer. These choices were made with two objectives in mind. Firstly, preservation of readability—the LEAD metamodel contains 147 two-way semantic relations for the chosen metaobjects—and secondly, the promotion of accessibility for inexperienced EA users within the case study organisation. Thus, the salient semantic relations were selected to develop a robust and digestible narrative for those users. The metamodel was created to facilitate the deconstruction of its abstract concepts and their subsequent relation to known real-world organisational elements.

3   Activating and Layering the Metamodel

The CGtoFCA algorithm implemented in the CG-FCA application translates the ternary relations of CGs into binary relations, thereby preparing them for processing by FCA [1]. The concepts are then presented in a Formal Concept Lattice (FCL), which visualises the mathematical rigour of FCA. CG-FCA was augmented with an algorithm to create a graph of active verbs that supports a chain of command, highlighting objects that act upon other objects [2]. However, this approach took little account of LEAD's layers, adversely impacting the readability of the active direction graph. The proposed revised algorithm

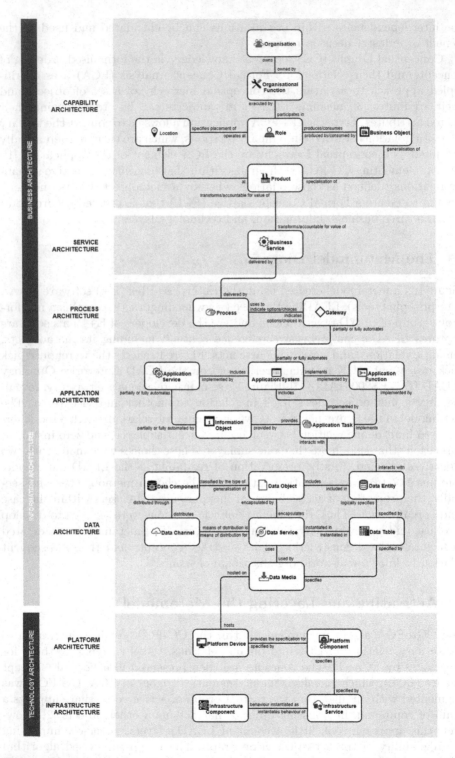

Fig. 1. Warehouse pick pack metamodel (based on LEADing Practice Meta Model)

introduces LEAD layering, delivering a more lucid, mathematically validated representation of the metamodel.

3.1 Methodology

The proposed algorithm is depicted in Fig. 2. The stages are identification of active semantic relations, resolution of cycles, then the introduction of layering. The variables are A active model, B bidirectional model, o triple object, s triple subject, and v triple verb. While the human interpretation required by the algorithm renders it more of a 'pseudo-algorithm' at present, it remains suitable for our current purposes.

```
 1  begin
 2      A = ∅
 3      foreach ((o, v, s), (s, v', o)) ∈ B do
 4          if isPassive(v) then
 5              A = A ∪ (s, v', o)|((o, v, s), (s, v', o)) ∈ B
 6          else
 7              A = A ∪ (o, v, s)|((o, v, s), (s, v', o)) ∈ B
 8      C = TriplesInCycles(A)
 9      foreach (o, v, s) ∈ C do
10          if inMultipleCycles(o, v, s)) or isImplicityPassive(v)) then
11              A = A\(o, v, s)
12              A = A ∪ (s, v', o)|((o, v, s), (s, v', o)) ∈ B
13          if isTransitive((o, v, s)) then
14              A = A\(o, v, s)
15      S = ConceptsInSupremum(A)
16      foreach (o, v, s) ∈ A|o ∈ S and Count((o, α, β) ∈ A) > 1 do
17          A = A\(o, v, s)
18          A = A ∪ (s, v', o)|((o, v, s), (s, v', o)) ∈ B
19      I = ConceptsInInfimum(A)
20      foreach (o, v, s) ∈ A|s ∈ I and Count((α, β, s) ∈ A) > 1 do
21          A = A\(o, v, s)
22          A = A ∪ (s, v', o)|((o, v, s), (s, v', o)) ∈ B
23  end
```

Fig. 2. Layered active semantic relations algorithm

The initial steps mirror an earlier study, whereby an active direction graph is created by determining the active relations and resolving any unwanted semantic cycles [2]. Subsequently, LEAD layering was introduced by examining and modifying the compositions of the supremum (the top-most formal concept) and infimum (the bottom-most formal concept) in the FCL. Beginning with the supremum, the triples containing the incorrectly layered metaobject were reviewed so that the triple determined to be the least active could be inverted. Encompassed within this stage was the consideration of the wider data set. We were mindful that the number of instances of a metaobject could be either a source or a target in a triple. Therefore, we could avoid a scenario whereby resolving one metaobject's erroneous presence in the supremum or infimum would see it replaced by another. Such a situation could lead to a cycle of layering issues (incidentally, not to be confused with a cycle defined by the CG-FCA application). In situations where a least active triple could not be determined (e.g., due to identical semantic relations), the relation furthest down the LEAD index would be inverted. We now describe our findings from the algorithm in Fig. 2 according to the EA layering and usability principles highlighted in Fig. 1.

3.2   Findings

The 30 active semantic relations were selected from the two-way relations included in the metamodel and compiled in the 00ActiveAll.csv file, which was then processed by the CG-FCA application. The subsequent '00ActiveAll_report' file presented two cycles, shown below:

1. Cycle: Data Object - includes - Data Entity - logically specifies - Data Table - instantiated in - Data Service - encapsulates - Data Object
2. Cycle: Data Table - instantiated in - Data Service - uses - Data Media - logically specifies - Data Table

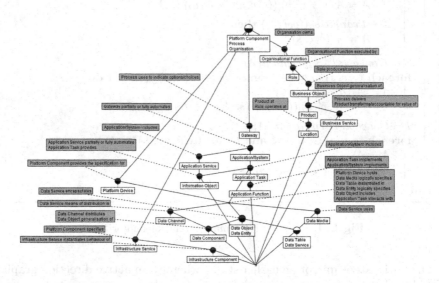

Fig. 3. 00ActiveAll lattice

Figure 3 shows the 00ActiveAll lattice, with a cycle indicated by the Data Table + Data Service object with no attributes. Furthermore, the Application

Task, Platform Device, Data Media, Data Channel, and Data Object + Data Entity concepts are linked to an infimum formal concept that is empty, i.e. one with no objects.

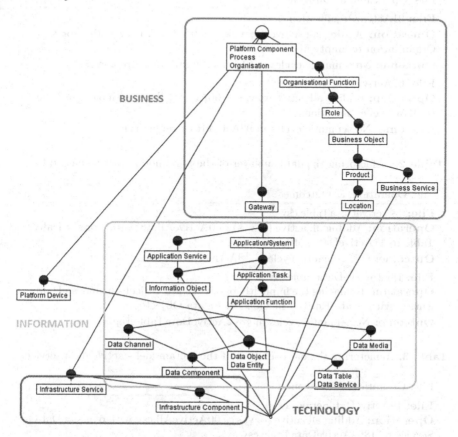

Fig. 4. 00ActiveAll lattice without attributes, LEAD layers indicated

Figure 4 reveals that LEAD layering is not a distant proposition for the 00ActiveAll lattice, although Platform Component and Platform Device are not presented in the appropriate LEAD layers. We note that while the 00ActiveAll lattice is (mostly) visually displayed in the LEAD layers, it is not so mathematically, e.g., Location and Business Service are positioned preceding the infimum at the bottom of the lattice (along with several other concepts). This outcome is evident by their direct line to the bottom-most empty concept. Overall, the 00ActiveAll lattice appears to suggest that LEAD layering is, to an extent, included in the activation of the semantic relations.

In Table 1, we initiate the refactoring of the lattice, whereby the 00ActiveAll file is broken down and rebuilt step-by-step to remove unwanted cycles[1].

---

[1] Due to space considerations and only two files presenting cycles, not all the steps are included in this paper.

Table 1. Refactoring the capability sublayer of the metamodel - active organisation and active role.

File, Operation, & Outcomes
File: 01ActiveOrganisation.csv **Operation:** Adding all active (o, v, s) ∈ 00ActiveAll.csv with o or s = Organisation to empty file **Outcome:** No semantic cycles in 01ActiveOrganisation_report.txt
File: 02ActiveRole.csv **Operation:** Adding all active (o, v, s) ∈ 00ActiveAll.csv with o or s = Role to 01ActiveOrganisation.csv **Outcome:** No semantic cycles in 02ActiveRole_report.txt

Table 2. Refactoring the data sublayer of the metamodel - active data table.

File, Operation, & Outcomes
File: 18ActiveDataTable.csv **Operation:** Adding all active (o, v, s) ∈ 00ActiveAll.csv with o or s = Data Table to 17ActiveDataEntity.csv **Outcome:** One semantic cycle in 18ActiveDataTable_report.txt
File: 18v2ActiveDataTable.csv **Operation:** Replacing the implicitly passive 'Data Object - includes - Data Entity' with 'Data Entity - included in - Data Object' **Outcome:** No semantic cycles in 18v2ActiveDataTable_report.txt

Table 3. Refactoring the data sublayer of the metamodel - active data service.

File, Operation, & Outcomes
File: 19ActiveDataService.csv **Operation:** Adding all active (o, v, s) ∈ 00ActiveAll.csv with o or s = Data Service to 18v2ActiveDataTable.csv **Outcome:** One semantic cycle in 19ActiveDataService_report.txt
File: 19v2ActiveDataService.csv **Operation:** Replacing the implicitly passive 'Data Table - instantiated in - Data Service' with 'Data Service - instantiated in - Data Table' **Outcome:** No semantic cycles in 19v2ActiveDataService_report.txt

18ActiveDataTable.csv and 19ActiveDataService.csv were the only two files to present any cycles, which were resolved using the operations documented in Tables 2 and 3.

Figure 5 displays the FCL for 25ActiveInfrastructureService, highlighting the effects of the refactoring process. Namely, both the Data Table + Data Service object without attributes and the empty formal concept linking various other formal concepts have been resolved. However, while the operation carried out in 19v2ActiveDataService (replacing 'Data Table - instantiated in - Data Service' with 'Data Service - instantiated in - Data Table') resolved an unwanted cycle, it also displaced Data Service from its appropriate position in the LEAD layers to within the supremum. This outcome suggests that the refactoring of the 00ActiveAll file has caused us to take a step backwards, away from our goal of an active, layered lattice. This position is supported by the continued presence of seven concepts (from all three layers) preceding the infimum, but with the addition of Data Service in the supremum. Furthermore, Fig. 5 overlays the 25ActiveInfrastructureService lattice with the LEAD layers, highlighting the absence of Data Service and Platform Component in the Information and Technology layers, respectively.

The absence of a metaobject as either a target or source metaobject in the triple composition—where the first triple element is the source, and the third is the target—corresponds with its presence in the FCL as either supremum or preceding infimum, respectively. To maintain the LEAD layer hierarchy, reorienting these metaobjects is the driving force behind the operations carried out and documented in Tables 4 and 5.

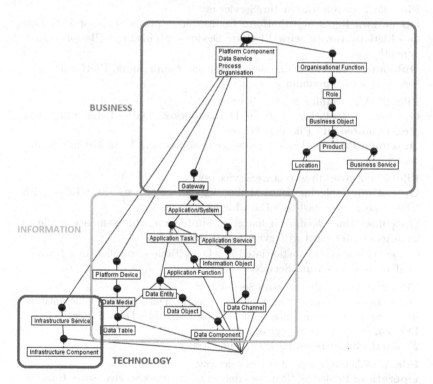

Fig. 5 25ActiveInfrastructureService lattice without attributes, LEAD layers indicated

Table 4 displays the operations performed to reposition Data Service and Platform Component to their appropriate LEAD layers while also removing Process from the supremum (as its presence there suggests it being equal to Organisation as a driving force). 25v2ActiveInfrastructureService and 25v7ActiveInfrastructureService are examples of operations that had active relations replaced with the passive relations ('Data Service - uses - Data Media' replaced with 'Data Media - used by - Data Service' and 'Process - delivers - Business Service' replaced with 'Business Service - delivered by - Process'). We also reversed the identical semantic relations in 25v6ActiveInfrastructureService (where distinguishing active/passive relations was not possible).

Table 4. Refactoring 25ActiveInfrastructureService lattice to achieve LEAD layering - supremum focus.

File, Operation, & Outcomes
File: 25v2ActiveInfrastructureService.csv **Operation:** Replacing 'Data Service - uses - Data Media' with 'Data Media - used by - Data Service' **Outcome:** Data Service no longer in supremum
File: 25v3ActiveInfrastructureService.csv **Operation:** Replacing 'Platform Component - provides the specification for - Platform Device' with 'Platform Device - specified by - Platform Component' **Outcome:** Platform Component no longer in supremum. Platform Device now in supremum
File: 25v4ActiveInfrastructureService.csv **Operation:** Replacing 'Platform Device - hosts - Data Media' with 'Data Media - hosted on - Platform Device' **Outcome:** Platform Device no longer in supremum. Data Media now in supremum
File: 25v5ActiveInfrastructureService.csv **Operation:** Replacing 'Data Media - logically specifies - Data Table' with 'Data Table - specified by - Data Media' **Outcome:** Data Media no longer in supremum. One semantic cycle in 25v5ActiveInfrastructureService_report.txt Cycle: Data Service - instantiated in - Data Table - specified by - Data Media - used by - Data Service
File: 25v6ActiveInfrastructureService.csv **Operation:** Replacing the implicitly passive 'Data Service - instantiated in - Data Table' with 'Data Table - instantiated in - Data Service' **Outcome:** No semantic cycles in 25v6ActiveInfrastructureService_report.txt
File: 25v7ActiveInfrastructureService.csv **Operation:** Replacing 'Process - delivers - Business Service' with 'Business Service - delivered by - Process' **Outcome:** Process no longer in supremum

Table 5 shows how we approached positioning a Technology-layer concept as the infimum. Active relations were again substituted for the passive rela-

Table 5. Refactoring 25ActiveInfrastructureService lattice to achieve LEAD layering–infimum focus.

File, Operation, & Outcomes
File: 25v8ActiveInfrastructureService.csv **Operation:** Replacing 'Product – at – Location' with 'Location – at – Product' **Outcome:** Location no longer preceding infimum
File: 25v9ActiveInfrastructureService.csv **Operation:** Replacing 'Application Task – implements – Application Function' with 'Application Function – implemented by – Application Task' **Outcome:** Application Function no longer preceding infimum
File: 25v10ActiveInfrastructureService.csv **Operation:** Replacing 'Application Task – provides – Information Object' with 'Information Object – provided by – Application Task' **Outcome:** Information Object no longer preceding infimum
File: 25v11ActiveInfrastructureService.csv **Operation:** Replacing 'Data Channel – distributes – Data Component' with 'Data Component – distributed through – Data Channel' **Outcome:** Data Component no longer preceding infimum. Data Channel now preceding infimum
File: 25v12ActiveInfrastructureService.csv **Operation:** Replacing 'Data Service – means of distribution is – Data Channel' with 'Data Channel – means of distribution for – Data Service' **Outcome:** Data Channel no longer preceding infimum. One semantic cycle in 25v12ActiveInfrastructureService_report.txt Cycle: Data Object - generalisation of - Data Component - distributed through - Data Channel - means of distribution for - Data Service - encapsulates - Data Object
File: 25v13ActiveInfrastructureService.csv **Operation:** Replacing the implicitly passive 'Data Service – encapsulates – Data Object' with 'Data Object – encapsulated by – Data Service' **Outcome:** Data Service now preceding infimum. No semantic cycles in 25v6ActiveInfrastructureService_report.txt
File: 25v14ActiveInfrastructureService.csv **Operation:** Replacing 'Data Table – instantiated in – Data Service' with 'Data Service – instantiated in – Data Table' **Outcome:** Data Service no longer preceding infimum. One semantic cycle in 25v14ActiveInfrastructureService_report.txt Cycle: Data Service - instantiated in - Data Table - specified by - Data Media - used by - Data Service
File: 25v15ActiveInfrastructureService.csv **Operation:** Replacing the implicitly passive 'Data Media – used by – Data Service' with 'Data Service – uses – Data Media' **Outcome:** No semantic cycles in 25v15ActiveInfrastructureService_report.txt

tion. There were two further instances of reversing identical semantic relations
(25v8ActiveInfrastructureService and 25v14ActiveInfrastructureService). Interestingly, the first operation performed is also the last, whereby reversing 'Data
Service - uses - Data Media' to remove Data Service from the supremum is then
itself reversed to complete the LEAD layered lattice. Other modellers could conceivably make different operation choices consistent with the algorithm, which
provides the overarching context under which such decisions can be made.

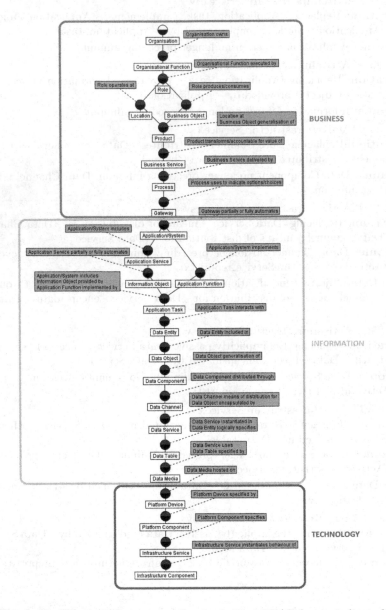

Fig. 6. 25v15ActiveInfrastructureService lattice, LEAD layers indicated

3.3   Layered Formal Concept Lattice

Figure 6, the visualisation of 25v15ActiveInfrastructureService, shows a successfully layered lattice. While the lattice is predominantly active, it includes various passive relations due to the operations performed to introduce LEAD layering.

For example, 'Business Service - delivered by - Process' is passive compared to 'Process - delivers - Business Service'. However, the other option was inverting 'Process - uses to indicate options/choices - Gateway', which would have removed Process from the supremum but replaced it with Gateway. This route would have an adverse effect on the link between the Business and Information layers ('Gateway - partially or fully automates -Application/System'), hence disrupting the layering.

4   Discussion

4.1   Implications

We have shown that an active direction graph can be rebuilt and visualised to display LEAD layering. While the initial 00ActiveAll graph and refactored 25ActiveInfrastructureService graph were largely layered, this demonstrates the contrast between how humans process information and how a computer does. Certain concepts in the 00ActiveAll and refactored 25ActiveInfrastructureService FCLs (Location, Business Service, Application Function, Information Object, Data Component, and Data Table), while not mathematically appropriately layered, could be positioned in a way that exhibits LEAD layering to the human eye. Our principled approach introduced this mathematical layering to narrow the gap between human and computer interpretation of the metamodel[2]. Readability is patently improved when contrasting the layered 25v15ActiveInfrastructureService graph with the purely active graphs (00ActiveAll and 25ActiveInfrastructureService), which has value for business decision-makers when identifying the levers required to effect change in an organisation. By attempting to create a directed graph that is both active and layered, we could elucidate that layering can be included in the remit of semantic relations. We also observed that LEAD's overall active flow is primarily top-down, nudged along by the occasional bottom-up active flow, suggesting that business mostly drives technology, with some instances where technology demonstrates that the reverse is possible.

4.2   Current Limitations

While a layered lattice was attained, there remains room for ongoing development of our approach. Firstly, the manual nature of the current approach means that there is room for interpretation and that the rigour in the execution of the

---

[2] Thus aligning information processing in mind and machine in accordance with the subtitle of Sowa's seminal text on Conceptual Structures [5].

pseudo-algorithm depends on the human executor. As the size of the data set increases, a human modeller can inadvertently stray from the proposed refactoring logic. While this challenge could be overcome by executing the logic in a computer-implemented algorithm, there are various considerations before such an approach can be developed. For example, the logical conclusion of selecting the 'least active' triple when applying FCL layering is that the semantic relations would need to be ranked to be interpreted by a computer, such as by using a passivity scale. However, other criteria could be included, such as the impact of the proposed operation on the lattice's intended (layered) structure. We created a layered lattice without introducing further relations to the metamodel portrayed by Fig. 1, but including other relations could add value. Within the omitted 117 two-way semantic relations possible with Fig. 1, other active relations may have resolved the supremum and infimum issues by other means while also minimising or even eradicating the need for the inclusion of semantically passive relations. Furthermore, there are more than 3,300 semantic relations in the LEAD ontology, thus fertile ground to explore.

4.3 Future Research

Given the above considerations, by inserting LEAD's integrated ontology elements that are only implicit in the case study metamodel, it would be possible to highlight further the levers that can be pulled to effect the desired change. This future work would also tease out more of LEAD's hitherto hidden insights. Furthermore, refinement of the algorithm could be pursued to integrate the activation and layering stages of the approach. We seek ways it can be more automated. One such method is by considering layering (and supremum and infimum composition) at the point of concept introduction. We could then conceivably resolve undesirable, complex-to-handle situations whereby the operations of one stage adversely impact another, contributing to expressive lattices dynamically modified according to any given organisational situation.

5 Conclusion

We have demonstrated a principled approach that successfully introduces LEAD layering to an active direction graph. Consequently, the outcome is an improved value proposition for industry, in the form of an inherently more readable illustration of change levers for business decision-makers. It would promote understanding of Layered Enterprise Architecture Development (LEAD) and the LEAD Enterprise Ontology, allowing organisations to exploit their information technology assets instead of being exploited by them.

References

1. Andrews, S., Polovina, S.: Exploring, reasoning with and validating directed graphs by applying formal concept analysis to conceptual graphs. In: Croitoru, M., Marquis, P., Rudolph, S., Stapleton, G. (eds.) GKR 2017. LNCS (LNAI), vol. 10775, pp. 3–28. Springer, Cham (2018). https://doi.org/10.1007/978-3-319-78102-0_1
2. Baxter, M., Polovina, S., Laurier, W., Rosing, M.: Active semantic relations in layered enterprise architecture development. In: Cochez, M., Croitoru, M., Marquis, P., Rudolph, S. (eds.) GKR 2020. LNCS (LNAI), vol. 12640, pp. 3–16. Springer, Cham (2021). https://doi.org/10.1007/978-3-030-72308-8_1
3. Ganter, B., Wille, R.: Formal Concept Analysis. Springer, Heidelberg (1999). https://doi.org/10.1007/978-3-642-59830-2
4. Polovina, S., von Rosing, M., Etzel, G.: Leading the practice in layered enterprise architecture. In: CEUR Workshop Proceedings, vol. 2574, pp. 62–69 (2020)
5. Sowa, J.F.: Conceptual Structures: Information Processing in Mind and Machine. Addison-Wesley Longman Publishing Co., Inc. (1984)
6. Sowa, J.F.: Conceptual Graphs, chap. 5, pp. 213–237. Elsevier (2008)
7. von Rosing, M., Laurier, W.: An introduction to the business ontology. Int. J. Conceptual Struct. Smart Appl. (IJCSSA) 3(1), 20–41 (2015)

An Approach to Identifying the Most Predictive and Discriminant Features in Supervised Classification Problems

Alexandre Bazin[✉], Miguel Couceiro, Marie-Dominique Devignes, and Amedeo Napoli

Université de Lorraine – CNRS – Inria, LORIA, 54000 Nancy, France
{alexandre.bazin,miguel.couceiro,
marie-dominique.devignes,amedeo.napoli}@loria.fr

Abstract. In this paper, we are interested in explaining datasets used in supervised classification problems by identifying the features that are most predictive and discriminant of the class. We first propose a definition of predictive and discriminant features based on the impact of the features on the performance of classification models. We then propose an approach to identifying the most predictive and discriminant features using multicriteria decision making. Finally, we present and discuss an experiment on a public dataset illustrating the potential of the approach.

1 Introduction

Biomedical sciences make increasing use of computer science methods. For instance, biologists wishing to study diabetes now collect data, in the form of biological features, from both diabetic and healthy patients and then use machine learning techniques to discriminate classes of patients and predict the disease. Provided that the patients are sufficiently numerous and the data correctly collected, most modern supervised classification approaches [1] are able to build models capable of diagnosing, or predicting the onset of, diabetes in new patients with good performances. While useful for the patients themselves, simply applying such models is not sufficient for biologists who rather need to understand the underlying causes of diabetes, i.e. they need meaning to be assigned to the biological features in terms of their roles in the development of the illness and its diagnostic. Which biological features can best be used to predict that a patient has diabetes? Which biological features can best be used to discriminate between having and not having diabetes? The answers to these questions go beyond the explanation of machine learning models [2,3] and, instead, constitute a form of explanation of the dataset itself, viewed as a supervised classification problem.

In this paper, we are interested in explaining datasets used in supervised classification problems. To do this, we propose a general approach for identifying the features that are the most important for different tasks related to supervised classification. Among possible tasks and as a case study, we consider *prediction*

© Springer Nature Switzerland AG 2021
T. Braun et al. (Eds.): ICCS 2021, LNAI 12879, pp. 48–56, 2021.
https://doi.org/10.1007/978-3-030-86982-3_4

and *discrimination*. We first discuss the nature of prediction and discrimination, and how the realisation of these tasks by machine learning models is quantified by different performance measures. We represent the knowledge conveyed by the measures as an ontological tree that is then used to characterise predictive and discriminant features based on their impact on the scores of models for the performance measures. We then propose an approach to identifying the most predictive and discriminant features through the use of multiple machine learning models, multicriteria decision making [4] and pattern mining. The supervised classification models are used to produce rankings of features according to their importance w.r.t measures of performance. Multiple models provide multiple different points of view on how the features can be used to predict and discriminate, so as to remain model-agnostic. The multicriteria decision making processes the rankings of features to select the "most important" features. Pattern mining, through the formal concept analysis (FCA) formalism [5,6], exploits the symbolic background knowledge about the measures of performance to transfer meaning to the selected features, and allows for an intuitive visual representation of the result. As a practical case, we analyse a public biomedical dataset and show that the application of the proposed method allows the user to gain an understanding of the data and the classification problem. To the best of our knowledge, this is one of the few papers discussing the discriminant and predictive nature of dataset features in a supervised classification problem thanks to decision making and FCA.

This paper is organised as follows. In Sect. 2, we propose a definition of discrimination and prediction and discuss how they can be measured using models. In Sect. 3, we present how to use multicriteria decision to identify the features we are interested in. In Sect. 4, we apply the proposed method to a public dataset to illustrate the capabilities of the framework introduced in this paper. In Sect. 5, we discuss the choices we made and present some directions for future work.

2   Prediction and Discrimination

The notions of "predictiveness" and "discriminativeness" of features are rarely discussed in the literature so we will first introduce working definitions. *To predict* means to assert that something will happen, is true or, in a classification problem, belongs to a class. *To discriminate* means to be able to perceive the differences between two things. Regarding features in a classification problem, a feature is said to be *predictive* when its value can be used to assert that an individual belongs to a particular class, and as *discriminant* when its value can be used to differentiate between the classes. For instance, fevers are predictive of being ill because their presence can be used by doctors to diagnose illnesses but they are not discriminant as they do not allow to separate between several possible diseases. The definitions of predictive and discriminant are thus linked to the existence of an external process that uses the features to make decisions. Here, we choose to use models built with classifiers as external processes.

We consider binary classification problems [7] in which individuals belong to one of two groups, the *positive* (or *target*) and *negative* classes. A *classifier* is a process that uses a set of individuals for which the classes are known (the *training set*) to create a *model* that is able to assign classes to a set of individuals for which the true classes are hidden (the *test set*) or unknown. In this work, we want to explain the dataset itself by identifying the features that are most important for prediction and discrimination, i.e. the features that are best used by the models trained on this dataset to predict and/or discriminate. We thus need an explanation approach that highlights features w.r.t. their importance in these two tasks. Many *measures* have been proposed [8–10] to quantify the performance of models with regard to various views of what a good model should be doing. The relations between these measures, as well as the role that they play in the evaluation of models [11–13], have been extensively studied. The subject is of particular importance in biostatistics where researchers are notably interested in the relations between performance measures and prediction and discrimination [14, 15]. In this paper, we consider measures that are combinations of four different scores obtained by guessing the classes of individuals in a test set. We argue that some measures quantify prediction while others quantify discrimination.

The *sensitivity* (or *recall*) measure, for instance, is the ratio of the number of positive individuals that have been correctly recognised as such by the model to the total number of positive individuals in the test set, i.e. sensitivity equals $\frac{TP}{TP+FN}$. Sensitivity quantifies the ability of the model to recognise the positive class. The *precision* measure is the ratio of the number of positive individuals that have been correctly recognised as such by the model to the total number of positive guesses, i.e. precision equals $\frac{TP}{TP+FP}$. It quantifies the ability of the model not to make mistakes when identifying the positive class. The *accuracy* measure is the ratio of the number of individuals whose class has been correctly guessed by the model to the total number of individuals, i.e. accuracy equals $\frac{TP+TN}{TP+TN+FP+FN}$. As such, it quantifies the ability of the model to recognise both positive and negative classes while not making mistakes.

These three measures represent different priorities. Sensitivity is maximised when the model is always predicting the positive class. Many errors can be made (false positive) but all individuals belonging to the positive class are recognised as such. Conversely, the precision can be maximised by being overly cautious with positive predictions. The accuracy can be considered as a compromise between the predictive power and the error avoidance that perceives both classes as equally important. We observe that two important notions are at play here: recognising classes and not making mistakes. We will consider that measures quantify the *prediction* power of models when they focus only on the recognition part (e.g. sensitivity, specificity), the *correctness* of models when they focus only on not making mistakes (e.g. precision, NPV), and the *discrimination* power of models when they mix both goals (e.g. accuracy, Fscore). This is similar to the inductive learning notions of characterization (prediction) and

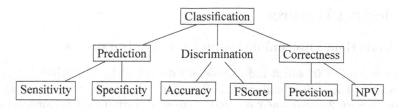

Fig. 1. Ontological tree of terms characterising performance measures and their role in a classification process.

discrimination [16]. Additionally, we see that the concept of prediction admits two subconcepts: prediction of the class 1, quantified by the sensitivity, and prediction of the class 0, quantified by the specificity. In order to represent this hierarchy a concepts, we build and introduce an ontological tree of concepts related to prediction and discrimination, from the concept of *Classification* itself to individual performance measures. This ontological tree is depicted in Fig. 1 and it shall serve as background knowledge for the interpretation of features in the remainder of this paper. It states, for instance, that sensitivity is related to prediction power which is in turn related to classification.

Let T be a test set, M a model, m a measure and f a feature used to describe the individuals in T. We denote by $m(M, T)$ the score of the model M for the measure m on the test set T, and denote by T_i^f the test set obtained by randomly permuting the values taken by f in T for a permutation i. The *impact* of the feature f on the score of the model M for the measure m is defined as the mean variation of the score of the model for m when the values taken by f in the test set are permuted [17], i.e., for a large enough k (number of permutations),

$$impact(f, M, m) \approx \sum_{i=1}^{k} \frac{m(M, T_i^f) - m(M, T)}{k}.$$

In other words, the impact reflects the importance that the feature has for the model w.r.t. the measure. This impact thus constitutes a form of explanation of the model. As it is a real number, the impact can be used to rank the features. A negative impact means that changing the values of the feature has a negative influence on the model's score, which means that the model makes use of the feature for whatever the measure is quantifying. Therefore, we consider a feature f as predictive whenever f has a negative impact on a measure related to prediction. In the same way, we consider a feature f as discriminant whenever f has a negative impact on a measure related to discrimination. Measures of correctness are not directly taken into account in this work but they are discussed again later.

3 Selecting Features

3.1 Prediction, Discrimination and Feature Importance

We have a dataset in which individuals are described by the values of a set $\mathcal{F}$ of features and a corresponding class (here we will assume that there are two classes). In Sect. 2, we defined predictive (resp. discriminant) features as those having a negative impact on the score of a model for a measure of prediction (resp. discrimination). All features in the dataset potentially have these characteristics but we want to identify the features that are important in that they are among *the most* predictive or discriminant.

We could argue that a feature f_1 is *more predictive* than a feature f_2 if it has a smaller impact value on a model's sensitivity score. However, if f_2 has a smaller impact value than f_1 on the same model's specificity score, which one is the most predictive? And if f_2 has a smaller impact value on another model's sensitivity score? As multiple measures are indicative of prediction or discrimination, and different models can result in different rankings of features, we represent the problem of identifying the most predictive and discriminant features as a multicriteria decision problem.

One of the goals of multicriteria decision making [4,18] is to model preferences. In this paper, we take a utility-based approach. Let $V_1, ..., V_n$ be attributes, and let $\mathbb{R}$ be the set of real numbers that we use as evaluation space. By a criterion we mean a pair $\mathcal{V}_i = (V_i, \phi_i)$, $i \in \{1, \ldots, n\}$, where $\phi_i \colon V_i \to \mathbb{R}$ is a utility function. Such a criterion naturally defines a local preference relation (reflexive and transitive) $\preceq_i$ on V_i: for all $x, y \in V_i$, $x \preceq_i y$ if $\phi_i(x) \geq \phi_i(y)$. Let $a = (a_1, \ldots, a_n)$ and $b = (b_1, \ldots, b_n)$ be two alternatives in $V_1 \times \cdots \times V_n$. We say that a *is preferred to* b *on the ith criterion* when $a_i \succeq_i b_i$. For instance, when buying a new car, two criteria could be based on the price and the maximum speed: price-wise, one would prefer a cheaper car whereas Speed-wise, one would prefer a faster car. However, preferences on those two criteria do not necessarily coincide and compromises must be made. When faced with a set of alternatives and multiple criteria, we will refer to the problem of identifying the "best" alternatives according to the criteria as a multicriteria decision problem.

Let $a = (a_1, \ldots, a_n)$ and $b = (b_1, \ldots, b_n)$ be two alternatives. Alternative a is said to *dominate* b, denoted by $a \succeq b$, if $a_i \succeq_i b_i$ for all $i \in \{1, \ldots, n\}$. The *Pareto front* of the multicriteria decision problem over a set $Crit$ of criteria and a set Alt of alternatives is denoted by $Pareto(Crit, Alt)$ and it is defined as the set of alternatives that are not dominated by any other alternative. In other words, an alternative is in the Pareto front if it is better than all the others on at least one criterion. A car that is both slower and more expensive than another is surely not preferred and thus it does not constitute a better choice. Having excluded all the alternatives that are clearly worse than others, the Pareto front contains only alternatives for which one cannot improve on a criterion without losing on another.

Let $\mathcal{M}o$ be a set of models and let $\mathcal{M}e$ be a set of performance measures quantifying either prediction or discrimination. We represent the problem of identifying the most predictive and discriminant features as the multicriteria decision problem in which the set of alternatives is the set $\mathcal{F}$ of features and the set of attributes is the set $\mathcal{M}o \times \mathcal{M}e$ of the pairs composed of a model and a measure. The value of the attribute $(m_o, m_e) \in \mathcal{M}o \times \mathcal{M}e$ for the feature $f \in \mathcal{F}$ is $impact(f, m_o, m_e)$. The criteria are the pairs $((m_o, m_e), id)$ where id is the identity function. A feature f_1 is preferred to a feature f_2 for a criterion $((m_o, m_e), id)$ if and only if $impact(f_1, m_o, m_e) \leq impact(f_2, m_o, m_e)$. In order to simplify the notations, we thereafter identify the criteria with their attributes and use "the criterion (m_o, m_e)" to refer to $((m_o, m_e), id)$, as well as $\mathcal{M}_o \times \mathcal{M}_e$ to refer to the set of criteria.

Definition 1 *(IMPORTANT FEATURES). A feature f is said to be important if*

$$f \in Pareto(\mathcal{M}o \times \mathcal{M}e, \mathcal{F}).$$

3.2 Identifying Important Features

Important features are defined w.r.t. a multicriteria decision problem that involves models and measures. As it is impossible to consider all possible models and measures, we have to make choices and restrict ourselves to finite sets.

Let $\mathcal{C}$ be a finite set of classifiers (e.g. Random Forests [19], Naive Bayes, Neural Networks, Support Vector Machines [20]) and $\mathcal{M}e$ be a finite set of measures of a model's performance (e.g. accuracy, specificity, sensitivity). As a running example, we will use

- $\mathcal{F} = \{f_1, f_2, f_3, f_4, f_5\}$
- $\mathcal{C} = \{$Random Forests (RF), Neural Networks (NN)$\}$
- $\mathcal{M}e = \{Specificity, Sensitivity, Accuracy\}$

Our assumption is that different types of classifiers learn, and thus perceive and use features, differently so the most important features for accuracy are not necessarily the same in models learned with neural networks and random forests. With each classifier $C \in \mathcal{C}$, we create a model that represents the classifier. The training and test sets are of fixed sizes and randomly drawn from the dataset at each new training phase. This process results in the creation of the set $\mathcal{M}o$ of models. From there, for each model M and measure m, we associate to each feature f its impact on M's m score. This results in the creation of a $|\mathcal{C} \times \mathcal{M}e| \times |\mathcal{F}|$ matrix that quantifies the importance that each classifier's representative model assigns to each feature w.r.t. each measure. We use the matrix of impacts of features to compute $Pareto(\mathcal{M}o \times \mathcal{M}e, \mathcal{F})$, i.e. the important features.

Once the important features are identified, we want to interpret their importance in terms of prediction and discrimination. To do this, we use the multicriteria decision explanation approach described in [21].

4 Experimental Results

The Pima Indians Diabetes Database is a public dataset available on the Kaggle machine learning repository[1]. It contains 768 instances, 8 features and two classes

---

[1] https://www.kaggle.com/uciml/pima-indians-diabetes-database.

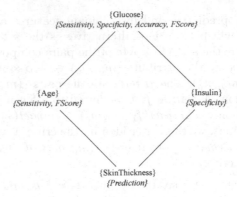

Fig. 2. The interpretation of the 4 important features in the Pima Indians Diabetes dataset. For the sake of legibility, only the most specific terms describing the sets of features are depicted. Terms are written in blue if they are related to prediction and in red if they are related to discrimination.

: having diabetes (positive class) or not (negative class). We chose to consider four types of classifiers $C = \{$Random Forests, Naive Bayes, Neural Networks, Support Vector Machines$\}$ and four measures $M = \{$Sensitivity, Specificity, Accuracy, FScore$\}$, the first two quantifying prediction and the last two discrimination so as to preserve a good balance of criteria. The background knowledge used in the multicriteria decision explanation approach is the one presented in Fig. 1. The 16 criteria created by the classifiers and measures produce a Pareto front, and thus a set of important features, of size 4. The interpretation of those 4 important features is presented in Fig. 2.

We observe that the feature *Glucose* is good for every measure and so is both predictive (of both classes) and discriminant. The feature *Age* is good for FScore and so it is discriminant. *Age* is also good for sensitivity, which is a measure of the ability of a model to predict the positive class (having diabetes), so we can say that *Age* is predictive of having diabetes. The feature *Insulin* is good for specificity, which is a measure of the ability of a model to predict the negative class (not having diabetes), so we can say that *Insulin* is predictive of not having diabetes. The feature *SkinThickness* is deemed good for prediction in general, which means it is worse than *Age* at predicting the positive class and worse than *Insulin* at predicting the negative class but it represents a good compromise between the two.

One can use these results to understand that, in the population described by this particular dataset, the plasma glucose concentration is the most important value to look at when trying to diagnose diabetes. After the plasma glucose concentration, the age is the most important value for diagnosing diabetes and the insulin level is the most important value for diagnosing not having diabetes. If these features are not enough to decide, the triceps skin fold thickness can also be looked at.

5   Discussion and Conclusion

Our approach explains a dataset by identifying important features and labeling them in terms of prediction and discrimination. To reach this result, we have made a number of choices. First of all, we defined predictive and discriminant features through their usage by models learned from data. Whether it be from the selection of the training and test sets or the classifier algorithm itself, nondeterminism is introduced in the first step of the approach. The output is therefore not always the same. For the definition of *"most* predictive or discriminant features"*, we used the membership to the Pareto front of a multicriteria decision problem. We believe that this makes sense but other methods could be considered. Finally, the objective of this work is to identify predictive and discriminant features but, in defining these notions, we also mentioned the existence of measures that quantify the *correctness* of models, i.e. the model's ability not to make mistakes. It would be interesting, as a future work, to integrate this notion into the approach and study the differences between features that are good for avoiding mistakes and features that are good for predicting classes.

Acknowlegdement. This work was supported partly by the french PIA project «Lorraine Université d'Excellence», reference ANR-15-IDEX-04-LUE.

References

1. Friedman, J., Hastie, T., Tibshirani, R.: The Elements of Statistical Learning. Springer Series in Statistics, vol. 1, no. 10. Springer, New York (2001)
2. Adadi, A., Berrada, M.: Peeking inside the black-box: a survey on explainable artificial intelligence (XAI). IEEE Access **6**, 52 138–52 160 (2018)
3. Guidotti, R., Monreale, A., Ruggieri, S., Turini, F., Giannotti, F., Pedreschi, D.: A survey of methods for explaining black box models. ACM Comput. Surv. (CSUR) **51**(5), 93 (2018)
4. Bouyssou, D., Dubois, D., Prade, H., Pirlot, M.: Decision Making Process: Concepts and Methods. Wiley, Hoboken (2013)
5. Ganter, B., Wille, R.: Formal Concept Analysis: Mathematical Foundations. Springer, Heidelberg (1999)
6. Poelmans, J., Ignatov, D.I., Kuznetsov, S.O., Dedene, G.: Formal concept analysis in knowledge processing: a survey on applications. Expert Syst. Appl. **40**(16), 6538–6560 (2013)
7. Flach, P.: Machine Learning: The Art and Science of Algorithms that Make Sense of Data. Cambridge University Press, Cambridge (2012)
8. Sokolova, M., Lapalme, G.: A systematic analysis of performance measures for classification tasks. Inf. Process. Manag. **45**(4), 427–437 (2009)
9. Fawcett, T.: An introduction to ROC analysis. Pattern Recogn. Lett. **27**(8), 861 874 (2006)
10. Sokolova, M., Japkowicz, N., Szpakowicz, S.: Beyond accuracy, F-score and ROC: a family of discriminant measures for performance evaluation. In: Sattar, A., Kang, B. (eds.) AI 2006. LNCS (LNAI), vol. 4304, pp. 1015–1021. Springer, Heidelberg (2006). https://doi.org/10.1007/11941439_114

11. Powers, D.M.: Evaluation: from precision, recall and F-measure to ROC, informedness, markedness & correlation. J. Mach. Learn. Technol. **2**(1), 37–63 (2011)
12. Davis, J., Goadrich, M.: The relationship between precision-recall and ROC curves. In: Proceedings of the 23rd International Conference on Machine Learning, pp. 233–240 (2006)
13. Japkowicz, N., Shah, M. (eds.): Evaluating Learning Algorithms: A Classification Perspective. Cambridge University Press, Cambridge (2011)
14. Pencina, M.J., D'Agostino, R.B.: Evaluating discrimination of risk prediction models: the C statistic. JAMA **314**(10), 1063–1064 (2015)
15. Steyerberg, E.W., et al.: Assessing the performance of prediction models: a framework for some traditional and novel measures. Epidemiology **21**(1), 128–138 (2010)
16. Michalski, R.S.: A theory and methodology of inductive learning. In: Machine Learning, pp. 83–134. Elsevier (1983)
17. Fisher, A., Rudin, C., Dominici, F.: All models are wrong but many are useful: variable importance for black-box, proprietary, or misspecified prediction models, using model class reliance. arXiv preprint arXiv:1801.01489 (2018)
18. Bouyssou, D., Marchant, T., Pirlot, M., Tsoukias, A., Vincke, P.: Evaluation and Decision Models with Multiple Criteria: Stepping Stones for the Analyst, vol. 86. Springer, Heidelberg (2006)
19. Breiman, L.: Random forests. Mach. Learn. **45**(1), 5–32 (2001)
20. Vapnik, V.N.: Statistical Learning Theory. Wiley, Hoboken (1998)
21. Bazin, A., Couceiro, M., Devignes, M.-D., Napoli, A.: Explaining multicriteria decision making with formal concept analysis. In: Concept Lattices and Applications 2020 (2020)

Combining Implications and Conceptual Analysis to Learn from a Pesticidal Plant Knowledge Base

Lina Mahrach[1,2], Alain Gutierrez[3], Marianne Huchard[3(✉)], Priscilla Keip[1,2],
Pascal Marnotte[1,2], Pierre Silvie[1,2,4], and Pierre Martin[1,2]

[1] CIRAD, UPR AIDA, 34398 Montpellier, France
`{lina.mahrach,priscilla.keip,pascal.marnotte,`
`pierre.silvie,pierre.martin}@cirad.fr`
[2] AIDA, Univ Montpellier, CIRAD, Montpellier, France
[3] LIRMM, Univ Montpellier, CNRS, Montpellier, France
`{alain.gutierrez,marianne.huchard}@lirmm.fr`
[4] PHIM Plant Health Institute, Montpellier University, IRD, CIRAD, INRAE,
Institut Agro, Montpellier, France

Abstract. Supporting organic farming aims to find alternative solutions to synthetic pesticides and antibiotics, using local plants, to protect crops. Moreover, in the One Health approach (OHA), a pesticidal plant should not be harmful to humans, meaning it cannot be toxic if the crop is consumed or should have a limited and conscious use if it is used for medical care. Knowledge on plant use presented in the scientific literature was compiled in a knowledge base (KB). The challenge is to develop a KB exploration method that informs experts (including farmers) about protection systems properties that respect OHA. In this paper, we present a method that extracts the Duquenne-Guigues basis of implications from knowledge structured using Relational Concept Analysis (RCA). We evaluate the impact of three data representations on the implications and their readability. The experimentation is conducted on 562 plant species used to protect 15 crops against 29 pest species of the Noctuidae family. Results show that consistently splitting data into several tables fosters less redundant and more focused implications.

Keywords: Relational concept analysis · Duquenne-Guigues basis · Implication rules · Life sciences knowledge base · One health · Formal concept analysis

1 Introduction

Reducing the use of synthetic pesticides and antibiotics is a major challenge for the environment and living organisms. Moreover, for the Global South countries, it is also crucial to preserve biodiversity and design sustainable production systems (SPS) that respect the One Health approach (OHA) [4]. OHA calls for

© Springer Nature Switzerland AG 2021
T. Braun et al. (Eds.): ICCS 2021, LNAI 12879, pp. 57–72, 2021.
https://doi.org/10.1007/978-3-030-86982-3_5

an interdisciplinary and intersectoral action in the public management of health problems at the interface between humans, animals, and their shared environment. An alternative solution to synthetic pesticides and antibiotics accepted by OHA is the use of local plants, in the form of essential oil or aqueous solution, with a pesticidal or anti-parasitic effect. Using such plants requires ensuring that they are not harmful to humans. Some plants can indeed be toxic to humans when inhaled during their spray in the field or ingested through crop consumption. Other plants, also used by humans for medical care, can induce a resistance to certain molecules through excessive absorption. One challenge for the scientific experts and for the farmers is to understand the properties and constraints of the already known **protection systems**, composed of a **crop** to be protected against a **pest** using a protecting **plant**, with respect to OHA.

A significant number of protection systems have been extracted in the scientific literature and gathered in the Knomana knowledge base [13]. Knomana includes several datasets. Among them, PPAf (Pesticide Effect Plant of Africa) currently gathers 44270 descriptions of plants used for plant, animal, human, and public health. In PPAf, each use is described using 70 data, such as the protected organism (e.g. crop, fish, human being), the target organism (e.g. insect, fungus, bacterium), the location, and the usage domain (plant, animal, environmental, human, or public health). Knomana also includes PAL (Edible plants), which informs whether plants are consumed by humans as food or drink.

In this paper, we make the assumption that implications are a relevant formalism for delivering information on protection systems relative to OHA. We choose to build the Duquenne-Guigues basis (DGB) of implications for its quality of being a non redundant implication set of minimal cardinality. Besides, we assess the impact of three data representations on the implication form and readability. These three representations reconcile the two datasets and split them into one or several data tables. When the representation has several data tables, we build the DGB of implications from the extended formal contexts computed by Relational Concept Analysis (RCA) [7] with AOC-posets. An experimentation is conducted on a Knomana excerpt composed of 562 plants species used to protect 15 crops against 29 pest species of the Noctuidae family. Results show that consistently reconciling datasets and splitting the data into several tables fosters less redundant and more focused implications.

Section 2 introduces the background and outlines the approach. Section 3 describes the Knomana excerpt and the three studied representations. Section 4 reports and discusses the experiment. Section 5 exposes related research and Sect. 6 concludes and draws future work.

2   Approach

This section introduces the approach, which combines RCA and the computation of the DGB of implications.

RCA. RCA is designed to analyze a dataset conforming to the entity-relationship model [7]. RCA is an extension of Formal Concept Analysis (FCA) [5]. FCA seeks to extract *formal concepts* from a formal context (FC) $\mathcal{K} = (G, M, I)$ where G is an object set, M is an attribute set and $I \subseteq G \times M$. Two operators, both denoted by $'$, associate object sets with attribute sets. For $O \subseteq G$, the set of attributes shared by the objects of O is $O' = \{m | \forall g \in O, (g, m) \in I\}$. For $A \subseteq M$, the set of objects that share the attributes of A is $A' = \{g | \forall m \in A, (g, m) \in I\}$. A formal concept $\mathcal{C} = (Extent(\mathcal{C}), Intent(\mathcal{C}))$ associates a maximal object group (extent) with their maximal shared attribute group (intent): $Extent(\mathcal{C}) = Intent(\mathcal{C})'$. More generally, we denote by $\preceq_C$ the concept order: $\mathcal{C}_1 \preceq_C \mathcal{C}_2$ when $Intent(\mathcal{C}_2) \subseteq Intent(\mathcal{C}_1)$ and $Extent(\mathcal{C}_1) \subseteq Extent(\mathcal{C}_2)$. The set of all concepts, provided with $\preceq_C$, forms the concept lattice. The lowest (w.r.t. $\preceq_C$) concept owning one object is its introducer concept. The highest (w.r.t. $\preceq_C$) concept owning one attribute is its introducer concept. The suborder of the concept lattice restricted to these introducer concepts is called the AOC-poset (Attribute-Object Concept poset). For instance, in Table 1, the FC *OrganismInfo* describes plant (pl_i), crop ($prot_i$), and pest ($pest_i$) organisms using their genus ($genus_i$) and their non-use in medical care (*no-medical*). Plants $pl1$ and $pl2$ are grouped as a concept being both from *genus1* and not used in medical care. $pl1$ and $pl2$ can as well be grouped with $prot1$ and $prot2$ as they are not used in medical care. As presented in Fig. 1, these two concepts, respectively named C_Org_15 and C_Org_22, are ordered by inclusion of their object sets from bottom to top, or equivalently by inclusion of their attribute sets from top to bottom. This figure shows that C_Org_15 is a subconcept of C_Org_22 where C_Org_15 introduces *genus1*, C_Org_22 introduces *no-medical*, C_Org_15 inherits *no-medical* from C_Org_22, and C_Org_22 inherits $pl1$ and $pl2$ from C_Org_15.

Table 1. Example of RCF made of 2 FCs (i.e. *OrganismInfo* and *ProtSystem*) on the top and 3 RCs (i.e. *uses*, *protects*, and *treats*) on the bottom. The attribute set of FC *ProtSystem* is empty.

OrganismInfo	genus1	...	genus4	...	genus6	...	no-medical	...	ProtSystem
plant1 (pl1)	x	...		...		...	x	...	1
plant2 (pl2)	x	...		...		...	x	...	2
prot1		...		...	x	...	x	...	3
prot2		...		...	x	...	x	...	4
pest1		...	x	...		...		...	5
pest2		...	x	...		...		...	6
...		...	...	...	...	...	...	...	7

uses	pl1	pl2	pl3	pl4	...	protects	...	prot1	prot2	...	treats	...	pest1	pest2	...
1			x		...	1	...			...	1	...			...
2		x			...	2	...			...	2	...			...
3	x				...	3	...	x		...	3	...	x		...
4	x				...	4	...	x		...	4	...	x		...
5		x			...	5	...		x	...	5	...		x	...
6		x			...	6	...		x	...	6	...		x	...
7				x	...	7	...			...	7	...			...

RCA takes a *Relational Context Family* (RCF) as input. A RCF is a pair $(\mathbf{K}, \mathbf{R})$ where $\mathbf{K}$ is a set of FCs ($\mathbf{K} = \{\mathcal{K}_i = (G_i, M_i, I_i)\}_{i=1,2,...,n}$), and each FC describes an object category. $\mathbf{R}$ is a set of relational contexts (RC) between the objects of the FCs. $\mathbf{R} = \{r_j\}_{j=1,2,...,p}$ and $r_j \subseteq G_k \times G_l$ for $k, l \in \{1, 2, ..., n\}$.

To compute the concepts for each FC considering the RCs, RCA builds *relational attributes* $qr(\mathcal{C})$, where q is a quantifier (e.g. the existential quantifier $\exists$ or the universal quantifier $\forall$), r is a RC, and $\mathcal{C}$ is a concept on the objects of the co-domain of r. These attributes thus group the individual-to-individual relationships into individual-to-concept relationships. To compute the final conceptual structure family, RCA alternates between building conceptual structures associated with FCs (such as a concept lattice or an AOC-poset) and extending the FCs with relational attributes, including the concepts of these structures, until a fix-point is reached. Table 1 presents a RCF, composed of the FCs *OrganismInfo* and *ProtSystem* and 3 RCs, i.e. *uses*, *protects*, and *treats*. These 3 RCs respectively indicate the plant, the crop, and the pest for each protection system. In this example, the FC *ProtSystem* is finally extended with relational attributes formed with the quantifier $\exists$, a RC (i.e. *uses*, *protects*, or *treats*) and a concept of *OrganismInfo* as shown in Table 2. In Fig. 1, the concepts built on the extended FC (EFC) *ProtSystem* group and organize protection systems by considering the relational attributes.

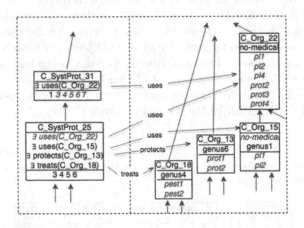

Fig. 1. Partial view of a lattice family, of the RCF presented in Table 1, with the protection system lattice to the left and an organism one to the right. A plain or dashed arrow represents respectively a subconcept-superconcept relation or a cross-lattice link materialized by a relational attribute. Concept $C\_SystProt\_31$ groups 6 protection systems $(1,3,4,5,6,7)$ using a plant from concept C_Org_22, i.e. $pl1$, $pl2$, or $pl4$, not used in medical care. $C\_SystProt\_25$, which is a subconcept of $C\_SystProt\_31$, groups 4 protection systems $(3,4,5,6)$, informing that they use a plant from $genus1$ $(\exists uses(C\_Org\_15))$, not used in medical care $(\exists uses(C\_Org\_22))$ to protect a crop from $genus6$ $(\exists protects(C\_Org\_13))$ against a pest of $genus4$ $(\exists treats(C\_Org\_18))$.

Implications. An implication, denoted by $A \implies B$, is a pair of attribute sets $(A,B), A, B \subseteq M$ where all the objects that own the attributes of A (premise) also own the ones of B (conclusion): $A' \subseteq B'$. For example, the implication (I1) indicates that no plant of $genus1$ is used in medical care:

Table 2. Excerpt of the EFC *ProtSystem* presenting relational attributes formed with the existential quantifier ∃, a relation (*uses*, *protects*, or *treats*), and a concept from FC *OrganismInfo*.

ProtSystem	...	∃*uses* (*C_Org_*15)	∃*uses* (*C_Org_*22)	...	∃*protects* (*C_Org_*13)	...	∃*treats* (*C_Org_*18)	...
1	...		x	...		...		...
2	...			...		...		...
3	...	x	x	...	x	...	x	...
4	...	x	x	...	x	...	x	...
5	...	x	x	...	x	...	x	...
6	...	x	x	...	x	...	x	...
7	...		x	...		...		...

$$\{genus1\} \implies \{no-medical\} \quad (I1)$$

There are several types of implication sets and bases [1] that can be computed from a FC. Binary implications such as (I1) can also be obtained from $\preceq_C$ and the introducing attributes' concepts, e.g. in Fig. 1: C_Org_15 introduces $genus1$, while its superconcept C_Org_22 introduces $no\text{-}medical$. The Duquenne-Guigues Basis (DGB) of implications can be defined upon pseudo-intents [6]. A pseudo-intent is an attribute set $P_i \subseteq M$ such that: P_i is not an intent ($P_i'' \neq P_i$); for any other pseudo-intent $P_j \subset P_i$, $P_j'' \subset P_i$. The DGB is the implication set $\{P_i \implies P_i'' | P_i$ is a pseudo-intent$\}$. It is canonical and a cardinality minimal set of non redundant implications, from which all implications can be produced.

Our Approach. In our work, we compute the DGB of implications, that is usually built for an FC. When using RCA, implications are extracted when the fix-point is reached. For a FC which is not extended, because it is not the object set of a RC, the DGB of implications is directly computed on itself. For a FC which is extended, the DGB is built from its extension (EFC). In our approach, AOC-posets are built at each RCA step. For an easier interpretation of the implications extracted from the EFCs, the concepts in the relational attributes are recursively replaced by the 'non-relational' attributes that serve as seeds for these concepts [15,16]. For instance, the implication *(I2)* becomes *(rewritten I2)*:

$$\{\exists treats(C\_Org\_18)\} \implies \{\exists uses(C\_Org\_22)\} \quad (I2)$$
$$\{\exists treats(genus4)\} \implies \{\exists uses(no-medical)\} \quad (rewritten\ I2)$$

Both *(I2)* and *(rewritten I2)* stipulate that for the protection systems treating a pest of $genus4$ ($pest1$ or $pest2$ grouped in C_Org_18), we then observe the use of one of the plants ($pl1, pl2, pl4$) grouped in concept C_Org_22, these plants not being used in medical care as indicated by C_Org_22 intent. Implication (I2) can also be read from: $C\_SystProt\_25 \preceq_C C\_SystProt\_31$; $C\_SystProt\_25$ introduces $\exists treats(C\_Org\_18)$; and $C\_SystProt\_31$ introduces $\exists uses(C\_Org\_22)$. The *scope (S)* of an implication informs on the number of objects verifying the implication premise, the *support* being the proportion of EF or EFC objects verifying the implication premise: Let $Imp = A \implies B$, we have $S(Imp) = |A'|$. $Support(Imp) = S(Imp)/|G|$. Figure 2 summarizes this computation process for the running example.

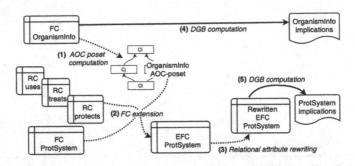

Fig. 2. Overview of the process for the running example. (1) The AOC-poset is built from FC *OrganismInfo*. (2) The EFC *ProtSystem* is built using the relational attributes $\exists r(C)$, where r is *uses*, *treats* or *protects*, and C is a concept from the *OrganismInfo* AOC-poset. (3) The relational attributes are rewritten for easier reading. (4) and (5) The DGBs of implications are built for FC *OrganismInfo* and EFC *ProtSystem*.

3   Three Representations of the Datasets

This section presents the datasets and their combination through three representations splitting the data differently. Our objective is to assess the impact of the splitting on the form and the readability of the implications.

The Datasets. The datasets concern 29 pest species belonging to 15 genera of the Noctuidae family [12]. To control these species on 15 crops (e.g. tomato, maize, cotton) belonging to seven families, 562 plant species, belonging to 352 genus and to 94 families, are identified.

The first dataset, which is an excerpt of PPAf, contains 721 protection systems, i.e. triplets *(plant, pest, crop)* describing the use of a plant to protect a crop against a Noctuidae pest at the species taxonomic level. The modeling interest of the Noctuidae family raises on the polyphagous or highly polyphagous nature of some of its pest species' diet. A polyphagous pest, such as *Trichilia pallida*, attacks crops from various genera of the same family, while a highly polyphagous pest, such as *Spodoptera frugiperda*, attacks crops from various families. In this first dataset, some publications do not specify the crop but the plant and the pest, mainly because of the polyphagous nature of the pest diet. To obtain a triplet in this case, a generic name was provided to the crop. Five generic species names were adopted, namely CropBrasS, CropFabaS, CropMalvS, CropPoacS, and CropS. The first four correspond to a crop attacked by a polyphagous pest, respectively from Brassicaceae, Fabaceae, Malvaceae, and Poaceae family. CropS corresponds to a crop attacked by a highly polyphagous pest. To the best of our knowledge, and to be as cautious as possible, we consider that they are all consumed by humans, and that only CropMalvS and CropS are used for medical care. Finally, in this PPAf excerpt, six organism species (e.g. pepper, chickpea, and castor bean) are both described as a crop and a protecting plant.

The second dataset is another excerpt of PPAf and informs on the plants used for medical care. This information was extracted for each protecting plant and each crop listed in the first dataset. None of the pests is used for human and public health.

The last dataset, an excerpt of PAL, informs on the consumption of plants and crops by humans. This excerpt includes only plants and crops present in the first dataset. In this work, we consider that none of the pests are consumed by human or used in medical care.

The Three Representations. Combining the three datasets enables to representing SPSs that respect OHA. Three representations, leading to three different RCFs, were developed according to the reification of different entities and roles.

The *Relational* representation (Fig. 3a) considers five different entities. The three first represent the biological organisms. The first entity is *crop*. It is described using three attributes, i.e. *crSpecies*, *crGenus*, and *crFamily*, which respectively correspond to its species, its genus, and its family. The second entity is *Pest*, i.e. an aggressor of a crop. It contains three attributes, i.e. *peSpecies*, *peGenus*, and *peFamily*, which respectively correspond to its species, its genus, and its family. The third entity is *Plant*. Plants are described using three attributes, i.e. *plSpecies*, *plGenus*, and *plFamily*, which respectively correspond to its species, its genus, and its family. The fourth entity represents the protection systems (*ProtSystem*). *ProtSystem* reifies the ternary relation linking *plSpecies*, *crSpecies*, and *peSpecies*. The last entity is *OrganismInfo* in which each organism is described using its name at the species, genus, and family taxonomic levels using respectively the attributes *species*, *genus*, and *family*. In addition *OrganismInfo* indicates whether the organism is consumed (attribute *food*) and whether it is used for medical care (attribute *medical*). *ProtSystem* includes the data from PPAf knowledge set, and *OrganismInfo* compiles the two other knowledge sets. The RCF for this representation is thus composed of five FCs (*ProtSystem, Plant, Crop, Pest, OrganismInfo*). Boolean attributes are obtained through a nominal scaling of the attributes [5]. The RCF also contains six RCs: *uses, protects, treats, pl_CharactBy, cr_CharactBy,* and *pe_CharactBy*.

The *TwoTables* representation (Fig. 3b) comports two entities. *ProtSystem* and *OrganismInfo* respectively represent the protection systems and the organisms, as in the *Relational* representation. This representation does not reify the role of the organisms in the protection systems, as does the *Relational* representation. The RCF for this representation is thus composed of two FCs (i.e. *ProtSystem, OrganismInfo*). The native (Boolean) attributes are obtained

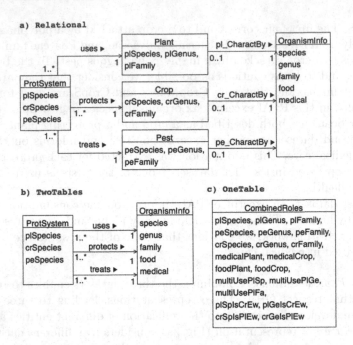

Fig. 3. Data model of the three datasets' representations.

through a nominal scaling of the attributes. The RCF also contains three RCs: *uses*, *protects*, and *treats*.

The *OneTable* representation (Fig. 3c) reifies protection systems in an entity named *CombinedSystem*. This entity includes the attributes of entities *Plant*, *Crop*, and *Pest* of the *Relational* representation. It also contains the medical and food attributes related to the protecting plant and to the crop, respectively named *medicalPlant*, *foodPlant*, *medicalCrop*, and *foodCrop*. Additional attributes were included to express relationships between data not formalized by this representation. *plSpIsCrEw* and *plGeIsCrEw* indicate respectively that a protecting species is a crop species in another triplet, and a protecting genus is a crop genus in another triplet. The attributes *crSpIsPlEw* and *crGeIsPlEw* indicate respectively that a crop species is a protecting species in another triplet, and a crop genus is a protecting genus in another triplet. *multiUsePlSp*, *multiUsePlGe*, and *multiUsePlFa* indicate whether the protecting plant, respectively at the species, genus, and family taxonomic levels, is both consumed and used for medical care. The RCF is here reduced to a single FC *CombinedSystem*, with attributes obtained by a nominal scaling of the *CombinedSystem* entity attributes.

Table 3 presents the size of the different representations, in terms of number of objects and attributes, number of relational attributes, and size of the AOC-posets at the initial and at the last steps of RCA process.

Table 3. Quantitative description of the RCFs and AOC-posets.

Representation	Formal context	#objects	#attributes	#relational attributes	#concepts AOC Poset (initial step)	#concepts AOC Poset (last step)
OneTable	FC CombinedRoles	721	1113	0	1005	1005
TwoTables	*All formal contexts*	1321	1078	2250	751	1750
	EFC ProtSystem	721	0	2250	1	1000
	FC OrganismInfo	600	1078	0	750	750
Relational	*All formal contexts*	1927	2169	3017	1507	2517
	EFC ProtSystem	721	0	767	1	1000
	EFC Plant	562	1008	750	700	705
	EFC Pest	29	45	750	36	37
	EFC Crop	15	38	750	20	25
	FC OrganismInfo	600	1078	0	750	750

Table 4. Implications (implic.) from the Duquenne-Guigues basis per scope (S) and maximum scope (Smax).

Representation	Formal context	#implic. S = 0	#implic. S = 1	#implic. S= 2	#implic. S = 3	#implic. S = [4–10] (avg)	#implic. S >10 (avg)	#total implic.S > 0	Smax (#implic.)
OneTable	FC CombinedRoles	3360	1105	281	125	236 (33.71)	173 (2.34)	1920	721 (1)
TwoTables	EFC ProtSystem	4891	827	234	95	165 (23.57)	74 (1.90)	1395	721 (1)
	FC OrganismInfo	6069	1007	76	37	42 (7.00)	6 (1.2)	1168	35 (1)
	All FCs	10960	1834	310	132	207	80	2571	
Relational	EFC ProtSystem	3414	825	234	95	164 (23.42)	73 (1.87)	1391	721 (1)
	EFC Plant	5698	1509	132	64	85 (14.17)	25 (2.08)	1815	87 (2)
	EFC Pest	855	67	8	0	4 (2)	1	80	29 (1)
	EFC Crop	740	58	8	4	0	0	70	3 (4)
	FC OrganismInfo	6069	1007	76	37	42 (7)	6 (1.2)	1168	35 (1)
	All FCs	16776	3466	450	208	295	105	4532	

4 Evaluation

This section presents (Sect. 4.1) and discusses (Sect. 4.2) the results obtained for the three data structures. The experiments were conducted using Cogui software platform[1], which includes Java implementations of RCA and LinCbO [8]. Running times for the Java LinCbO implementation remain below 3229 ms for the most complex case (relational data model), summing the running times for all the EFCs.

4.1 Analysis of the Implications Obtained for the 3 Representations

In this section, we analyze the DGB of implications for the three representations (cf. Table 4). For each one, we present a quantitative and a qualitative analysis describing the main implication patterns, and provide selected examples. To consider implications applicable to OHA, we focus on the ones with scope > 0.

Implications in *Relational* Representation

OrganismInfo. The DGB contains 1168 implications: 1007 are held by one object ($S = 1$) and thus are very specific. Four types of implications are observed. The

---

[1] http://www.lirmm.fr/cogui/.

first one informs about the uses in medical care and food care for a species, a genus, or a family, e.g. the Meliaceae are not consumed (with $S = 35$)[2]:

$Family\_Meliaceae \implies Food\_$

The second type gives more specific information about subsets of species in families and genus, e.g. the species of Annonaceae, which are not consumed, are also not used in medical care. The third type reflects taxonomy: a genus implies a family or a species implies a genus, e.g. Genus Salvia implies Family Lamiaceae (with $S = 18$):

$Genus\_Salvia \implies Family\_Lamiaceae$

The fourth implication type reveals data variety in the dataset. For instance species of Lythraceae family are not consumed and not used for care, and are exclusively from Genus Lythrum.

Crop. The DGB contains 70 implications. The small value of $Smax$ (3), indicates that the implications are rather specific. The implications focus on the role of the organisms as crop. A first implication type describes the taxonomy. They come from FC $OrganismInfo$. A second implication type describes the bijection between the taxonomic information encoded in FCs $Crop$ and $OrganismInfo$, as the attributes are duplicated in both contexts, completed by information on food and medical care if appropriate. For instance, the following implication (with $S = 2$) indicates that a crop belonging to family Fabaceae ($CrFamily\_Fabaceae$) is connected to the $OrganismInfo$ objects representing this family, and is also consumed and not used in medical care:

$CrFamily\_Fabaceae \implies \exists cr\_CharactBy(Medical\_), \exists cr\_CharactBy(Food\_X),$
$\exists cr\_CharactBy(Family\_Fabaceae)$

A third implication type informs on the organisms role as crop, such as the following implication (with $S = 1$) named *Rel1*, which indicates that crops, used in medical care and not consumed, are from the Ricinus Communis species:

$\exists cr\_CharactBy(Food\_), \exists cr\_CharactBy(Medical\_X) \implies CrSpecies\_RicinusCommunis,$
$CrGenus\_Ricinus, CrFamily\_Euphorbiaceae, \exists cr\_CharactBy(Family\_Euphorbiaceae),$
$\exists cr\_CharactBy(Species\_RicinusCommunis\&Genus\_Ricinus)$ *(Rel1)*

The next example of implication (with $S = 1$), indicates that Malvaceae crops, not used in medical care, are restricted to Gossypium Genus and not consumed:

$CrFamily\_Malvaceae, \exists cr\_CharactBy(Medical\_), \exists cr\_CharactBy(Family\_Malvaceae) \implies$
$CrSpecies\_GossypiumHirsutum, CrGenus\_Gossypium, \exists cr\_CharactBy(Food\_),$
$\exists cr\_CharactBy(Species\_GossypiumHirsutum\&Genus\_Gossypium)$

Pest. The DGB contains 80 implications. Some implications reflect the taxonomy, already highlighted in $OrganismInfo$, and add no information for the experts. The Smax implication ($Smax = 29$) indicates that all pests are from the Noctuidae family, not consumed, and not used in medical care.

---

[2] *Food_X means is consumed; Food_ means is not consumed*, and similarly for *Medical_X* and *Medical_*.

Plant. The DGB contains 1815 implications. Most of the implications (1509) hold for a single plant. As for crops and pests, the implications either reflect taxonomy or information about human consumption and medical care usage (restricted to organisms that play the role of protecting plant). Some other implications are true for protecting plants only, such as the following one, indicating that family Poaceae plants not used in medical care, are also not consumed (with $S = 2$):

$$PlFamily\_Poaceae, \exists pl\_CharactBy(Medical\_), \exists pl\_CharactBy(Family\_Poaceae)$$
$$\implies \exists pl\_CharactBy(Food\_)$$

ProtectionSystem. The DGB contains 1391 implications, among which 566 held by more than one object. This result informs the expert on the numerous combinations of information existing in the datasets. The implication with $Smax = 721$, i.e. held by all objects, indicates that all systems treat Noctuidae. Within the 1391 implications, many implications types are present. They gather knowledge on the various roles of the organisms. We present some representative examples with diverse S values. The following implication (with $S = 380$), named *Rel2*, informs that when the studied protection systems treat Spodoptera Genus (Noctuidae Family), with a plant not consumed and not used in care, then the crop is used in medical care:

$$\exists treats(PeFamily\_Noctuidae), \exists treats(PeGenus\_Spodoptera), \exists uses(pl\_CharactBy(Food\_)),$$
$$\exists uses(pl\_CharactBy(Medical\_)) \implies \exists protects(cr\_CharactBy(Medical\_X)) \quad \textbf{(Rel2)}$$

The next implication (with $S = 8$) indicates that when studied protection systems treat Noctuidae Family with Genus Cymbopogon plants, then this is with Poaceae plants on consumed crops and the plants are used in medical care. Poaceae are also crops, and thus subject to implications for both roles:

$$\exists treats(PeFamily\_Noctuidae), \exists uses(PlGenus\_Cymbopogon) \implies$$
$$\exists uses(PlFamily\_Poaceae),$$
$$\exists protects(cr\_CharactBy(Food\_X)), \exists uses(pl\_CharactBy(Medical\_X))$$

The next implication (with $S = 4$) indicates that when the protection systems protect Poaceae crops consumed and not used in medical care, to treat Noctuidae pests, using non consumed plants, then this is with Meliaceae plants used in medical care:

$$\exists protects(CrFamily\_Poaceae), \exists treats(PeFamily\_Noctuidae), \exists uses(pl\_CharactBy(Food\_))$$
$$\exists protects(cr\_CharactBy(Food\_X)), \exists protects(cr\_CharactBy(Medical\_)),$$
$$\implies \exists uses(PlFamily\_Meliaceae), \exists uses(pl\_CharactBy(Medical\_X))$$

Implications in *TwoTables* Representation. As the FC *OrganismInfo* is similar to the one of *Relational*, it thus provides the same implication set. The DGB contains 1395 implications for the FC *ProtSystem*. This implication number is very similar to the one of the *ProtSystem Relational* representation. As an illustration, two implications are compared. The first one, *TT1*, focuses on the crop role:

$$\exists protects(Food\_), \exists protects(Medical\_X), \exists treats(Family\_Noctuidae)$$
$$\exists treats(Food\_), \exists treats(Medical\_) \implies \exists protects(Family\_Euphorbiaceae),$$
$$\exists protects(Species\_RicinusCommunis\&Genus\_Ricinus), \exists treats(Genus\_Spodoptera),$$
$$\exists treats(Species\_SpodopteraLitura), \exists uses(Food\_), \exists uses(Medical\_), \exists uses(Family\_Asteraceae),$$
$$\exists uses(Species\_WollastoniaDentata\&Genus\_Wollastonia) \quad \textbf{(TT1)}$$

It is one of the 5 implications that mention *Ricinus Communis*. Compared to its *Relational* representation formulation, i.e. *Rel1*, it mixes information proper to *Ricinus Communis* as a crop with additional information on the protection systems, in particular the usage of *Wollastonia Dentata* as the protecting plant. In this case, implications of the *Relational* representation are easier to read, as they focus on organism roles. The second implication, *TT2*, is held by Noctuidae that are not consumed and not used in medical care:

$\exists treats(Food\_), \exists treats(Medical\_), \exists treats(Family\_Noctuidae), \exists treats(Genus\_Spodoptera),$
$\exists uses(Food\_), uses(Medical\_) \implies \exists protects(Medical\_X)$ *(TT2)*

This information is not provided in its corresponding *Relational* representation formulation *Rel2* because it is not needed: in *Relational* representation it indeed appears in a separate and more precise way through the *Pest* implication indicating that Noctuidae are never consumed, nor used in medical care. *Rel2* is more focused and more synthetic.

Implications in *One Table* Representation. The DGB contains 1920 implications. Its *Smax* value is identical to the one of FCs *ProtSystem* of *TwoTables* and *Relational*. Its *S* value is lower, and the total number of implications is low (1920), compared to respectively 2571 and 4532 for *TwoTables* and *Relational*. This representation thus provides less implications, but with a higher diversity of implication formulations. As illustration, let us consider the implication *OT1* that corresponds to *Rel1* and *TT1*:

$PeFamily\_Noctuidae, MedicalCrop\_X, FoodCrop\_ \implies PeGenus\_Spodoptera, FoodPlant\_,$
$MedicalPlant\_, MultiUsePlSp\_, MultiUsePlGe\_, MultiUsePlFa\_, PlSpIsCrEw\_, PlGeIsCrEw\_,$
$PlFamily\_Asteraceae, PeSpecies\_SpodopteraLitura, CrSpIsPlEw\_X,$
$CrGeIsPlEw\_X, PlSpecies\_WollastoniaDentata, PlGenus\_Wollastonia,$
$CrSpecies\_RicinusCommunis, CrGenus\_Ricinus, CrFamily\_Euphorbiaceae$ *(OT1)*

The role has been encoded in the attribute name (e.g. *MedicalCrop*), rather than in the relations. Compared to *Rel1*, attributes about the protection system are included, e.g. *PeGenus_Spodoptera*. Compared to both *Rel1* and *TT1*, additional attributes indicate multi-use purpose, e.g. that the crop *Ricinus Communis* is used elsewhere as a protecting plant (*CrSpIsPlEw_X*), and the protecting plant *Wollastonia Dentata* is not used as a crop (*PlSpIsCrEw_*). Another example is *OT2*, where roles appear as attributes rather than through relations:

$PeGenus\_Spodoptera, PeFamily\_Noctuidae, FoodPlant\_, MedicalPlant\_, MultiUsePlSp\_,$
$MultiUsePlGe\_, MultiUsePlFa\_ \implies MedicalCrop\_X$ *(OT2)*

Information on food and medical care has not been encoded for pests in *OneTable* representation to simplify, being identical for all Noctuidae. Compared to both *Rel2* and *TT2*, additional attributes complete the premise to indicate that the plant has no multiple uses, e.g. *MultiUsePlGe_*.

4.2 Discussion

Lessons Learned. There is many taxonomic information in the implications, and some are duplicated in several tables. Although this duplication helps reading separately the implications (not considering several FCs at the same time), it complicates the reading of implications. Some other taxonomic information, such as indicating species, genus, and family may seem redundant too, as the latter two can be deduced from the species. Nevertheless, it may be useful for the readers who are not totally familiar with the taxonomy. In addition, some implications only precise the taxonomy, such as *species implies genus*. These implications could be automatically discarded, as they correspond to initial data encoding. Different settings of the implication formulation could be proposed to the user depending on the expected information.

Effect of Splitting the Representations. As shown in Table 4, dividing data into separate FCs, which introduces RCs, produces more implications. This may be explained by the fact that, for a relation (e.g. *uses* in *TwoTables*), concepts grouping target objects (e.g. *OrganismInfo*) induce concepts grouping source objects (e.g. *ProtSystem*) via the relational attributes. The implications include the result of this propagation schema. As a counterpart, in *Relational* representation, the implications are divided into coherent subsets, i.e. one per FC, simplifying their analysis. As the examples show, having few or no separate roles limits the relational attribute number and complexity. E.g., an advantage of *TwoTables* over *Relational* may be that the *TwoTables* implications contain one-level relational attributes (one RC), when the *Relational* ones contain relational attributes composing two RCs. But in return, when reducing the splitting, technical attributes, such as *plSpIsCrEw* in *OneTable* (plant species is crop elsewhere), have to be added to express multi-use and role, giving longer implications. This building and the formulation are not easier to understand by the expert. Moreover, as it has been highlighted by *TwoTables* and *OneTable*, the less the dataset is split, the more the implications mix information. This situation occurs with organism roles and protection systems, that are mixed in the implications of *CombinedRole* in *OneTable*, and of *ProtSystem* in *TwoTables*.

Threats to Validity. With regard to internal validity, the Knomana knowledge sets have been manually collected by many participants but controlled by two domain experts that are co-authors of this paper. The software used in this evaluation, i.e. RCA algorithms implemented in Cogui and Conexp, have already been used in other case studies with validated results. LinCbO has been implemented in Java and inserted in the Cogui framework. To confirm the correctness of this implementation, the results have been compared with those of Conexp. Construct validity can be appreciated through the metrics and the qualitative analysis adopted to evaluate the effect of representation splitting. The metrics have been chosen in order to evaluate the feasibility in terms of structure size and implication number. The running time obtained thanks to LinCbO is very low. The obtained implications have been exhaustively examined, a task made easier by the substitution of the concept number by the seed attributes. Some recurring schemes and representative implications have been reported in the paper as a result of this analysis. Conclusion validity is concerned with the possibility of generalizing the observations. Knomana knowledge set has its own particularities, such as being organized around a ternary relation $Plant \times Pest \times Crop$ (protection system). Other secondary relations gravitate around this central relation. This has the effect of centralizing, for protection systems, the information coming from the other contexts. The implications reflect this organization. Using another dataset, not organized this way, conclusions may be different.

5 Related Work

Modeling complex data with the objective of extracting knowledge is part of the Knowledge Discovery and Data Mining processes (KDD) [3]. This issue is addressed in FCA through various encoding schemes and extensions, starting with conceptual scaling [5]. In the case of RCA, data modeling includes choosing a kind of entity-relationship model with binary relationships and Boolean attributes. This requires deciding how data are separated in formal and relational contexts, and how to represent n-ary relations, e.g. ternary relations, a topic we studied in [10]. Life sciences data raise other issues, such as indeterminate species [9].

Association and Implication extraction is closely connected to FCA [1,11]. Implications with premises restricted to one attribute, have been extracted from the result of RCA combined with AOC-posets [2]. More recently, M. Wajnberg et al. extracted implications together with RCA, using generators [15,16]. The approach is applied to detect anomalies in manufacturing by aluminum die casting. The relational context is composed of machined parts, problems and the relation *generates* between parts and problems. Relational attributes and then concepts are built using the existential quantifier. Then in relational attributes, concepts are rewritten using their initial intent (the intent they had at their creation). This rewriting is made recursively.

In this paper, we build the DGB, and we use AOC-posets rather than concept lattices. We rewrite the relational attributes, as inspired by [15,16], to analyze the implications. In addition, we compare several encodings of our data to investigate the impact of this encoding on the implication sets.

6 Conclusion

This paper explores the combination of RCA and the Duquenne-Guigues basis of implications on an environmental knowledge set in order to render knowledge suitable to experts. Our case study gathers information on plants that can replace synthetic pesticides and antibiotics, and be consumed or used in medical care. The guiding research question was to assess whether splitting the datasets could have a positive or negative impact on the implications' readability by the experts. We identified advantages of this splitting to enable the separate analysis of coherent, simpler, implication subsets, not mixing information types. This is strengthened by the relational attribute rewriting that makes the implication easier to read and to interpret.

As future work, we plan to evaluate the impact of using concept lattices and Iceberg rather than AOC-posets for building the implications, as well as using other quantifiers provided by RCA. We will analyze the complete Knomana knowledge base, which includes additional descriptors such as location and plant chemical compounds. Finally, we will post-process the implications. In particular, we plan to present implications by categories and order them by relevance, using standard metrics or metrics specific to the experts' questions. A preliminary work [14] investigates the potential of using patterns on implication premise and conclusion for categorizing the implications. These patterns are based on multi-valued attributes (before nominal scaling) describing species, genera and families, and on a 'meta-attribute' representing the presence of information on *medical* or *food*.

Acknowledgments. This work was supported by the French National Research Agency under the Investments for the Future Program, referred as ANR-16-CONV-0004.

References

1. Bertet, K., Demko, C., Viaud, J.F., Guérin, C.: Lattices, closures systems and implication bases: a survey of structural aspects and algorithms. Theor. Comput. Sci. **743**, 93–109 (2018)
2. Dolques, X., Ber, F.L., Huchard, M., Grac, C.: Performance-friendly rule extraction in large water data-sets with AOC posets and relational concept analysis. Int. J. Gener. Syst. **45**(2), 187–210 (2016)
3. Fayyad, U.M., Piatetsky-Shapiro, G., Smyth, P.: The KDD process for extracting useful knowledge from volumes of data. Commun. ACM **39**(11), 27–34 (1996)
4. Frank, D.: One world, one health, one medicine. Can. Vet. J. **49**(11), 1063–1065 (2008)
5. Ganter, B., Wille, R.: Formal Concept Analysis - Mathematical Foundations. Springer, Heidelberg (1999)
6. Guigues, J.L., Duquenne, V.: Famille minimale d'implications informatives résultant d'un tableau de données binaires. Math. et Sci. Hum. **24**(95), 5–18 (1986)
7. Hacene, M.R., Huchard, M., Napoli, A., Valtchev, P.: Relational concept analysis: mining concept lattices from multi-relational data. Ann. Math. Artif. Intell. **67**(1), 81–108 (2013)
8. Janostik, R., Konecny, J., Krajča, P.: Pruning techniques in LinCbO for computation of the Duquenne-Guigues basis. In: Braud, A., Buzmakov, A., Hanika, T., Le Ber, F. (eds.) ICFCA 2021. LNCS (LNAI), vol. 12733, pp. 91–106. Springer, Cham (2021). https://doi.org/10.1007/978-3-030-77867-5_6
9. Keip, P., Ferré, S., Gutierrez, A., Huchard, M., Silvie, P., Martin, P.: Practical comparison of FCA extensions to model indeterminate value of ternary data. In: CLA 2020, CEUR Workshop Proceedings, vol. 2668, pp. 197–208 (2020)
10. Keip, P., et al.: Effects of input data formalisation in relational concept analysis for a data model with a ternary relation. In: Cristea, D., Le Ber, F., Sertkaya, B. (eds.) ICFCA 2019, LNCS (LNAI), vol. 11511, pp. 191–207. Springer, Cham (2019). https://doi.org/10.1007/978-3-030-21462-3_13
11. Kuznetsov, S.O., Poelmans, J.: Knowledge representation and processing with formal concept analysis. Wiley Interd. Rev. Data Min. Knowl. Disc. **3**(3), 200–215 (2013)

12. Martin, P., et al.: Dataset on noctuidae species used to evaluate the separate concerns in conceptual analysis: application to a life sciences knowledge base (2021). https://doi.org/10.18167/DVN1/HTFE8T
13. Martin, P., Silvie, P., Sarter, S.: Knomana - usage des plantes á effet pesticide, antimicrobien, antiparasitaire et antibiotique (patent APP IDDN.FR.001.130024.000.S.P.2019.000.31235) (2019)
14. Braud, A., Buzmakov, A., Hanika, T., Le Ber, F. (eds.): ICFCA 2021. LNCS (LNAI), vol. 12733. Springer, Cham (2021). https://doi.org/10.1007/978-3-030-77867-5
15. Wajnberg, M.: Analyse relationnelle de concepts: une méthode polyvalente pour l'extraction de connaissance. Ph.D. thesis, Université du Québec à Montréal (2020)
16. Wajnberg, M., Valtchev, P., Lezoche, M., Massé, A.B., Panetto, H.: Concept analysis-based association mining from linked data: a case in industrial decision making. In: Proceedings of the Joint Ontology Works. 2019 Episode V: The Styrian Autumn of Ontology. CEUR Workshop Proceedings, vol. 2518. CEUR-WS.org (2019)

Ranking Schemas by Focus: A Cognitively-Inspired Approach

Mattia Fumagalli[1], Daqian Shi[2(✉)], and Fausto Giunchiglia[2]

[1] Conceptual and Cognitive Modeling Research Group (CORE),
Free University of Bozen-Bolzano, Bolzano, Italy
mattia.fumagalli@unibz.it
[2] Department of Information Engineering and Computer Science (DISI),
University of Trento, Trento, Italy
daqian.shi@unitn.it, fausto.giunchiglia@unitn.it

Abstract. The main goal of this paper is to evaluate *knowledge base schemas*, modeled as a set of *entity types*, each such type being associated with a set of *properties*, according to their *focus*. We model the notion of focus as *"the state or quality of being relevant in storing and retrieving information"*. This definition of focus is adapted from the notion of *"categorization purpose"*, as first defined in cognitive psychology. In turn, this notion is formalized based on a set of knowledge metrics that, for any given focus, rank knowledge base schemas according to their quality. We apply the proposed methodology on a large data set of state-of-the-art knowledge base schemas and we show how it can be used in practice (Data and scripts are available at https://github.com/knowdive/Focus).

Keywords: Knowledge base schema · Schema ranking · Categorization purpose · Knowledge representation · Mental representation

1 Introduction

Following contemporary psychology, the purpose of what we call categorization can be reduced to *"...a means of simplifying the environment, of reducing the load on memory, and of helping us to store and retrieve information efficiently"* [1, 2]. According to this perspective, categorizing consists of putting things (like events, items, objects, ideas or people) into categories (e.g., classes or types) based on their similarities, or common features. Without categorization we would be overwhelmed by the huge amount of diverse information coming from the external environment and our mental life would be chaotic [3, 4]. In the context of Artificial Intelligence (AI), the purpose of categorization is usually implemented by well defined and effective information objects, namely knowledge base schemas (KBSs), where prominent examples include *knowledge graphs (KGs), schema layers* [5] and *ontologies* [6]. KBSs offer many pivotal benefits [7], such as: *i)*. human understandability; *ii)*. a fixed and discrete view over a stream of multiple and diverse data; *iii)*. a tree or a grid structure, so that each information

© Springer Nature Switzerland AG 2021
T. Braun et al. (Eds.): ICCS 2021, LNAI 12879, pp. 73–88, 2021.
https://doi.org/10.1007/978-3-030-86982-3_6

can be located by answering a determinate set of questions in order; and *iv)*. an encoding in a formal language, which is a fragment of the first first-order predicate calculus. These benefits allow representing high-performance solutions to large-scale categorization problems, namely problems of efficient information storage and retrieval.

KBSs are the backbone of many semantic applications and play a central role in improving the efficiency of many "categorization systems" (like digital libraries or online stores). Their construction usually involves a huge effort in terms of time and domain-specific knowledge (see for instance well-known problems as "knowledge acquisition bottleneck" [8]). So far, in order to minimize the effort in building KBSs, a huge number of search engines, catalogs, and metrics have been produced, to also facilitate their reuse [9]. As the number of available KBSs increases, the definition of approaches for facilitating their reuse becomes an even greater issue [10], also considering new areas of application, see, for instance, *Relational Learning* [11] or *Transfer Learning* [12].

The main goal of this paper is to provide a quantifiable and deterministic way to assess KBSs according to their *categorization purpose*, by means of what we call their *focus*. Here we take a KBS as a set of *entity types*, each such type being associated with a set of *properties*, and we model the notion of focus as *"the state or quality of being relevant in storing and retrieving information"*. We measure focus via a set of metrics that we ground on the notion of *categorization*, as first defined in cognitive psychology [13]. We then show how focus can be used to rank: *i)*. the concepts inside a KBS which are more/less informative; *ii)*. the concepts across multiple KBS which are more/less informative; and *iii)*. the KBSs which are more/less informative. As final step, in order to test the utility of the focus measures we show how it can be used to support engineers in measuring the relevance[1] of KBSs. That is, *a)*. we verify how the KBSs ranking provided by the focus metrics reflects the ranking of the KBSs provided by a group of knowledge engineers, according to guidelines inspired by a well-known experiment in cognitive psychology; *b)*. we verify how focus can help scientists in selecting better KBSs to train a classifier and address an *Entity Type Recognition (ETR)* task, as it is defined in [15].

The paper main contributions can be then summarized as follows: *i)*. a cognitive psychology grounded account of the notion of focus (Sect. 2); *ii)*. a set of metrics that apply to KBSs, their entity types, and their properties, which can be used to rank KBSs according to their focus (Sect. 3); *iii)*. an analysis of the application of the metrics over ~50 state-of-the-art (SoA) data sets (Sect. 4). Based on these results, in the second part of the paper, the scope of Sect. 5 is to describe the feasibility and practical utility of the approach; Sect. 6 discusses the related work, while Sect. 7 reports the conclusions.

---

[1] *"Something (A) is relevant to a task (T) if it increases the likelihood of accomplishing the goal (G), which is implied by T"* [14].

2   Defining Focus

Imagine that, by saying "the green book on my desk in my office", someone wants someone else to bring her that book. This will happen only if the two subjects share *a way of describing objects* into those that are offices and those that are not, those that are books and those that are non-books, desks, and non-desks. These "object descriptions" are what is meant to convey for retrieving the intended objects. The point is *to draw sharp lines around the group of objects to be described.* That is *the categorization purpose* of an object description. These object descriptions, also called types, categories, or classes, are the basis of the organization of our mental life. Meaning and communication heavily depend on this categorization [3,4,13,16].

Following the contemporary descriptions by psychologists, and, in particular, the seminal work by Eleanor Rosch [1], the categorization purpose of objects descriptions or categories, can be explained according to two main dimensions, namely: *i). the maximization of the number of features that describe the members of the given category* and *ii). the minimization of the number of features shared with other categories.*

To evaluate these dimensions Eleanor Rosch introduces the central notion of *cue validity* [17]. This notion was defined as *"the conditional probability $p(c_j|f_j)$ that an object falls in a category c_j given a feature, or cue, f_j"*, and then used to define the set of basic level categories, namely those categories which maximize the number of characteristics (i.e., features or attributes like "having a tail" and "being colored") shared by their members and minimize the number of characteristics shared with the members of their sibling categories. The intuition is that *basic level categories* have higher cue validity and, because of this, they are *more relevant in categorization.*

Rosch's definitions were designed for experiments where humans were asked to score objects as members of certain given categories. We adapt Rosch's original methodology to the context of KBS engineering. In our setting, each available KBS (see, for instance, *schema.org*[2] or *DBpedia*[3]) plays the role of a categorization, which is modeled as a set of *entity types* associated to a set of *properties*, whose main function is to *draw sharp lines around the types of entities it contains, so that each member in its domain falls determinately either in or out of each entity type* [15,18]. The knowledge engineers play a role similar to the persons involved in Rosch's experiment. Each knowledge base schema provides a rich set of categorization examples. Each entity type plays the role of a category and all entity type properties play the role of features. The categorization purpose of the KBS is what we call *focus*. We then model the notion of focus as *"the state or quality of being relevant in storing and retrieving information"* and we quantify the degree of this relevance by adapting Rosch's notion of cue validity as follows:

---

[2] http://schema.org/.
[3] https://wiki.dbpedia.org/.

- we take each property to have the same "cue validity" (which we assume to be normalized to one);
- for each KBS we equally divide the property "cue validity" across the entity types the properties are associated to;
- by checking the wide-spreading of "cue validity" we quantify the relevance of the KBS and entity types in storing and retrieving information.

The "focus" can be then calculated in relation to this analysis and, in turn, it can be functionally articulated in:

- *the entity types focus*, namely, what allows to identify the entity types that are maximally informative categories, which have a *higher categorization relevance*, or, more precisely, which maximize the number of properties and minimize the number of properties shared with other categories. These entity types being, to some extent, related to what expert users consider as "core entity types" or central entity types for a given domain;
- *the KBSs focus*, namely, what allows to identify the KBSs that maximize the number of maximally informative (focused) entity types. These KBSs being described, to some extent, as *"clean"* or *"not-noisy"* and being related to what expert users classify as well-designed KBSs [7].

3 Focus Metrics

Taking inspiration by the research results presented in [15, 18], we assume that a KBS can be formalized as: $K = \langle E_K, P_K, I_K \rangle$, with $E_K = \{e_1, ..., e_n\}$ being the set of *entity types* of K, $P_K = \{p_1, ..., p_n\}$ being the set of *properties* of K, and I_K being a binary relation $I_K \subseteq E_K \times P_K$ that expresses specific entity types that *are associated* with specific properties. We describe that an entity type e is *associated with* a property p when e is being in the domain of the p, in formula e $\in$ *dom(p)*. For instance, the entity type *Person* can be in the domain of properties such as *address* or *name*, while the property *address* may be associated with entities such as *Person*, or *Building*. It is worth noticing that the proposed formalization of entities and properties is different from, e.g., the encoding that can be provided by the OWL[4] representational language. The key difference can be clarified by considering our formalism very similar to what is proposed by the *Formal Concept Analysis* (FCA) methods [19]. Our commitment to this model is motivated not only on foundational considerations but also on pragmatic grounds. Once properties and entity types are formalized as described above, data can be indeed analyzed and processed with few limitations in practice.[5]

Given the above formalization, we define a main set of metrics, namely the focus of an entity type, $Focus_e$ and the focus of a KBS, $Focus_k$.

---

[4] https://www.w3.org/2001/sw/WebOnt/.
[5] See [20] for an overview of the multiple available approaches and applications.

3.1 $Focus_e$

According to the notion of *entity type focus* which is introduced in Sect. 2, we model *entity type focus* metric $Focus_e$ as:

$$Focus_e(e) = Cue_e(e) + \eta Cue_{er}(e) = Cue_e(e)(1 + \frac{\eta}{|prop(e)|}) \, , \, \eta > 0 \qquad (1)$$

In the above function, e represents an entity type. The $Focus_e$ results from the summation of Cue_e and Cue_{er}. Cue_e represents the *cue validity* of the entity type. Cue_{er} represents a normalization of Cue_e. η represents a constraint factor to be applied over Cue_{er}. The constraint factor η is used to manipulate the weight of the metric Cue_{er}, thereby affecting the value of the metric $Focus_e$. Specifically, two parts of the function can also be combined, in which $|prop(e)|$ is the number of properties associated with the specific entity type e. Notice that, in this setting, we assume that the weight of η is equal to 1, postponing the analysis on how to derive the best constraint factors to the immediate future work.

To model Cue_e and Cue_{er} we mainly adapted the work presented in [21]. In order to calculate Cue_e, firstly, we define the *cue validity* of a property p associated with an entity type e, also called Cue_p, as:

$$Cue_p(p, e) = \frac{PoE(p, e)}{|dom(p)|} \in [0, 1] \qquad (2)$$

$|dom(p)|$ presents the cardinality of entity types that are the domain of the specific property p. $PoE(p, e)$ is defined as:

$$PoE(p, e) = \begin{cases} 1, if e \in dom(p) \\ 0, if e \notin dom(p) \end{cases} \qquad (3)$$

$Cue_p(p, e)$ returns 0 if p is not associated with e. Otherwise returns $1/n$, where n is the number of entity types in the domain of p. In particular, Cue_p takes the maximum value 1 if p is associated with only one entity type.

Given the notion of Cue_p we provide the notion of *cue validity* of an entity type. Cue_e, is related to the sum of the *cue validity* of the properties associated with the specific entity type e and is modeled as follows:

$$Cue_e(e) = \sum_{i=1}^{|prop(e)|} Cue_p(p_i, e) \in [0, |prop(e)|] \qquad (4)$$

Cue_e provides the *centrality* of an entity in a given KBS, by summing all its properties Cue_p. Cue_e refers to the maximization of the properties associated with entity type e with the members it categories.

Given the notion of Cue_e, we capture the minimization level of the number of properties shared with other entity types, inside a KBS with the notion of Cue_{er}, which we define as:

$$Cue_{er}(e) = \frac{Cue_e(e)}{|prop(e)|} \in [0, 1] \qquad (5)$$

After deriving Cue_e and Cue_{er} it is possible to calculate $Focus_e$. Notice that, to normalize the range of the metrics, we applied *log normalization* [22] on Cue_e since $|prop(e)|$ can be significantly unbalanced between entity types and *min-max normalization* [23] on Cue_{er}.

3.2 $Focus_k$

Following the *KBSs focus* notion we introduced in Sect. 2, we model the *KBSs focus*, namely $Focus_k$, as follows:

$$Focus_k(K) = Cue_k(K) + \mu Cue_{kr}(K) = Cue_k(K)(1 + \frac{\mu}{|prop(K)|}), \mu > 0 \qquad (6)$$

where we take K as an input KBS and we take $Focus_k$ as a summation of Cue_k and Cue_{kr}. Cue_k represents the *cue validity* of the KBS. Cue_{kr} represents a normalization of Cue_k. μ represents a constraint factor for Cue_{kr}, which we assume being equal to 1, as for Cue_{er} above. $|prop(K)|$ refers to the number of the properties in K.

The notions and terminology used for entity types, i.e., the notions of Cue_e and Cue_{er}, can be straightforwardly generalized to KBSs, generating the following metrics:

$$Cue_k(K) = \sum_{i=1}^{|E_K|} Cue_e(e_i) \in [0, |prop(K)|] \qquad (7)$$

The $Cue_k(K)$ is calculated as a summation of the *cue validity* of all the entity types in a given KBS, which in the function is represented by E_K. $|prop(K)|$ refers to the number of the properties in the KBS, as the maximization of Cue_k.

Following the formalization of Cue_{er} we capture the minimization level of the number of properties shared across the entity types inside the schema with the notion of Cue_{kr}, which we define as:

$$Cue_{kr}(K) = Cue_k(K)/ \sum_{i=1}^{|E_K|} prop(e_i) \in [0, 1] \qquad (8)$$

Cue_k and Cue_{kr} can be used then to assess the focus of a whole KBS. Notice that to normalize the metric $Focus_k$, we applied *log normalization* on Cue_k, since $|prop(K)|$ may be significantly higher in some KBSs than others KBSs and *min-max normalization* on Cue_{kr}.

4   Ranking KBSs

We started to put into use the above metrics by measuring the focus of state-of-the-art KBSs.

We collected a data set of 700 KBSs, expressed in the *Terse RDF Triple Language (Turtle)*[6] format. Most of these resources have been taken from the

---

[6] https://www.w3.org/TR/turtle/.

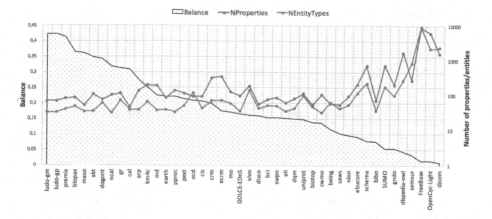

Fig. 1. KBSs selected for the analysis

LOV catalog[7]. The remaining ones, see for instance *freebase*[8] and *SUMO*[9] have been added to collect more data.

For the sake of the analysis, all the data sets have been flattened into a set of sets of triples (one set per entity type, or etype), where each triple encodes information about "etype-property" associations $I_K(e)$ (e.g., the triple "Person-domainOf-friend" encodes the "Person-friend" $I_K(e)$ association). Moreover, in order to generate the final output data sets we processed properties labels via NLP pipeline which performs various steps, including, for instance: *i)*. split a string every time a capital letter is encountered (e.g., *birthDate* → birth and date); *ii)*. lower case all characters; *iii)*. filter out stop-words (e.g., *hasAuthor* → author). This allowed us to run a more accurate analysis. For instance, if "Person" and "Place" have properties like "globalLocationNumberInfo" and "LocationNumber", respectively, by processing the labels as we have done, it is possible to find some overlapping (see "location" and "number") otherwise no.

We selected a subset of the starting data set after the above processing, by discharging all the KBSs with less than 30 entity types. An overall view of the final output data set is provided by Fig. 1, where, for each of the remaining 44 KBSs, the number of properties, the number of entity types, and the balance are provided. The balance returns the value of a simple distribution of the properties of a KBS across its entity types and it is calculated as:

$$Balance(K) = \frac{|prop(K_i)|}{|E_{K_i}|} * \frac{1}{|prop(e_i)|_{max}} \tag{9}$$

---

[7] https://lov.linkeddata.es/dataset/lov.

[8] https://developers.google.com/freebase.

[9] http://www.adampease.org/OP/.

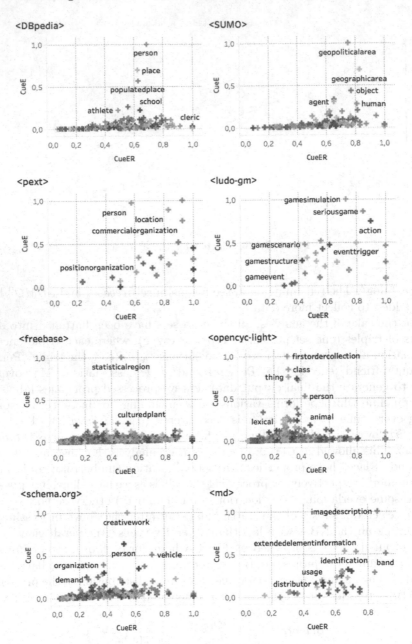

Fig. 2. Entity types categorization relevance for eight example KBSs

with $|prop(K_i)|$ being the cardinality of the set of properties of the KBS, $|E_{K_i}|$ being the cardinality of the set of entities of the KBS and $|prop(e_i)|_{max}$ being the cardinality of the set of properties associated to the entity with the major number of properties in the KBS.

Table 1. KBSs ranking

KBS	$Cue_k(K)$	$Cue_{kr}(K)$	$Focus_k(K)$
freebase	8981	0,21	1,15
cal	46	0,98	0,92
bibo	71	0,97	0,92
opencyc-l	6266	0,26	0,90
swpo	87	0,88	0,83
cwmo	107	0,85	0,80
eli	62	0,84	0,78
ncal	103	0,80	0,75
mo	124	0,79	0,74
akt	106	0,79	0,74

Table 2. Entity types ranking

KBS	Entity type	$Cue_e(e)$	$Cue_{er}(e)$	$Focus_e(e)$
DBpedia	person	169,02	0,69	1,42
opencyc-l	firstordercoll.	230,59	0,30	1,30
freebase	statisticalreg.	161,53	0,48	1,17
opencyc-l	class	194,95	0,31	1,15
dicom	ieimage	158,90	0,44	1,13
DBpedia	place	116,97	0,63	1,13

Table 3. Ranking for the entity type person from different KBSs

KBS	Entity type	$Cue_e(e)$	$Cue_{er}(e)$	$Focus_e(e)$
DBpedia	person	169,02	0,69	1,42
akt	person	8,00	1,00	1,03
opencyc-l	person	122,14	0,43	0,95
vivo	person	10,60	0,88	0,92
swpo	person	3,50	0,88	0,88
cwmo	person	5,83	0,83	0,85

By applying the cue entity metrics, i.e., $Cue_e(e)$ and $Cue_{er}(e)$ to the KBSs of the resulting list, we obtained the scores to evaluate the categorization relevance of the entity types for each KBS. Let us take, for instance the values provided by KBSs in Fig. 2. We randomly selected eight KBSs from the starting set and we listed them according to the number of entity types. The selected KBSs are: *Freebase*, *OpenCyc*[10], *DBpedia*, *SUMO*, *schema.org*, *md*[11], *pext*[12] and *ludo-gm*.[13]

The corresponding scattered plots provide the correlations between (a *min-max normalization* of) $Cue_e(e)$ and $Cue_{er}(e)$ for each entity type of each of the selected KBSs. The top-right entity types are the ones with the higher categorization relevance according to our metrics. For instance, in *SUMO* we have entity types like *GeopoliticalArea* and *GeographicalArea* and in *DBpedia* we have *Person* and *Place*.

By applying the $Focus_k(K)$ over the set of 44 KBSs we obtained the KBS ranking, where the top 11 KBSs are reported in Table 1. By applying $Focus_e(e)$ over the set of 44 KBSs we obtained the entity types ranking, where the top 6 entity types in terms of categorization relevance are reported in Table 2. Finally, by selecting a given entity type, by applying $Focus_e(e)$, it is possible to find the best KBS for that entity type. Table 3 provides an example for the entity type *Person*.

5   Validating Focus

To validate the focus metrics we use two types of assessment. In Sect. 5.1 we analyze the accuracy of the $Focus_e(e)$ metric in weighting the categorization relevance of entity types, namely their centrality in the maximization of information. This will be done by applying our metrics and some related SoA ranking algorithms over a set of example KBSs. Then we compare the results with a reference data set generated by 5 knowledge engineers, to which we provided a set of instructions/guidelines to rank the entity types, taking inspiration from Rosch's experiment [1]. The main goal of the assessment run in this subsection is to show how Focus reflects the judgment of engineers in measuring the relevance of a given KBS, w.r.t. a set of entity types. This also suggests a possible application of Focus in supporting search facilities in KBSs catalogs, where queries run by the users may be in the form of *"give me the most relevant KBS for the eType x and y"*.

In Sect. 5.2, given the lack of baseline metrics for calculating the overall score of a KBS on similar functions, and the lack of reference gold standards, we analyze the effects that the $Focus_k(K)$ of a KBS may have on the prediction performance of a relational classification task. The main goal of the assessment run in this subsection is to show how focus can support scientists in reusing KBSs in new application areas, like, for instance, *statistical relational learning* or, more precisely, in tasks like *entity type recognition*.

---

[10] https://pythonhosted.org/ordf/ordf_vocab_opencyc.html.
[11] http://def.seegrid.csiro.au/isotc211/iso19115/2003/metadata.
[12] http://www.ontotext.com/proton/protonext.html.
[13] http://ns.inria.fr/ludo/v1/docs/gamemodel.html.

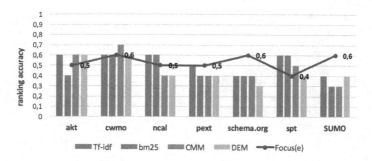

Fig. 3. $Focus_e(e)$ experiment results

5.1 $Focus_e$ Validation

The target here is to check how $Focus_e(e)$ allows to rank entity types in KBSs according to their categorization relevance, as described in Sect. 2. To assess our metric we firstly selected a subset of the KBSs discussed in the previous section, namely akt[14], $cwmo$[15], $ncal$, $pext$, $schema.org$, spt[16] and $SUMO$.

We selected these KBSs because they provide very different examples in terms of the number of properties and entity types. Moreover almost all their entity types labels are human understandable[17]. As second step we selected four SoA ranking algorithms, namely *TF-IDF* [24], *BM25* [25], *Class Match Measure (CMM)* and *Density Measure (DEM)* [26]. We used the performance of these rankings as a baseline, by selecting their scores for the top 10 entity types, for each of the given KBSs, and we compared them with the rankings provided by $Focus_e(e)$. The relevance of our approach was then measured in terms of accuracy (from 0 to 1) by checking how many entity types of the ranking results are in the entity types ranking lists provided by the knowledge engineers. The output of this experiment is represented by the data in Fig. 3.

As Fig. 3 shows, the blue line represents the accuracy of the ranking trend provided by $Focus_e(e)$. Each bar represents the accuracy of the ranking for the corresponding selected algorithm. All the accuracy results are grouped by the reference KBS.

The first main observation is that all the reference SoA metrics show a very similar trend, with higher accuracy for akt, $cwmo$, $ncal$ and spt, and lower accuracy for $schema.org$ and $SUMO$. This is not the case for $Focus_e(e)$. Our metric, indeed, even if it is not the best for all the KBSs, performs best with huge and very noisy (with lower entity types Cue_{er}) KBSs, as it is the case for $schema.org$ and $SUMO$ (just check the visualization of $SUMO$ and $schema.org$ as in Fig. 2 to observe the phenomenon). This, as we expected, depends on the pivotal role

---

[14] https://lov.linkeddata.es/dataset/lov/vocabs/akt.

[15] https://gabriel-alex.github.io/cwmo/.

[16] https://github.com/dbpedia/ontology-tracker/tree/master/ontologies/spitfire-project.eu.

[17] A lot of KBSs have entity types labels codified by an ID.

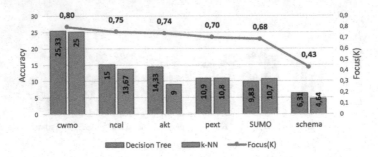

Fig. 4. $Focus_k(K)$ experiment results

we gave to the minimization of the number of overlapping properties. The Cue_{er} for each entity type provides indeed essential information about the categorization relevance that, giving more importance to the number of properties of an entity type, may not be properly identified. Thus, given small and not-noisy (or "clean" in terms of number of overlapping properties) KBSs, other approaches, very focused on the number of properties of entity types pay very well (see the good performance of the *TF-IDF* algorithm). Differently, when KBSs present a huge amount of entity types, with low Cue_{er}, $Focus_e$ allows to better identify the categorization relevance.

The second main observation is that *TF-IDF* and $Focus_e(e)$ are the best metrics in terms of average performance, namely 0.52 (both *TF-IDF* and $Focus_e(e)$) mean accuracy vs. 0.47 for *bm25* and *CMM*, and 0.44 for *DEM*. This score being motivated by the fact that *TF-IDF* is almost always the best when the given KBS is small and not-noisy and $Focus_e(e)$ compensates the standard performance with small and clean KBSs, with a high performance with huge and noisy KBSs.

5.2 $Focus_k$ Validation

The target of the second task is to check whether $Focus_k(K)$ helps to predict the performance of KBSs in their ability to predict their own entity types. In this experiment, we used the same KBSs we selected in the previous experiment to address relational classification, where entity types have an associated label and the task is to predict those labels. Notice that we addressed a specific type of relational classification, namely an *entity type recognition task (ETR)*, as defined in [15]. We set-up the experiment as follows: *i).* we trained machine learning models by the FCA-format KBS as training set (In this experiment we choose *decision tree* and *k-NN* [27,28]); *ii).* we reported the relative performance of the models in terms of differences in accuracy and compared the performances with the $Focus_k(K)$ for each of the given KBSs.

As shown in Fig. 4, the accuracy is reported as a proportion of correct predictions, within the range of [0%,100%]. The $Focus_k(K)$ is reported by the values of the line. The *cwmo* KBS is the one with the best scores, in terms of accuracy (for both the trained models) and $Focus_k(K)$. *schema.org* is the worst.

The main observation is that, as expected, the trend in terms of accuracy, considering both the two models, follows the $Focus_k(K)$ ranking for most of the given KBSs. However, it can be noticed that k-NN, with the *pext* KBS represents an exception, it is indeed worse than *akt* in terms of $Focus_k(K)$, but performs better with k-NN. Going deep into the analysis, this phenomenon can be explained by the relationship between the number of properties and the number of entity types, more specifically by the balance of the KBS. This value can indeed affect the performance of the model in prediction. The more the balance the more the probability of having entity types with a low focus. This effect being quite evident if we consider two KBSs with extremely similar $Focus_k(K)$, but disparate balance. This experiment, while showing how $Focus_k(K)$ can be a concrete explanation of the categorization relevance of a KBS, suggests the possibility of a practical application of $Focus_k(K)$ to measure the potential performance of a KBS or a set of KBSs in a relational classification task. The results may be used, e.g., to fine-tune KBSs in an open-world data integration scenario.

6   Related Work

Our work shares with the research on *ontology* and *knowledge graph (KG) schema* (functional) evaluation [7,9,29] the goal of facilitating the reuse of these knowledge structures. This work has been extensive and has exploited a huge amount of methods and techniques including, e.g. *DWRank* [30] and the *NCBO* [31] (the former being a high precision recommender for biomedical ontology, the latter being a "learning to rank approach" based on search queries).

Our proposal differs from this related work in two major respects. The first is that we ground our approach and the notion of focus on the notion of categorization purpose from cognitive psychology. The theoretical underpinning of our formalization of the metrics and the experimental setup is then inspired by the analysis of human behavior in categorization, and in particular by the seminal work by E. Rosch. Our goal is not to redefine terminology already in use in the related work, but rather to propose a both theoretically and practically useful formalization of the central activity of categorization, which can be considered as the baseline of each knowledge engineering task. The second difference, which is actually a consequence of the first, is that, while most of the functional evaluation approaches are related to the intended use of a given KBS, and consider functional dimensions, like task and domain, which are very context-dependent, this is not the case with our approach. The notion of focus we adapted, indeed, aims to model a privileged level of categorization, independently from the tasks and the domain of application of the data structure. This in turn allows us to devise a somewhat opposite approach. In fact, the domain of a KBS can be then identified through the focus scores. For instance, the fact that a KBS has a high focus for entity types like *CreativeWork* or *Product*, will help the user to understand what is the real potential of that KBS for a given domain of application.

As a final remark, it is important to observe how the notion of cue validity has been widely studied in the context of feature engineering. Together with other similar measures as "category utility" or "mutual information" and, it has been used to measure the informativeness of a category [32]. Our approach differs from the related work in the application of Rosch's notion at the KBS level, rather than on data. Moreover, the introduction of the "overall" *Focus* metrics to rank categorization relevance is a novel contribution.

7   Conclusion

In this paper, we have proposed a formal method to evaluate KBSs according to their focus, namely, what cognitive psychologists call categorization purpose. This in turn has allowed us to describe how this evaluation plays an important role in supporting an accurate level of KBSs understanding and reuse.

In this regard, as preliminary validation of the proposed metrics we are showing: *a)*. how focus KBSs ranking reflects the ranking of the KBSs provided by a group of knowledge engineers, following the guidelines inspired by a well-known experiment in cognitive psychology; *b)*. how focus can help scientists in selecting better KBSs to train a classifier and address an *Entity Type Recognition (ETR)* task.

The future work will concentrate on an extension of the proposed metrics, possibly by considering the hierarchical structure of KBSs, an extension of the experimental set-up, and an implementation of the metrics for supporting the search engine of a large number of existing high-quality KBSs.

Acknowledgement. The research conducted by Mattia Fumagalli is supported by the *"NEXON - Foundations of Next-Generation Ontology-Driven Conceptual Modeling"* project, funded by the *Free University of Bozen-Bolzano*. The research conducted by Fausto Giunchiglia and Daqian Shi has received funding from the *"DELPhi - DiscovEring Life Patterns"*, funded by the MIUR Progetti di Ricerca di Rilevante Interesse Nazionale (PRIN) 2017 – DD n. 1062.

References

1. Rosch, E.: Principles of categorization. Concepts: Core Readings **189** (1999)
2. Harnad, S.: To cognize is to categorize: cognition is categorization. In: Handbook of Categorization in Cognitive Science, pp. 21–54. Elsevier (2017)
3. Millikan, R.G.: On Clear and Confused Ideas: An Essay About Substance Concepts. Cambridge University Press, Cambridge (2000)
4. Giunchiglia, F., Fumagalli, M.: Concepts as (recognition) abilities. In: FOIS, pp. 153–166 (2016)
5. Qiao, L., Yang, L., Hong, D., Yao, L., Zhiguang, Q.: Knowledge graph construction techniques. J. Comput. Res. Dev. **53**(3), 582–600 (2016)
6. Guarino, N., Oberle, D., Staab, S.: What is an ontology? In: Staab, S., Studer, R. (eds.) Handbook on Ontologies. IHIS, pp. 1–17. Springer, Heidelberg (2009). https://doi.org/10.1007/978-3-540-92673-3_0
7. Paulheim, H.: Knowledge graph refinement: a survey of approaches and evaluation methods. Semant. web **8**(3), 489–508 (2017)

8. Shadbolt, N., Smart, P.R., Wilson, J.R., Sharples, S.: Knowledge elicitation. Eval. Hum. Work 163–200 (2015)
9. McDaniel, M., Storey, V.C.: Evaluating domain ontologies: clarification, classification, and challenges. ACM Comput. Surv. (CSUR) $52(4)$, 1–44 (2019)
10. Degbelo, A.: A snapshot of ontology evaluation criteria and strategies. In: Proceedings of the 13th International Conference on Semantic Systems, pp. 1–8 (2017)
11. Nickel, M., Murphy, K., Tresp, V., Gabrilovich, E.: A review of relational machine learning for knowledge graphs. Proc. IEEE $104(1)$, 11–33 (2015)
12. Fumagalli, M., Bella, G., Conti, S., Giunchiglia, F.: Ontology-driven cross-domain transfer learning. In: Formal Ontology in Information Systems, pp. 249–263. IOS Press (2020)
13. Millikan, R.G.: Beyond Concepts: Unicepts, Language, and Natural Information. Oxford University Press (2017)
14. Hjørland, B., Christensen, F.S.: Work tasks and socio-cognitive relevance: a specific example. J. Am. Soc. Inform. Sci. Technol. $53(11)$, 960–965 (2002)
15. Giunchiglia, F., Fumagalli, M.: Entity type recognition-dealing with the diversity of knowledge. In: Proceedings of the International Conference on Principles of Knowledge Representation and Reasoning, vol. 17, pp. 414–423 (2020)
16. Fumagalli, M., Bella, G., Giunchiglia, F.: Towards understanding classification and identification. In: Nayak, A.C., Sharma, A. (eds.) PRICAI 2019. LNCS (LNAI), vol. 11670, pp. 71–84. Springer, Cham (2019). https://doi.org/10.1007/978-3-030-29908-8_6
17. Rosch, E., Mervis, C.B.: Family resemblances: studies in the internal structure of categories. Cogn. Psychol. $7(4)$, 573–605 (1975)
18. Giunchiglia, F., Fumagalli, M.: On knowledge diversity. In: Proceedings of the 2019 Joint Ontology Workshops, WOMoCoE (2019)
19. Ganter, B., Wille, R.: Formal Concept Analysis: Mathematical Foundations. Springer, Heidelberg (2012)
20. Goyal, P., Ferrara, E.: Graph embedding techniques, applications, and performance: a survey. Knowl.-Based Syst. 151, 78–94 (2018)
21. Giunchiglia, F., Fumagalli, M.: On knowledge diversity. In: JOWO (2019)
22. Bornemann, E., Doveton, J.H., et al.: Log normalization by trend surface analysis. Log Anal. $22(04)$ (1981)
23. Kumar Jain, Y., Bhandare, S.K.: Min max normalization based data perturbation method for privacy protection. Int. J. Comput. Commun. Technol. $2(8)$, 45–50 (2011)
24. Salton, G., Buckley, C.: Term-weighting approaches in automatic text retrieval. Inf. Process. Manag. $24(5)$, 513–523 (1988)
25. Robertson, S.E., Walker, S., Jones, S., Hancock-Beaulieu, M.M., Gatford, M., et al.: Okapi at TREC-3. NIST Special Publication SP, 109:109 (1995)
26. Alani, H., Brewster, C.: Metrics for ranking ontologies (2006)
27. Kamiński, B., Jakubczyk, M., Szufel, P.: A framework for sensitivity analysis of decision trees. CEJOR $26(1)$, 135–159 (2017). https://doi.org/10.1007/s10100-017-0479-6
28. Dasarathy, B.V.: Nearest Neighbor (NN) Norms: NN Pattern Classification Techniques. IEEE Computer Society Tutorial (1991)
29. Gangemi, A., Catenacci, C., Ciaramita, M., Lehmann, J.: A theoretical framework for ontology evaluation and validation. In: SWAP, vol. 166, p. 16. Citeseer (2005)
30. Butt, A.S., Haller, A., Xie, L.: DWRank: learning concept ranking for ontology search. Semant. Web $7(4)$, 447–461 (2016)

31. Martínez-Romero, M., Jonquet, C., O'connor, M.J., Graybeal, J., Pazos, A., Musen, M.A.: NCBO ontology recommender 2.0: an enhanced approach for biomedical ontology recommendation. J. Biomed. Semant. **8**(1), 21 (2017)
32. Peng, H., Long, F., Ding, C.: Feature selection based on mutual information: criteria of max-dependency, max-relevance, and min-redundancy. IEEE Trans. Pattern Anal. Mach. Intell. **8**, 1226–1238 (2005)

Theory on Conceptual Structures

Improving the Performance
of Lindig-Style Algorithms
with Empty Intersections

Petr Krajča[(✉)] [iD]

Department of Computer Science, Palacký University Olomouc,
17. listopadu 12, 77146 Olomouc, Czech Republic
petr.krajca@upol.cz

Abstract. The building of a concept lattice and its line diagram from
a set of formal concepts is an important task in formal concept analysis
(FCA), since it allows one to express relationships among formal concepts in a concise and comprehensible form. One may enumerate direct
neighbors of each formal concept and build a concept lattice or its line
diagram in a straightforward way. This is the main idea behind the algorithm proposed by Lindig. This algorithm, as well as other algorithms
in FCA, must contend with the fact that some formal concepts are enumerated multiple times. In practice a substantial amount of redundant
computations is related to the top (or bottom) formal concept. The In-
Close4 algorithm came up with an optimization technique that allows one
to eliminate such redundant computations and significantly improves the
performance of algorithms from the Close-by-One family. We show that
this technique can be used in the Lindig-type algorithms to improve their
performance as well.

Keywords: Algorithm · Formal concept analysis · Formal concepts ·
Concept lattice · Hasse diagram

1 Introduction

Formal concept analysis (FCA) allows us to extract rectangular patterns, so
called formal concepts, from object-attribute data, i.e. from data tables where
rows describe objects, columns correspond to attributes, and crosses in the table
indicate if an object possesses a given attribute. Formal concepts are particularly
interesting, since each formal concept represents a collection of objects sharing
common attributes and a set of attributes that are common to these objects. In
a manner of speaking, formal concepts can be seen as an analogy to the ordinary
concepts we deal with on a daily basis. Formal concepts, similarly to ordinary
concepts, can be ordered, in the sense that one concept is more general (or more

The research was supported by the grant JG 2019 of Palacký University Olomouc,
No. JG_2019_008.

T. Braun et al. (Eds.): ICCS 2021, LNAI 12879, pp. 91–104, 2021.
https://doi.org/10.1007/978-3-030-86982-3_7

specific) than the other. Using this ordering one may organize formal concepts into a so-called concept lattice that provides an important insight into data.

The concept lattice and its line diagram can be used to present the results of the formal concept analysis to the end users if the lattice is of a reasonable size, or it can be used for further applications that utilize relationships among concepts. Such applications include, for instance, information retrieval [10] or selecting interesting concepts [7], to name a few.

Numerous algorithms for enumerating formal concepts were proposed; see, for instance, a survey [15]. Particularly efficient algorithms are from the CbO-family (CbO [14], FCbO [19], In-Close(1–5) [1–5]). The algorithms from the CbO-family use a lexicographical (or similar) order to enumerate formal concepts, along with various techniques to avoid redundant computations. Unfortunately, the order in which formal concepts are enumerated is not compatible with the natural ordering of formal concepts. Hence, if we want to obtain a concept lattice, we need to enumerate formal concepts first and reorder them afterwards. Alternatively, we may use other, often less efficient (from the viewpoint of enumerating formal concepts), algorithms that enumerate formal concepts and build a concept lattice in the same time, e.g. Lindig's UpperNeighbors [16], Bordat's algorihtm [8], AddIntent [17], or Nourine's algorithm [18].

We show that the efficiency of Lindig's UpperNeighbors algorithm [16] can be significantly improved by the technique proposed in In-Close4 [4]. Our interest in improving the performance of Lindig's algorithm is motivated by several appealing features it has. (i) It is not necessary to maintain a complete concept lattice in the main memory. (ii) It is easy to parallelize or distribute the computation. These two features make the algorithm suitable for processing large datasets. Besides this, there also exists a variant of Lindig's algorithm for graded setting [6] that could possibly benefit from our results.

The paper is organized as follows. First, necessary notions from FCA are introduced (Sect. 2). Then, the main idea of Lindig's algorithm is described along with the pruning technique from In-Close4 (Sects. 3.1 and 3.2). Then, the new algorithm is presented along with notes on implementation (Sects. 3.3 and 3.4). The paper concludes with experimental evaluation (Sect. 4) and several concluding remarks (Sect. 5).

2   Preliminaries

We shall recall the basic notions of the formal concept analysis. Interested readers may find more details, for instance, in monographs [11,12] and [9].

Definition 1. Let X and Y denote finite nonempty sets of objects and attributes, respectively. A *formal context* is a triplet $\langle X, Y, I \rangle$ where $I \subseteq X \times Y$, i.e. I is a binary relation between X and Y. The fact $\langle x, y \rangle \in I$ can be interpreted that the object x has the attribute y.

	2 legs	4 legs	6 legs	can fly	spine	feathers	fur
ant			×				
butterfly			×	×			
chicken	×					×	×
dog		×			×		×
eagle	×			×	×	×	
falcon	×			×	×	×	
giraffe		×			×		×

$c_1 = \langle \{a,b,c,d,e,f,g\}, \emptyset \rangle$
$c_2 = \langle \{a,b\}, \{6\ \text{legs}\} \rangle$
$c_3 = \langle \{b,e,f\}, \{\text{can fly}\} \rangle$
$c_4 = \langle \{c,d,e,f,g\}, \{\text{spine}\} \rangle$
$c_5 = \langle \{b\}, \{6\ \text{legs}, \text{can fly}\} \rangle$
$c_6 = \langle \{c,e,f\}, \{2\ \text{legs}, \text{spine}, \text{feathers}\} \rangle$
$c_7 = \langle \{e,f\}, \{2\ \text{legs}, \text{can fly}, \text{spine}, \text{feathers}\} \rangle$
$c_8 = \langle \{d,g\}, \{4\ \text{legs}, \text{spine}, \text{fur}\} \rangle$
$c_9 = \langle \emptyset, \{2\ \text{legs}, 4\ \text{legs}, 6\ \text{legs}, \text{can fly}, \text{spine},$
$\qquad\qquad \text{feathers}, \text{fur}\} \rangle$

Fig. 1. Example of a formal context with a highlighted formal concept c_6 (left), list of all formal concepts in this formal context (right)

In fact, the formal context $\langle X, Y, I \rangle$ can be seen as a two-dimensional data table where rows correspond to objects and columns to attributes. Crosses in the intersections of rows and columns indicate if a given object has a given attribute. See Fig. 1 (left) for an example of a formal context.

Definition 2. Each formal context $\langle X, Y, I \rangle$ induces a pair of *concept-forming operators* [11] $^\uparrow: 2^X \to 2^Y$ and $^\downarrow: 2^Y \to 2^X$ defined, for each $A \subseteq X$ and $B \subseteq Y$, by

$$A^\uparrow = \{y \in Y \mid \text{for each } x \in A: \langle x,y \rangle \in I\}, \tag{1}$$

$$B^\downarrow = \{x \in X \mid \text{for each } y \in B: \langle x,y \rangle \in I\}. \tag{2}$$

By definition (1), $A^\uparrow$ is the set of all attributes shared by all objects from A and, by definition (2), $B^\downarrow$ is the set of all objects sharing all attributes from B.

Definition 3. A *closure operator* on a set X is a mapping $C: 2^X \to 2^X$ satisfying for each $A, A_1, A_2 \subseteq X$

$$A \subseteq C(A) \tag{3}$$

$$A_1 \subseteq A_2 \text{ implies } C(A_1) \subseteq C(A_2) \tag{4}$$

$$C(A) = C(C(A)). \tag{5}$$

Compositions $^{\uparrow\downarrow}$ and $^{\downarrow\uparrow}$ of concept-forming operators are closure operators $^{\uparrow\downarrow}: 2^X \to 2^X$ and $^{\downarrow\uparrow}: 2^Y \to 2^Y$, respectively.

Definition 4. A *formal concept* in $\langle X, Y, I \rangle$ is a pair $\langle A, B \rangle$ such that $A^\uparrow = B$ and $B^\downarrow = A$, where $^\uparrow$ and $^\downarrow$ are concept-forming operators induced by $\langle X, Y, I \rangle$. A and B are called the *extent* and *intent*, respectively.

Formal concepts in $\langle X, Y, I \rangle$ correspond to *maximal rectangles* full of crosses present in $\langle X, Y, I \rangle$ and may be interpreted as natural concepts hidden in the data. For instance, in the formal context from Fig. 1 (left), a pair $\langle \{c, e, f\},$

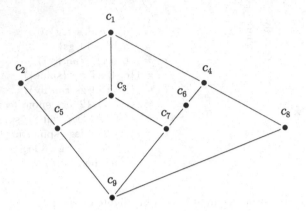

Fig. 2. Concept lattice for the data from Fig. 1

$\{2 \text{ legs}, \text{spine}, \text{feathers}\}\rangle$ is a formal concept that can be interpreted as *a bird*. A list of all nine formal concepts in this formal context is presented in Fig. 1 (right).

The set of all formal concepts of a given formal context $\langle X, Y, I \rangle$ is denoted by $\mathcal{B}(X, Y, I)$ and can be equipped with a partial order $\leq$ defined as follows:

$$\langle A_1, B_1 \rangle \leq \langle A_2, B_2 \rangle \text{ iff } A_1 \subseteq A_2 \text{ (or, equivalently, iff } B_2 \subseteq B_1). \qquad (6)$$

The partial order $\leq$ models a subconcept-superconcept hierarchy. This order has a natural interpretation. Let A and B be formal concepts such that $A \leq B$, then the formal concept B can be interpreted as a more general concept than A or, in other words, the formal concept A can be seen as a more specific concept than B. For example, it holds $c_7 < c_6$ (see Fig. 1), which means that the formal concept c_6 (*a bird*) is more general than the formal concept c_7 (*a raptor*). Further, a set of formal concepts together with $\leq$ forms a complete lattice, so called *concept lattice*. A concept lattice for the formal context from Fig. 1 is depicted as a line diagram (Hasse diagram) in Fig. 2.

In practical applications, we are often interested in a cover relation of $\mathcal{B}(X, Y, I)$ and $\leq$. The *cover relation* is a reduct of $\leq$, such that for any two formal concepts $c_1, c_2 \in \mathcal{B}(X, Y, I)$, a formal concept c_2 covers c_1 if $c_1 < c_2$ and there is no formal concept $c_3 \in \mathcal{B}(X, Y, I)$ such that $c_1 < c_3 < c_2$. In essence, the cover relation describes lower (or dually upper) neighbors of formal concepts in a line diagram of a concept lattice. Therefore, we say that a formal concept c_1 is *a lower neighbor* of c_2 (and dually c_2 is *an upper neighbor* of c_1) if c_2 covers c_1.

Remark 1. Algorithms for computing concept lattices in fact compute only a cover relation, since it has direct applications, for instance, it is essential for building a line a diagram of a concept lattice.

3   Lindig's Algorithm and Its Enhancement

We shall recall the basic idea of Lindig's algorithm [16] first. Then, we will show how empty intersections can be used to eliminate redundant computations and present a novel and more efficient algorithm for computing concept lattices. The section concludes with notes related to the implementation of the algorithm.

3.1 Lindig's Algorithm

The central idea of Lindig's algorithm is very straightforward. The algorithm starts with the topmost formal concept and recursively computes its lower neighbors, their lower neighbors, etc. Naturally, a formal concept may be a lower neighbor of multiple formal concepts. Therefore, in order to avoid enumerating formal concepts multiple times and to properly determine the relationship between formal concepts, the algorithm maintains a data structure that contains already obtained formal concepts.

A crucial part of the algorithm is a procedure that computes lower neighbors, see Algorithm 1 for its pseudo-code. The procedure NEIGHBORS takes a formal concept $\langle A, B \rangle$ and for each attribute $i \notin B$, a new formal concept $\langle C, D \rangle = \langle (B \cup \{i\})^{\downarrow}, (B \cup \{i\})^{\downarrow\uparrow} \rangle$ is computed; i.e. the current formal concept is extended with the attribute i. Note that the extent C can be computed more efficiently as $A \cap \{i\}^{\downarrow}$, since the intersection operator is usually faster than the concept-forming operator $^{\downarrow}$. Further, note that even though $\langle C, D \rangle < \langle A, B \rangle$, it does not mean that $\langle C, D \rangle$ is a lower neighbor of $\langle A, B \rangle$. To ensure that $\langle C, D \rangle$ is a lower neighbor, the NEIGHBORS procedure maintains a variable min, which is a minimal set of attributes generating lower neighbors. Initially, all attributes not in B are assumed to generate lower neighbors (line 1). For each attribute $i \notin B$, a formal concept $\langle C, D \rangle$ is obtained (lines 4 and 5). Then, the intent D is checked for a presence of an attribute j that possibly generates a lower neighbor (i.e. $j \in min, j \neq i$) with an intent containing attribute i (line 6). If there is such attribute j, then $\langle C, D \rangle$ is not considered as a lower neighbor and i, is removed from min (line 9). Otherwise, $\langle C, D \rangle$ is a lower neighbor of $\langle A, B \rangle$ (line 7). For more details, see [16].

Algorithm 1: NEIGHBORS(A, B)

Input: A is an extent, B is an intent
Output: a set of lower neighbors $\mathcal{N}$

```
1  min ← Y\B;
2  N ← ∅;
3  foreach i ∈ Y and i ∉ B do
4  │   C ← A ∩ {i}↓;
5  │   D ← C↑;
6  │   if (min ∩ (D\B\{i}) = ∅) then
7  │   └   N ← N ∪ {⟨C, D⟩};
8  │   else
9  │   └   min ← min\{i};
10 return N;
```

Remark 2. The original description of Lindig's algorithm starts with the least formal concept and computes its upper neighbors. We describe the dual variant of the algorithm, since the number of attributes is usually significantly smaller than the number of objects, and thus, the dual variant of the algorithm is usually more efficient, see Remark 4.

3.2 Use of Empty Intersections

Algorithms from the CbO-family compute new formal concepts in a similar way as the NEIGHBORS procedure (Algorithm 1). This means that they take an existing concept $\langle A, B \rangle$ and add one attribute i at a time and form a new formal concept $\langle A \cap \{i\}^{\downarrow}, (B \cup \{i\})^{\downarrow\uparrow} \rangle$. Andrews in [4] observed that for formal contexts which do not contain any row full of crosses

(o1) often a substantial amount of a newly formed formal concepts is $\langle \emptyset, Y \rangle$ (bottom formal concept);

(o2) if the addition of an attribute i to an intent B leads to the bottom formal concept, then the addition of an attribute i to every superset of B also leads to the bottom formal concept $\langle \emptyset, Y \rangle$.

More formally, let $\langle A, B \rangle, \langle C, D \rangle$ be formal concepts such that $B \subseteq D \subseteq Y$ and attribute $i \notin B$. Due to the monotony of closure operators, if $\langle A \cap \{i\}^{\downarrow}, (B \cup \{i\})^{\downarrow\uparrow} \rangle = \langle \emptyset, Y \rangle$, then $\langle C \cap \{i\}^{\downarrow}, (D \cup \{i\})^{\downarrow\uparrow} \rangle = \langle \emptyset, Y \rangle$. This can be further simplified. Apparently, if the intersection $A \cap \{i\}^{\downarrow}$ is empty, then also the intersection $C \cap \{i\}^{\downarrow}$ is empty and consequently the corresponding intent is equal to Y.

This means, if during the processing of a formal concept $\langle A, B \rangle$ an attribute i leading to the bottom concept is encountered, we may store this information for future use. Subsequently, when processing any lower neighbor of $\langle A, B \rangle$, we may skip the computation of the closure for attribute i and use $\langle \emptyset, Y \rangle$ immediately.

Remark 3. The bottom formal concept has an empty extent if and only if the formal context contains no rows full of crosses. Therefore, the condition proposed in In-Close4 [4] has limited use. This can be resolved either (i) by eliminating all rows full of crosses from the formal context (note that this does not affect structure of the concept lattice), or (ii) by considering a more general condition. Note that the extent of the bottom formal concept consists solely of rows full of crosses. This means, we found the bottom formal concept if and only if $|A \cap \{i\}^{\downarrow}| = |Y^{\downarrow}|$. Obviously, it is sufficient to obtain the value of $|Y^{\downarrow}|$ only once, before the enumeration of the formal concepts starts. Thus, the check of this condition can be as fast as a check for an empty extent.

3.3 Computing a Concept Lattice

Both observations discussed in the previous section are applicable to Lindig's algorithm as well, even though it uses a different order to enumerate formal concepts than CbO. We show how the discussed ideas may be combined together into an algorithm we shall call FastLattice.

Algorithm 2: FASTNEIGHBORS(A, B, S)

Input: A is an extent, B is an intent, S is a set of attributes to skip
Output: $\mathcal{N}$ is a set of lower neighbors, S' is a new set of attributes to skip
1   $min \leftarrow Y \backslash B$;
2   $\mathcal{N} \leftarrow \emptyset$;
3   $S' \leftarrow S$;
4   **foreach** $i \in Y$ and $i \notin B$ and $i \notin S$ **do**
5      $C \leftarrow A \cap \{i\}^{\downarrow}$;
6   **if** $|C| > |Y^{\downarrow}|$ **then**
7         $D \leftarrow C^{\uparrow}$;
8   **if** $(min \cap (D \backslash B \backslash \{i\}) = \emptyset)$ **then**
9            $\mathcal{N} \leftarrow \mathcal{N} \cup \{\langle C, D \rangle\}$;
10   **else**
11           $min \leftarrow min \backslash \{i\}$;

12   **else**
13        $S' \leftarrow S' \cup \{i\}$;

14 **return** $\mathcal{N}, S'$;

First, we present a modified version of the NEIGHBORS procedure called FASTNEIGHBORS, see Algorithm 2 for its pseudo-code. This procedure differs from the original one in the following steps:

- It accepts an additional argument S containing attributes leading to the bottom formal concept.
- It creates a copy S' of this argument (line 3).
- Attributes from S are skipped (line 4).
- Whenever an extent of the bottom formal concept is obtained (line 6), computation of an intent is skipped and the given attribute is inserted into S' (lines 12 and 13).
- The procedure returns not only the set of all lower neighbors of $\langle A, B \rangle$, but also the set of attributes S' leading to the bottom formal concept (line 14).

The main procedure of the algorithm is also similar to what was proposed by Lindig. However, it has to (i) handle sets of attributes to skip and (ii) deal with the fact that the FASTNEIGHBORS procedure never returns the bottom formal concept. Thus, this case has to be treated separately. The pseudo-code of the main procedure can be seen in Algorithm 3.

The procedure accepts a formal context $\langle X, Y, I \rangle$ and returns a collection of all formal concepts along with its cover relation.

First, data structures are initialized. Namely, data structure Q is initialized with a triplet that contains an extent and intent of the topmost formal concept and an empty set of attributes (lines 1 and 4). The purpose of the structure Q is twofold. (i) It is a queue of formal concepts that have not yet been processed. (ii) It is a structure that allows one to store and lookup formal concepts that

---

Algorithm 3: FASTLATTICE(X, Y, I)

Input: formal context $\langle X, Y, I \rangle$
Output: set of all formal concepts $\mathcal{B}$

1   $\mathcal{Q} \leftarrow \emptyset$;
2   $\mathcal{R} \leftarrow \emptyset$;
3   $\mathcal{B} \leftarrow \emptyset$;
4   store $\langle \langle X, X^{\uparrow} \rangle, \emptyset \rangle$ to $\mathcal{Q}$;
5   while $\langle c, S \rangle \leftarrow$ NEXT($\mathcal{Q}$) do
6      $\mathcal{B} \leftarrow \mathcal{B} \cup \{c\}$;
7      $\mathcal{N}, S' \leftarrow$ FASTNEIGHBORS(c, S);
8   if $|\mathcal{N}| > 0$ then
9   foreach $c' \in \mathcal{N}$ do
10   if $x \leftarrow$ LOOKUP($c', \mathcal{Q}$) is found then
11                $\mathcal{LN}(c) \leftarrow \mathcal{LN}(c) \cup \{x\}$;
12                $\mathcal{UN}(x) \leftarrow \mathcal{UN}(x) \cup \{c\}$;
13   else
14   store $\langle c', S' \rangle$ to $\mathcal{Q}$;
15                $\mathcal{LN}(c) \leftarrow \mathcal{LN}(c) \cup \{c'\}$;
16                $\mathcal{UN}(c') \leftarrow \mathcal{UN}(c') \cup \{c\}$;
17   else
18          $\mathcal{R} \leftarrow \mathcal{R} \cup \{c\}$;
19   if $X^{\uparrow} \neq Y$ then
20      $c_b \leftarrow \langle Y^{\downarrow}, Y \rangle$;
21      $\mathcal{B} \leftarrow \mathcal{B} \cup \{c_b\}$;
22   foreach $c \in \mathcal{R}$ do
23          $\mathcal{LN}(c) \leftarrow \mathcal{LN}(c) \cup \{c_b\}$;
24          $\mathcal{UN}(c_b) \leftarrow \mathcal{UN}(c_b) \cup \{c\}$;
25   return $\mathcal{B}$;

---

have been obtained so far. This data structure is discussed more thoroughly in Sect. 3.4. Further, a set $\mathcal{R}$ of formal concepts without lower neighbors is initialized to an empty set (line 2). This set is used to deal with the missing bottom formal concept. The set $\mathcal{B}$ of all formal concepts is empty at the beginning (line 3).

The main loop of the algorithm (lines 5 to 18) takes one unprocessed formal concept c from $\mathcal{Q}$, along with the set S of attributes to skip. The concept is inserted into the set $\mathcal{B}$ (line 6). Then, its set of lower neighbors is computed with the FASTNEIGHBORS procedure (see Algorithm 2) which returns also a set S' of attributes to skip (line 7).

If the set of lower neighbors is nonempty, each lower neighbor c' is looked up in $\mathcal{Q}$ (line 10). If it is found, it means that the concept was already obtained, hence the existing formal concept x from $\mathcal{Q}$ becomes a lower neighbor of c (line 11), and dually, c becomes an upper neighbor of x (line 12). Otherwise, if the formal concept c' has not been encountered yet, it is inserted into Q along with S' containing attributes that can be skipped since they are leading to the bottom formal concept (line 14). Naturally, c' is a lower neighbor of c (line 15), and dually, c is an upper neighbor of c' (line 16). If the set of lower neighbors is empty, the formal concept is inserted into $\mathcal{R}$ (line 18) for further processing.

It remains to deal with the bottom formal concept (lines 19 to 24). Since the FASTNEIGHBORS procedure never returns the bottom formal concept, it is present in $\mathcal{B}$ only in the trivial cases where the bottom and top formal concepts coincide. Otherwise, it has to be explicitly inserted (lines 20 and 21). Further, if there are some formal concepts without lower neighbors, they clearly have exactly one lower neighbor—the bottom formal concept. Thus, we establish relationships between them and the bottom formal concept (lines 22 to 24).

Remark 4. Since FASTLATTICE retains the same structure as Lindig's algorithm, it has also the same asymptotic worst case complexity, i.e. $O(|\mathcal{B}(X,Y,I)| \times |Y|^2 \times |X|)$. A closure is computed in $O(|X| \times |Y|)$ and for each formal concept we need to compute up to $|Y|$ of its lower neighbors. Note that if an appropriate data structure (e.g. search tree) is used to store and lookup formal concepts in Q, it does not affect the complexity of the algorithm.

3.4 Implementation Aspects

The choice of the data structure used to store formal concepts has with no doubt a crucial impact on the performance of the algorithm. Lindig [16] assumes the use of a search tree where the total order $\trianglelefteq$ of formal concepts (in the tree) is related to the order of formal concepts $\leq$ as follows:

$$c_1 \trianglelefteq c_2 \quad \text{implies} \quad c_1 \leq c_2. \tag{7}$$

The purpose of this order is to ensure that when processing a particular formal concept, all its upper neighbors are already processed.

In fact, Lindig's algorithm does not require the data structure holding formal concepts to be a tree. It may be an arbitrary data structure which serves as a queue returning formal concepts with respect to the order (7) having sufficiently efficient operations NEXT, STORE, and LOOKUP.

We suggest using alternative data structure that could be characterized as a priority queue with an efficient lookup operation. More specifically, we suggest decomposing a single data structure Q into $|Y|+1$ independent data structures $Q_0, \ldots, Q_{|Y|}$, where each Q_i contains formal concepts with the same cardinality of an intent. This means, each data structure Q_i contains only formal concepts $\langle A, B \rangle$ such that $|B| = i$. The choice of data structure for Q_i is open and an arbitrary data structure with an efficient lookup operation (e.g., search tree or hash table) will serve the purpose.

When processing formal concepts, we proceed from the formal concepts in Q_0 to concepts in $Q_{|Y|}$. This ensures a proper ordering of processed concepts, i.e.

first are processed concepts with the intent with no attribute, then with a single attribute, etc. Once the formal concept is processed, we never return to it, hence it can be removed from the main memory and safely stored in the external storage for further processing. Depending on the selected data structure, formal concepts may be removed from the main memory one by one, or *en bloc* when all concepts in $\mathcal{Q}_i$ are processed. This way the memory footprint of the algorithm may be reduced. This makes it suitable for processing large datasets.

Moreover, this organization of unprocessed formal concepts has a further important consequence. Formal concepts with the same cardinality of an intent can be processed in an arbitrary order. This implies, (i) a wider range of data structures may be used to store and lookup formal concepts, (ii) formal concepts in a single data structure $\mathcal{Q}_i$ may be easily processed in parallel. This is of an eminent importance with the onset of multi-core computers.

4   Evaluation

We prepared a collection of experiments that evaluates performance of the proposed algorithm. Namely, we compared its performance with the original Lindig's algorithm [16], with the AddIntent algorithm [17], and with the variant of CbO [14] which builds a concept lattice.

4.1   Real World Datasets

The first set of experiments shows the efficiency of the algorithm on real world datasets from the UCI Machine Learning repository – *mushrooms, anonymous web, tic-tac-toe, breast cancer wisconsin, votes* and our own dataset, *debian tags*. Properties of these datasets are presented in Table 1 and computation times of the algorithms are presented in Table 2. In all cases, the new algorithm is faster than the original Lindig's algorithm. The most significant performance improvement can been seen on sparse datasets. Note that due to the data structure described in Sect. 3.4, which evicts already processed concepts from the main memory, the memory footprint is reduced and data locality is improved, and thus, our implementations of Lindig's algorithm and FastLattice outperform AddIntent and CbO.

Table 1. Properties of the selected datasets

Dataset	Objects	Attributes	Density (%)	Concepts	Edges
debian tags	14,315	496	1	38,977	132,582
anonymous web	32,710	296	1	129,009	588,933
mushrooms	8124	119	19	238,710	1,370,991
votes	435	50	34	264,035	1,617,903
breast cancer wisconsin	683	95	10	9569	36,743
tic-tac-toe	958	29	34	59,505	316,945

4.2 Synthetic Data

Table 2. Computation times in milliseconds of algorithms for the selected datasets

Dataset	FastLattice	Lindig	AddIntent	CbO
debian tags	587	4141	5433	26,397
anonymous web	1930	5731	18,708	30,709
mushrooms	5269	8530	104,853	97,637
votes	2416	2897	101,783	117,545
breast cancer wisconsin	73	158	123	274
tic-tac-toe	296	348	4982	5240

The experiments with the real world data offer an important but limited insight on the real performance of the algorithm. Therefore, we have designed another set of experiments involving synthetic datasets. We have created two collections of synthetic datasets that simulate data one may encounter in FCA. These collections of data can be characterized as

- transactional data, i.e. data used in market-basket analysis or recommender systems; for this purpose, IBM Quest Synthetic Data Generator has been used.
- questionnaire-like data, i.e. context consisting of attribute groups where each object has exactly one attribute from each group; note that similar properties have datasets created with nominal scaling. Therefore, we call these datasets *nominal*. Our own tool has been used to generate this type of data.

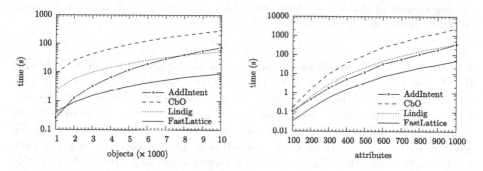

Fig. 3. Computation time in seconds (logarithmic scale) for transactional datasets having 500 attributes, 2 % density, and a varying number of objects (left) and 5000 objects, 2% density and a varying number of attributes (right)

For transactional data, we have investigated how the increasing number of objects and attributes affects the performance of the algorithm. We have used datasets with 500 attributes and varying numbers of objects and datasets with 5000 objects and varying numbers of attributes. In all scenarios, the density of data is 2%. Results of this experiment are shown in Fig. 3. The FastLattice algorithm significantly outperforms other algorithms (note that the logarithmic scale is used). The original Lindig's algorithm with the enhancement proposed in Sect. 3.4 is similarly fast as the AddIntent, especially for higher numbers objects.

Synthetic data simulating nominally scaled datasets have varying numbers of objects and ten groups of attributes of four or ten binary attributes where each object has exactly one attribute from each group. Computation times for these datasets can be seen in Fig. 4. From these experiments, it follows that for the dense datasets (Fig. 4, left), FastLattice brings only a small performance improvement. For the sparse datasets (Fig. 4, right), one can see a significant improvement over the original algorithm, again, a logarithmic scale is used to present the results. Note that in case of the nominal data, AddIntent is almost equally as fast as CbO and both of them are, by an order of magnitude, slower than our implementations of FastLattice and Lindig's algorithm.

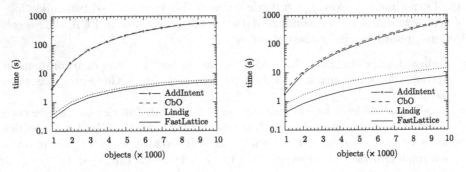

Fig. 4. Computation time in seconds (logarithmic scale) for nominal datasets having varying number of objects and ten groups of attributes each consisting of 4 (left) and 10 (right) binary attributes

Remark 5. All experiments were conducted on a computer equipped with 64 GiB RAM, two Intel Xeon E5-2680 CPUs, 2.80 GHz, and Debian Linux 10.9 with GNU GCC 8.3.0. All algorithms have been implemented from scratch in C++ with the same data structures. Namely, bit vectors are used to represent sets of attributes, and ordered arraylists are used to represent sets of objects. To store and retrieve already processed formal concepts (in FastLattice and CbO), a hash table from the STL is used. All implementations print out results in the same form, which consists of two types of lines (i) $\langle nodeId \rangle \langle intent \rangle$ and (ii) $\langle nodeId \rangle \rightarrow \langle nodeId \rangle$ describing a line diagram of a concept lattice.

5   Conclusions and Future Research

Redundant closure computations is a common issue affecting the performance of many algorithms for computing formal concepts. Interestingly, a substantial number of redundant closure computations lead to the bottom formal concept, especially if the input formal context is sparse. This type of redundant computations can be easily identified and eliminated. Even though the optimization deals with a single particular corner case, it has a significant impact on the performance of the algorithms. Besides In-Close4 [4], this optimization has already found its use in In-Close5 [5] or in the map-reduce variant of CbO [13].

We have shown that this optimization, originally proposed for the CbO-based algorithms, serves well in Lindig's algorithm and significantly improves its performance. Since Lindig's algorithm belongs to a different family of algorithms, it opens up an interesting question: can other algorithms benefit from this optimization as well? The answer to this question is left for future research. How this optimization may be incorporated into the other algorithms for computing concept lattices is to be discussed in the extended version of this paper.

References

1. Andrews, S.: In-close, a fast algorithm for computing formal concepts. In: Rudolph, S., Dau, F., Kuznetsov, S.O. (eds.) Proceedings of ICCS 2009. CEUR Workshop Proceedings, vol. 483. CEUR-WS.org (2009)
2. Andrews, S.: In-Close2, a high performance formal concept miner. In: Andrews, S., Polovina, S., Hill, R., Akhgar, B. (eds.) ICCS 2011. LNCS (LNAI), vol. 6828, pp. 50–62. Springer, Heidelberg (2011). https://doi.org/10.1007/978-3-642-22688-5_4
3. Andrews, S.: A 'best-of-breed' approach for designing a fast algorithm for computing fixpoints of Galois connections. Inf. Sci. **295**, 633–649 (2015). https://doi.org/10.1016/j.ins.2014.10.011
4. Andrews, S.: Making use of empty intersections to improve the performance of CbO-type algorithms. In: Bertet, K., Borchmann, D., Cellier, P., Ferré, S. (eds.) ICFCA 2017. LNCS (LNAI), vol. 10308, pp. 56–71. Springer, Cham (2017). https://doi.org/10.1007/978-3-319-59271-8_4
5. Andrews, S.: A new method for inheriting canonicity test failures in close-by-one type algorithms. In: Ignatov, D.I., Nourine, L. (eds.) Proceedings of the Fourteenth International Conference on Concept Lattices and Their Applications, CLA 2018, Olomouc, Czech Republic, 12–14 June 2018. CEUR Workshop Proceedings, vol. 2123, pp. 255–266. CEUR-WS.org (2018)
6. Belohlavek, R., De Baets, B., Outrata, J., Vychodil, V.: Lindig's algorithm for concept lattices over graded attributes. In: Torra, V., Narukawa, Y., Yoshida, Y. (eds.) MDAI 2007. LNCS (LNAI), vol. 4617, pp. 156–167. Springer, Heidelberg (2007). https://doi.org/10.1007/978-3-540-73729-2_15
7. Belohlávek, R., Trnecka, M.: Basic level of concepts in formal concept analysis 1: formalization and utilization. Int. J. Gen. Syst. **49**(7), 689–706 (2020)
8. Bordat, J.P.: Calcul pratique du treillis de galois d'une correspondance. Mathématiques et Sciences humaines **96**, 31–47 (1986)
9. Carpineto, C., Romano, G.: Concept Data Analysis: Theory and Applications. Wiley, Hoboken (2004)
10. Carpineto, C., Romano, G.: Exploiting the potential of concept lattices for information retrieval with CREDO. J. Univers. Comput. Sci. **10**(8), 985–1013 (2004)
11. Ganter, B., Wille, R.: Formal Concept Analysis: Mathematical Foundations. Springer, Heidelberg (1999). https://doi.org/10.1007/978-3-642-59830-2

12. Grätzer, G.: General Lattice Theory, 2nd edn. Birkhäuser, Basel (2003)
13. Konecny, J., Krajča, P.: Pruning in map-reduce style CbO algorithms. In: Alam, M., Braun, T., Yun, B. (eds.) ICCS 2020. LNCS (LNAI), vol. 12277, pp. 103–116. Springer, Cham (2020). https://doi.org/10.1007/978-3-030-57855-8_8
14. Kuznetsov, S.O.: Learning of simple conceptual graphs from positive and negative examples. In: Żytkow, J.M., Rauch, J. (eds.) PKDD 1999. LNCS (LNAI), vol. 1704, pp. 384–391. Springer, Heidelberg (1999). https://doi.org/10.1007/978-3-540-48247-5_47
15. Kuznetsov, S.O., Obiedkov, S.A.: Comparing performance of algorithms for generating concept lattices. J. Exp. Theor. Artif. Intell. **14**(2–3), 189–216 (2002)
16. Lindig, C., Gbr, G.: Fast concept analysis. In: Working with Conceptual Structures - Contributions to ICCS 2000 (2000)
17. van der Merwe, D., Obiedkov, S., Kourie, D.: AddIntent: a new incremental algorithm for constructing concept lattices. In: Eklund, P. (ed.) ICFCA 2004. LNCS (LNAI), vol. 2961, pp. 372–385. Springer, Heidelberg (2004). https://doi.org/10.1007/978-3-540-24651-0_31
18. Nourine, L., Raynaud, O.: A fast algorithm for building lattices. Inf. Process. Lett. **71**(5–6), 199–204 (1999)
19. Outrata, J., Vychodil, V.: Fast algorithm for computing fixpoints of Galois connections induced by object-attribute relational data. Inf. Sci. **185**(1), 114–127 (2012)

Quantifying the Conceptual Error
in Dimensionality Reduction

Tom Hanika[1,2] and Johannes Hirth[1,2]([✉])

[1] Knowledge and Data Engineering Group, University of Kassel, Kassel, Germany
{tom.hanika,hirth}@cs.uni-kassel.de
[2] Interdisciplinary Research Center for Information System Design,
University of Kassel, Kassel, Germany

Abstract. Dimension reduction of data sets is a standard problem in
the realm of machine learning and knowledge reasoning. They affect patterns in and dependencies on data dimensions and ultimately influence
any decision-making processes. Therefore, a wide variety of reduction
procedures are in use, each pursuing different objectives. A so far not
considered criterion is the conceptual continuity of the reduction mapping, i.e., the preservation of the conceptual structure with respect to
the original data set. Based on the notion scale-measure from formal
concept analysis we present in this work a) the theoretical foundations to
detect and quantify conceptual errors in data scalings; b) an experimental
investigation of our approach on eleven data sets that were respectively
treated with a variant of non-negative matrix factorization.

Keywords: Formal concept analysis · Dimension reduction ·
Conceptual measurement · Data scaling

1   Introduction

The analysis of large and complex data is presently a challenge for many data
driven research fields. This is especially true when using sophisticated analysis and learning methods, since their computational complexity usually grows at
least superlinearly with the problem size. One aspect of largeness and complexity
is the explicit data dimension, e.g., number of features, of a data set. Therefore,
a variety of methods have been developed to reduce exactly this data dimension to a computable size, such as *principal component analysis*, *singular value
decomposition*, or *factor analysis* [11]. What all these methods have in common
is that they are based on the principle of data scaling [8].

A particularly challenging task is to apply *Boolean factor analysis* (BFA) [15],
as the distinct feature values are restricted to either 0 (false) or 1 (true). For
example, given the binary data set matrix K, the application of a BFA yields
two binary data matrices S, H of lower dimension, such that $S \cdot H$ approximates

---

Authors are given in alphabetical order. No priority in authorship is implied.

© Springer Nature Switzerland AG 2021
T. Braun et al. (Eds.): ICCS 2021, LNAI 12879, pp. 105–118, 2021.
https://doi.org/10.1007/978-3-030-86982-3_8

K with respect to a previously selected norm $\|\cdot\|$. The factor S can be considered as a lower dimensional representation of K, i.e., a scaling of K. The connection between the scaling features of S and the original data features of K is represented by H. The quality of an approximation, and therewith the quality of a scale S, is usually scored through the Frobenius norm of $K - SH$, or other functions [3,9], such as the *Residual Sum of Squares* or, in the binary setting, the *Hemming distance*. These scoring functions give a good impression of the extent to which the linear operator K is approximated by $S \cdot H$, yet, they are incapable to detect the deviation of internal incidence structure of S with respect to K, which we want to call *conceptual scaling error*.

A well defined formalism from Formal Concept Analysis (FCA) [6] to analyze the resulting inconsistencies in (binary) data scaling is *scale-measures* [5,7]. In this work, we build up on this notion and introduce a comprehensive framework for quantification of quantifying the conceptual errors of scales. The so introduced mathematical tools are capable of determining how many conceptual errors arise from a particular scaling S and pinpoint which concepts are falsely introduced or lost. For this we overcome the potential exponential computational demands of computing complete conceptual structures by employing previous results on the scale-measures decision problem [8]. We motivate our results with accompanying examples and support our results with an experiment on eleven data sets.

2   Scales and Data

FCA Recap. In the field of Formal concept analysis (FCA) [6,14] the task for data scaling, and in particular feature scaling, is considered a fundamental step for data analysis. Hence, data scaling is part of the foundations of FCA [6] and it is frequently investigated within FCA [5,7].

The basic data structure of FCA is the *formal context*, see our running example $\mathbb{K}_W$ Fig. 1 (top). That is a triple (G, M, I) with non-empty and finite[1] set G (called *objects*), finite set M (called *attributes*) and a binary relation $I \subseteq G \times M$ (called *incidence*). The tuple (g, m) indicates "g has attribute m in $\mathbb{K}$", when $(g, m) \in I$. Any context $\mathbb{S} = (H, N, J)$ with $H \subseteq G, N \subseteq M$ and $J = I \cap (H \times N)$ we call *induced sub-context* of $\mathbb{K}$, and denote this relation by $\leq$, i.e., $\mathbb{S} \leq \mathbb{K}$.

The incidence relation $I \subseteq G \times M$ gives rise to *the* natural Galois connection between $P(G)$ and $P(M)$, which is the pair[2] of operators $\cdot' : P(G) \to P(M)$, $A \mapsto A' = \{m \in M \mid \forall a \in A : (a, m) \in I\}$, and $\cdot' : P(M) \to P(G), B \mapsto B' = \{g \in G \mid \forall b \in B : (g, b) \in I\}$, each called *derivation*. Using these operator, a *formal concept* is a pair $(A, B) \in P(G) \times P(M)$ with $A' = B$ and $A = B'$, where A and B are called *extent* and *intent*, respectively.

---

[1] This restriction is in general not necessary. Since data sets can be considered finite throughout this work and since this assumption allows a clearer representation of the results within this work, it was made.

[2] Both operators are traditionally denoted by the same symbol $\cdot'$.

$\mathbb{K}_W$	has limbs (L)	breast feeds (BF)	needs chlorophyll (Ch)	needs water to live (W)	lives on land (LL)	lives in water (LW)	can move (M)	monocotyledon (MC)	dicotyledon (DC)
dog	×	×		×	×		×		
fish				×		×	×		
leech				×		×	×		
corn			×	×	×			×	
bream	×			×		×	×		
water weeds			×	×		×		×	
bean			×	×	×				×
frog	×			×	×	×	×		
reed			×	×	×	×		×	

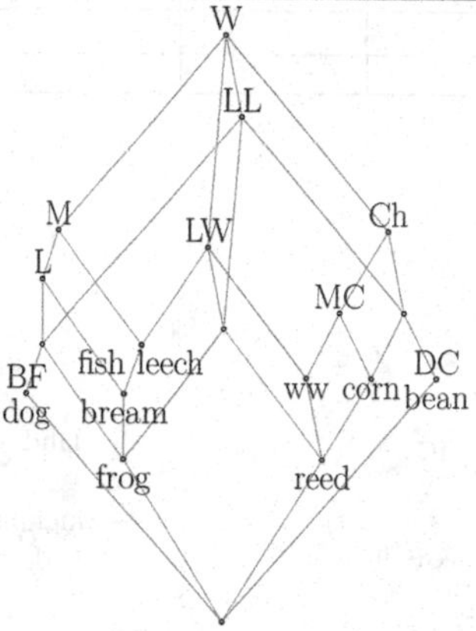

Fig. 1. This formal context of the *Living Beings and Water* data set (top) and its concept lattice (bottom).

The two possible compositions of the derivation operators lead to two *closure operators* $\cdot''\colon \mathcal{P}(G) \to \mathcal{P}(G)$ and $\cdot''\colon \mathcal{P}(M) \to \mathcal{P}(M)$, and in turn to two *closure spaces* $\mathrm{Ext}(\mathbb{K}) := (G, '')$ and $\mathrm{Int}(\mathbb{K}) := (M, '')$. Both closure systems are represented in the *(concept) lattice* $\mathfrak{B}(\mathbb{K}) = (\mathcal{B}(\mathbb{K}), \leq)$, where the set of all formal concepts is denoted by $\mathcal{B}(\mathbb{K}) := \{(A, B) \in \mathcal{P}(G) \times \mathcal{P}(M) \mid A' = B \wedge B' = A\}$ the order relation is $(A, B) \leq (C, D) :\Leftrightarrow A \subseteq C$. An example drawing of such a lattice is depicted in Fig. 1 (bottom).

2.1 Scales-Measures

The basis for quantifying the conceptual error of a data scaling is the continuity of the scaling map with respect to the resulting closure spaces. We say a map map $f : G_1 \to G_2$ is *continuous* with respect to the closure spaces (G_1, c_1) and (G_2, c_2) if and only if for all $A \in \mathcal{P}(G_2)$ we have $c_1(f^{-1}(A)) \subseteq f^{-1}(c_2(A))$. That is, a map is continuous iff the preimage of closed sets is closed. Within FCA this notion is captured by the following definition.

Definition 1 (Scale-Measure (cf. Definition 91, [6])). *Let* $\mathbb{K} = (G, M, I)$ *and* $\mathbb{S} = (G_{\mathbb{S}}, M_{\mathbb{S}}, I_{\mathbb{S}})$ *be a formal contexts. The map* $\sigma : G \to G_{\mathbb{S}}$ *is called an* $\mathbb{S}$*-measure of* $\mathbb{K}$ *into the scale* $\mathbb{S}$ *iff the preimage* $\sigma^{-1}(A) := \{g \in G \mid \sigma(g) \in A\}$ *of every extent* $A \in \mathrm{Ext}(\mathbb{S})$ *is an extent of* $\mathbb{K}$.

S	W	LW	plants := C	animals := M	land plants :=LL∧ plant	water plants := LW ∧ plant	land animal := LL ∧ animal	water animal := LW ∧ animal	mammal := animal ∧ BF
dog	×			×			×		×
fish leech	×	×		×				×	
corn	×		×		×				
bream	×	×		×				×	
water weeds	×	×	×			×			
bean	×		×		×				
frog	×	×		×			×	×	
reed	×	×	×		×	×			

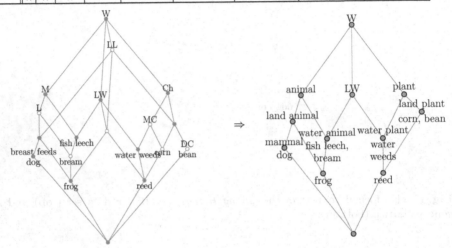

Fig. 2. A scale context (top), its concept lattice (bottom right) for which id_G is a scale-measure of the context in Fig. 1 and the reflected extents $\sigma^{-1}[\mathrm{Ext}(\mathbb{S})]$ (bottom left) indicated as in gray.

The (scaling-)map σ can be understood as an interpretation of the objects from $\mathbb{K}$ using the attribute (features) of $\mathbb{S}$. Hence, we denote $\sigma^{-1}[\mathrm{Ext}(\mathbb{S})] := \bigcup_{A \in \mathrm{Ext}(\mathbb{S})} \sigma^{-1}(A)$ as the set of extents that are *reflected* by the *scale context* $\mathbb{S}$.

In Fig. 2 we depicted an example scale-context $\mathbb{S}$, where the attributes of the scale-context are constructed by conjunctions of attributes from $\mathbb{K}_W$, as seen in Fig. 1. This scaling is based on the original object set G and we observe that $\mathbb{S}$ reflects twelve out of the nineteen concepts from $\mathfrak{B}(\mathbb{K}_W)$.

For any two scale-measures $(\sigma, \mathbb{S}), (\psi, \mathbb{T})$ we say [8] that $(\sigma, \mathbb{S})$ is *finer than* $(\psi, \mathbb{T})$, iff $\psi^{-1}(\mathbb{T}) \subseteq \sigma^{-1}[\mathrm{Ext}(\mathbb{S})]$. Dually we say then that $(\sigma, \mathbb{S})$ is *coarser than* $(\psi, \mathbb{T})$. From both relation an equivalence relation $\sim$ arises naturally. The set of all possible scale-measures for some $\mathbb{K}$, denoted by $\mathfrak{S}(\mathbb{K}) := \{(\sigma, \mathbb{S}) \mid \sigma$ is a $\mathbb{S}-$measure of $\mathbb{K}\}$, is therefore ordered. Furthermore, it is known [8] that factorizing $\mathfrak{S}(\mathbb{K})$ by $\sim$ leads to a lattice ordered structure $\underline{\mathfrak{S}}(\mathbb{K}) = (\mathfrak{S}(\mathbb{K})/\sim, \leq)$, called the *scale-hierarchy of* $\mathbb{K}$. This hierarchy is isomorphic to the set of all sub-closure systems of $\mathrm{Ext}(\mathbb{K})$, i.e. $\{Q \subseteq \mathrm{Ext}(\mathbb{K}) \mid Q$ is a Closure System on $G\}$, ordered by set inclusion $\subseteq$.

Every scale-measure $(\mathbb{S}, \sigma) \in \mathfrak{S}(\mathbb{K})$ does allow for a canonical representation [8], i.e., $(\sigma, \mathbb{S}) \sim (\mathrm{id}, \mathbb{K}_{\sigma^{-1}(\mathrm{Ext}(\mathbb{S}))})$. This representation, however, very often eludes human explanation to some degree. This issue can be remedied through a related approach called *logical scaling* [12] that is a representation of the scale-context attributes by conjunction, disjunction, and negation of the original attributes, formally $M_{\mathbb{S}} \subseteq \mathcal{L}(M, \{\wedge, \vee, \neg\})$. Such a representation does always exist:

Proposition 1 (CNF of Scale-measures (cf. Proposition 23, [8])). *Let $\mathbb{K}$ be a context, $(\sigma, \mathbb{S}) \in \mathfrak{S}(\mathbb{K})$. Then the scale-measure $(\psi, \mathbb{T}) \in \mathfrak{S}(\mathbb{K})$ given by*

$$\psi = \mathrm{id}_G \quad and \quad \mathbb{T} =|_{A \in \sigma^{-1}[\mathrm{Ext}(\mathbb{S})]} (G, \{\phi = \wedge A^I\}, I_\phi)$$

is equivalent to $(\sigma, \mathbb{S})$ and is called conjunctive normalform *of $(\sigma, \mathbb{S})$.*

3 Conceptual Errors in Data Scaling

Scaling and factorizations procedures are essential to almost all data science (DS) and machine learning (ML) approaches. For example, relational data, such as a formal context $\mathbb{K}$, is often scaled to a lower (attribute-) dimensional representation $\mathbb{S}$. Such scaling procedures, e.g., *principle component analysis, latent semantic analysis, non-negative matrix factorization*, however, do almost always not account for the conceptual structure of the original data $\mathbb{K}$. Hence, in order to comprehend the results of DS/ML procedures, it is crucial to investigate to what extent and which information is lost during the scaling process. In the following we want to introduce a first approach to quantify and treat *error* in data scalings through the notion of scale-measures. For this we need the notion of *context apposition* [6]. Given two formal contexts $\mathbb{K}_1 := (G_1, M_1, I_1)$, $\mathbb{K}_2 := (G_2, M_2, I_2)$ with $G_1 = G_2$ and $M_1 \cap M_2 = \emptyset$, then $\mathbb{K}_1 \mid \mathbb{K}_2 := (G, M_1 \cup M_2, I_1 \cup I_2)$. If $M_1 \cap M_2 \neq \emptyset$ the apposition is constructed disjoint union of the attribute sets.

Proposition 2. *Let $\mathbb{K}, \mathbb{S}$ be formal contexts, $\sigma : G_{\mathbb{K}} \to G_{\mathbb{S}}$ a map and let $\mathbb{A} = \mathbb{K} \mid (G_{\mathbb{K}}, M_{\mathbb{S}}, I_\sigma)$ with $I_\sigma = \{(g, \sigma(g)) \mid g \in G_{\mathbb{K}}\} \circ I_{\mathbb{S}}$, then $(\sigma, \mathbb{S})$ and $(\mathrm{id}_{G_{\mathbb{K}}}, \mathbb{K})$ are scale-measures of $\mathbb{A}$.*

Proof. It is to show that $\mathrm{id}_{G_{\mathbb{K}}}^{-1}[\mathrm{Ext}(\mathbb{K})]$ and $\sigma^{-1}[\mathrm{Ext}(\mathbb{S})]$ are subsets of $\mathrm{Ext}(\mathbb{A})$. The set $\mathrm{Ext}(\mathbb{A})$ is the smallest intersection closed set containing $\mathrm{Ext}(\mathbb{K})$ and $\mathrm{Ext}(G_{\mathbb{K}}, M_{\mathbb{S}}, I_\sigma)$. Thus $\mathrm{id}_{G_{\mathbb{K}}}^{-1}(\mathrm{Ext}(\mathbb{K})) \subseteq \mathrm{Ext}(\mathbb{A})$. Let $C \in \mathrm{Ext}(\mathbb{S})$, then there exists a representation $C = D^{I_{\mathbb{S}}}$ with $D \subseteq M_{\mathbb{S}}$. The derivation D^{I_σ} is an extent in $\mathrm{Ext}(G_{\mathbb{K}}, M_{\mathbb{S}}, I_\sigma)$ and is equal to $\sigma^{-1}(D^{I_{\mathbb{S}}})$, since $I_\sigma = \{(g, \sigma(g)) \mid g \in G_{\mathbb{K}}\} \circ I_{\mathbb{S}}$. Thus, $D^{I_\sigma} = \sigma^{-1}(C)$ and therefore we find $\sigma^{-1}(C) \in \mathrm{Ext}(G_{\mathbb{K}}, M_{\mathbb{S}}, I_\sigma)$.

The extent closure system of the in Proposition 2 constructed context $\mathbb{A}$, is equal to the join of $\mathrm{Ext}(\mathbb{K})$ and $\sigma^{-1}[\mathrm{Ext}(\mathbb{S})]$ in the closure system of all closure systems on G (cf. Proposition 13 [8]). Hence, $\mathrm{Ext}(A)$ is the smallest closure system on G, for which $\mathrm{Ext}(\mathbb{K})$ and $\sigma^{-1}[\mathrm{Ext}(\mathbb{S})]$ are contained.

In the above setting one can consider $\mathbb{K}$ and $\mathbb{S}$ as *consistent scalings* of $\mathbb{A}$. Based on this the question for representing and quantifying *inconsistencies* arises.

Definition 2 (Conceptual Scaling Error). *Let* $\mathbb{K}, \mathbb{S}$ *be formal contexts and* $\sigma : G_{\mathbb{K}} \to G_{\mathbb{S}}$, *then the* conceptual scaling error *of* $(\sigma, \mathbb{S})$ *with respect to* $\mathbb{K}$ *is the set* $\mathcal{E}_{\sigma,\mathbb{S}}^{\mathbb{K}} := \sigma^{-1}[\mathrm{Ext}(\mathbb{S})] \backslash \mathrm{Ext}(\mathbb{K})$.

The conceptual scaling error $\mathcal{E}_{\sigma,\mathbb{S}}^{\mathbb{K}}$ consists of all pre-images of closed object sets in $\mathbb{S}$ that are not closed in the context $\mathbb{K}$, i.e., the object sets that contradict the scale-measure criterion. Hence, $\mathcal{E}_{\sigma,\mathbb{S}}^{\mathbb{K}} = \emptyset$ iff $(\sigma, \mathbb{S}) \in \mathfrak{S}(\mathbb{K})$.

In the following, we denote by $\sigma^{-1}[\mathrm{Ext}(\mathbb{S})]|_{\mathrm{Ext}(\mathbb{K})} := \sigma^{-1}[\mathrm{Ext}(\mathbb{S})] \cap \mathrm{Ext}(\mathbb{K})$ the set of consistently reflected closed object sets of $\mathbb{S}$ by σ. This set can be represented as the intersection of two closure systems and is thereby a closure system as well. Using this notation together with the canonical representation Proposition 1 we can find the following statement.

Corollary 1. *For* $\mathbb{K}, \mathbb{S}$ *and* $\sigma : G_{\mathbb{K}} \mapsto G_{\mathbb{S}}$, *there exists a scale-measure* $(\psi, \mathbb{T}) \in \mathfrak{S}(\mathbb{K})$ *with* $\psi^{-1}(\mathrm{Ext}(\mathbb{T})) = \sigma^{-1}[\mathrm{Ext}(\mathbb{S})]|_{\mathrm{Ext}(\mathbb{K})}$.

The conceptual scaling error $\mathcal{E}_{\sigma,\mathbb{S}}^{\mathbb{K}}$ does not constitute a closure system on G, since it lacks the top element G. Moreover, the meet of elements $A, D \in \mathcal{E}_{\sigma,\mathbb{S}}^{\mathbb{K}}$ can be closed in $\mathbb{K}$ and thus $A \wedge D \notin \mathcal{E}_{\sigma,\mathbb{S}}^{\mathbb{K}}$.

To pinpoint the cause of the conceptual scaling inconsistencies we may investigate the scale's attributes using the following proposition.

Proposition 3 (Deciding Scale-Measures (cf. Proposition 20, [8])). *Let* $\mathbb{K}$ *and* $\mathbb{S}$ *be two formal contexts and* $\sigma : G_{\mathbb{K}} \to G_{\mathbb{S}}$, *then TFAE:*

i) σ *is a* $\mathbb{S}$-measure *of* $\mathbb{K}$
ii) $\sigma^{-1}(m^{I_{\mathbb{S}}}) \in \mathrm{Ext}(\mathbb{K})$ *for all* $m \in M_{\mathbb{S}}$

Based on this result, we can decide if $(\sigma, \mathbb{S})$ is a scale-measure of $\mathbb{K}$ solely based on the attribute extents of $\mathbb{S}$. In turn this enables us to determine the particular attributes n that cause conceptual scaling errors, i.e. $\sigma^{-1}(n^{I_{\mathbb{S}}}) \notin \mathrm{Ext}(\mathbb{K})$. We call the set of all these attributes the *attribute scaling error*.

Corollary 2. *For two formal contexts* $\mathbb{K}, \mathbb{S}$ *and map* $\sigma : G_{\mathbb{K}} \to G_{\mathbb{S}}$ *let the set* $O = \{m \in M_{\mathbb{S}} \mid \sigma^{-1}(m^{I_{\mathbb{S}}}) \in \mathrm{Ext}(\mathbb{K})\}$. *Then* $(\sigma, (G_{\mathbb{S}}, O, I_{\mathbb{S}} \cap G_{\mathbb{S}} \times O))$ *is a scale-measure of* $\mathbb{K}$.

Proof. Follows directly from applying Proposition 3.

The thus constructed scale-measure does not necessarily reflect all extents in $\sigma^{-1}[\mathrm{Ext}(\mathbb{S})]|_{\mathrm{Ext}(\mathbb{K})}$. For this, consider the example $\mathbb{K} = (\{1,2,3\}, \{1,2,3\}, =)$ with $\mathbb{S} = (\{1,2,3\}, \{1,2,3\}, \neq)$ and the map $\mathrm{id}_{\{1,2,3\}}$. The error set is equal to $\mathcal{E}_{\sigma,\mathbb{S}}^{\mathbb{K}} = \binom{\{1,2,3\}}{2}$. Hence, none of the scale-attributes $M_{\mathbb{S}} = \{1,2,3\}$ fulfills the scale-measure property. By omitting the whole set of attributes $M_{\mathbb{S}}$, we result in the context $(G, \{\}, \{\})$ whose set of extents is equal to $\{G\}$. The set $\sigma^{-1}[\mathrm{Ext}(\mathbb{S})]|_{\mathrm{Ext}(\mathbb{K})}$ however is equal to $\{\{\}, \{1\}, \{2\}, \{3\}, \{1,2,3\}\}$.

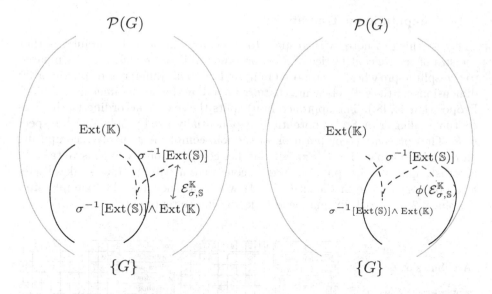

Fig. 3. The conceptual scaling error and the consistent part of $(\sigma, \mathbb{S})$ in $\underline{\mathfrak{S}}(\mathbb{K})$ (left). The right represents both parts as scale-measures of $\mathbb{S}$.

3.1   Representation and Structure of Conceptual Scaling Errors

So far, we apprehended $\mathcal{E}^{\mathbb{K}}_{\sigma,\mathbb{S}}$ as the set of erroneous preimages. However, the conceptual scaling error may be represented as a part of a scale-measure: i) The first approach is to analyze the extent structure of $\sigma^{-1}[\mathrm{Ext}(\mathbb{S})]$. This leads to a scale-measure $(\sigma, \mathbb{S})$ of the apposition $\mathbb{S} \mid \mathbb{K}$, according to Proposition 2. The conceptual scaling error $\mathcal{E}^{\mathbb{K}}_{\sigma,\mathbb{S}}$ is a subset of the reflected extents of $(\sigma, \mathbb{S})$. ii) The second approach is based on our result in Corollary 1. The conceptual scaling error $\mathcal{E}^{\mathbb{K}}_{\sigma,\mathbb{S}}$ cannot be represented as scale-measure of $\mathbb{K}$. However, since $\mathcal{E}^{\mathbb{K}}_{\sigma,\mathbb{S}} \subseteq \sigma^{-1}[\mathrm{Ext}(\mathbb{S})]$ there is a scale-measure of $\mathbb{S}$ that reflects $\mathcal{E}^{\mathbb{K}}_{\sigma,\mathbb{S}}$ (right, Fig. 3). Such a scale-measure can be computed using the canonical representation of scale-measures as highlighted by $\phi(\mathcal{E}^{\mathbb{K}}_{\sigma,\mathbb{S}})$ in Fig. 3. Since the scale-hierarchy is join-pseudocomplemented [8], we can compute a smaller representation of $\sigma^{-1}[\mathrm{Ext}(\mathbb{S})]|_{\mathrm{Ext}(\mathbb{K})}$ and $\mathcal{E}^{\mathbb{K}}_{\sigma,\mathbb{S}}$. In detail, for any $\sigma^{-1}[\mathrm{Ext}(\mathbb{S})]|_{\mathrm{Ext}(\mathbb{K})}$ there exists a least element in $\underline{\mathfrak{S}}(\mathbb{S})$ whose join with $\sigma^{-1}[\mathrm{Ext}(\mathbb{S})]|_{\mathrm{Ext}(\mathbb{K})}$ yields $\sigma^{-1}[\mathrm{Ext}(\mathbb{S})]$. Due to its smaller size, the so computed join-complement can be more human comprehensible than $\mathcal{E}^{\mathbb{K}}_{\sigma,\mathbb{S}}$. iii) The third option is based on splitting the scale context according to its consistent attributes, see Corollary 2. Both split elements are then considered as scale-measures of $\mathbb{S}$. This results in two smaller, potentially more comprehensible, concept lattices. Additionally, all discussed scale-measures can be given in conjunctive normalform.

3.2 Computational Tractability

The first thing to note, with respect to the computational tractability, is that the size of the concept lattice of $\mathbb{S}$, as proposed in i) (above) is larger compared to the split approaches, as proposed in ii) and iii). This difference results in order dimensions for the split elements that are bound by the order dimension of $\mathbb{S}$ (cf. Proposition 24, [8]). The approach in ii) splits the scale $\mathbb{S}$ according to the conceptual scaling error $\mathcal{E}_{\sigma,\mathbb{S}}^{\mathbb{K}}$, a potentially exponentially sized problem with respect to $\mathbb{S}$. The consecutive computation of the join-complement involves computing all meet-irreducibles in $\sigma^{-1}[\text{Ext}(\mathbb{S})]$, another computationally expensive task. In contrast, approach iii) splits $\mathbb{S}$ based on consistent attributes and is takes therefore polynomial time in the size of $\mathbb{S}$. However, as shown in the example after Corollary 2, approach iii) may lead to less accurate representations.

Attributes of $\mathbb{K}$

clearing land (CL), draft (Dr), dung (Du), education (Ed), eggs (Eg), feathers (Fe), fiber (F), fighting (Fi), guarding (He), horns (Ho), hunting (Hu), lawn mowing (LM), leather (Le), manure (Ma), meat (Me), milk (Mi), mount (Mo), narcotics detection (ND), ornamental (O), pack (Pa), pest control (PC), pets (Pe), plowing (Pl), policing (Po), racing (Ra), rescuing (R), research (Re), service (Se), show (Sh), skin (Sk), sport (Sp), therapy (Th), truffle harvesting (TH), vellum (V), weed control (WC), working (W)

$\mathbb{S}$	0	1	2	3	4	5	6	7	8	9
Brahman cattle		×					×			
European cattle		×					×	×	×	
Guppy				×						
alpaca					×			×	×	
bactrian camel			×							
bali cattle		×					×			
barbary dove										×
canary				×						
cat				×						×
chicken		×				×				
dog	×								×	×
donkey			×	×	×					
dromedary			×							
duck	×									
fancy mouse					×					
fancy rat					×					
ferret							×			
fuegian dog									×	
gayal		×								
goat		×			×				×	×

	0	1	2	3	4	5	6	7	8	9
goldfish								×		
goose		×								
guinea pig						×	×			×
guineafowl		×								
hedgehog										
horse				×		×		×		
koi							×			
lama						×			×	×
mink					×					
muscovy duck		×								
pig						×	×	×		×
pigeon							×			
rabbit						×	×			×
sheep				×		×	×	×		×
silkmoth						×				
silver fox						×				
society finch						×				
striped skunk						×				
turkey		×								
water buffalo				×				×		×
yak				×				×	×	

Fig. 4. Attributes of the *Domestic* data set (left) and a factor (right).

4 Experimental Evaluation

To provide practical evidence for the applicability of the just introduced conceptual scaling error, we conducted an experiment on eleven data sets. In those we compared the classical errors, such as Frobenius norm, to the conceptual scaling error. The data sets were, if not otherwise specified, nominally scaled to a binary representation. Six of them are available through the UCI[3] [4] data sets repository: i) *Diagnosis* [2] with *temperature* scaled in intervals of [35.0 37.5) [37.5

[3] i) https://archive.ics.uci.edu/ml/datasets/Acute+Inflammations,
   ii) https://archive.ics.uci.edu/ml/datasets/Hayes-Roth,
  iii) https://archive.ics.uci.edu/ml/datasets/zoo,
  iv) https://archive.ics.uci.edu/ml/datasets/mushroom,
   v) https://archive.ics.uci.edu/ml/datasets/HIV-1+protease+cleavage,
  vi) https://archive.ics.uci.edu/ml/datasets/Plants and https://plants.sc.egov.usda.gov/java/.

Table 1. Quantifying the conceptual scaling error for approximations $\mathbb{K}_{\approx} = \mathbb{S} \cdot H$ of data sets $\mathbb{K}$ by binary matrix factorization. Cells with '-' where not computed due to computational intractability. Density (D), Attribute Error (AE), Conceptual Scaling Error (CE), Hemming distance between $I_{\mathbb{K}}$ and $I_{\mathbb{S} \cdot H}$ relative to $|G| \cdot |M|$ (H%), Frobenius measure between $I_{\mathbb{K}}$ and $I_{\mathbb{S} \cdot H}$.

	Context $\mathbb{K}$				Approximated context $\mathbb{K}_{\approx} = \mathbb{S} \cdot H$					Respective Scale $\mathbb{S}$				
	$|G|$	$|M|$	D	$|\mathfrak{B}|$	Frob	H%	$|\mathfrak{B}|$	AE	CE	$|M|$	D	$|\mathfrak{B}|$	AE	CE
Diagnosis	120	17	0.471	88	13.04	8.3	26	6	7	4	0.250	6	0	0
Hayes-Roth	132	18	0.218	215	16.40	11.3	33	8	26	4	0.350	12	3	8
Domestic	41	55	0.158	292	8.49	3.2	148	14	68	10	0.183	34	6	15
Zoo	101	43	0.395	4579	15.52	5.5	442	13	347	7	0.315	25	2	4
Chess	346	683	0.473	3211381	82.01	2.8	229585	246	224673	26	0.767	4334	24	4280
Mushroom	8124	119	0.193	238710	243.86	6.2	10742	48	10598	11	0.277	139	7	116
HIV-1PC	6590	162	0.055	115615	221.38	4.6	303	32	229	13	0.154	330	12	236
Plant-Habitats	34781	68	0.127	-	322.16	4.4	-	68	-	8	0.128	256	8	255
Airbnb-Berlin	22552	145	0.007	-	130.29	0.5	-	0	0	12	0.057	8	1	1
UFC-Fights	5144	1915	0.001	-	101.43	0.1	2	0	1	44	0.932	2	44	1
Recipes	178265	58	0.057	-	492.8	2.3	-	7	-	8	0.236	256	4	187

40.0) [40.0 42.0], ii) *Hayes-Roth* iii) *Zoo* iv) *Mushroom* v) *HIV-1Protease Cleavage* [13] and vi) *Plant-Habitats* four kaggle[4] data sets vii) *Top-Chess-Players* with *rating, rank, games, bith_year* ordinally scaled, viii) neighbourhood data from the *Airbnb-Berlin* data sets, ix) *A_fighter* and *B_fighter* from the *UFC-Fights* data sets and x) *Recipes* [10]. The eleventh data set is generated from the Wikipedia list of *Domesticated Animals*.[5] This data set is also used for a qualitative analysis. We summarized all data sets in Table 1, first and second major column.

As dimension reduction method, we employ the *binary matrix factorization* [15] of the Nimfa [16] framework. Their algorithm is an adaption of the *non-negative matrix factorization*(NMF). In addition to the regular NMF a penalty and a thresholding function are applied to binarize the output. For any given data set $\mathbb{K}$ two binary factors $\mathbb{S}, H$ with $\mathbb{K} \approx \mathbb{S} \cdot H$ are computed.

The BMF factorization algorithm takes several parameters, such as convergence λ_w, λ_h, which we left at their default value of 1.1. We increased the maximum number of iterations to 500 to ensure convergence and conducted ten runs, of which took the best fit. The target number of attribute (features) in $|M_{\mathbb{S}}|$ was set approximately to $\sqrt{|M_{\mathbb{K}}|}$ to receive a data dimension reduction of one magnitude.

We depicted the results, in particular the quality of the factorizations, in Table 1 (major column three and four) where $\mathbb{K}_{\approx} = \mathbb{S} \cdot H$ is the BMF approximation of $\mathbb{K}$. Our investigation considers standard measures, such as Frobenius norm (*Frob*) and relative Hamming distance (*H%*), as well as the proposed conceptual scaling error (*CE*) and attribute scaling error (*AE*). For the large data

---

[4] https://www.kaggle.com/, i) https://www.kaggle.com/odartey/top-chess-players and https://www.fide.com/, ii) https://www.kaggle.com/brittabettendorf/berlin-airbnb-data/, iii) https://www.kaggle.com/rajeevw/ufcdata, iv) https://www.kaggle.com/shuyangli94/food-com-recipes-and-user-interactions.

[5] https://en.wikipedia.org/w/index.php?title=List_of_domesticated_animals, 25.02.2020.

sets, i.e., the last four in Table 1, we omitted computing the number of concepts due to its computational intractability, indicated by '-'. Therefore we were not able to compute the conceptual scaling errors of the approximate data sets $\mathbb{K}_{\approx}$. However, the conceptual scaling error of the related scales $\mathbb{S}$ is independent of the computational tractability of CE of $\mathbb{K}_{\approx}$.

We observe that the values for Frob and for H% differ vastly among the different data sets. For Example H% varies from 0.1 to 11.3. We find that for all data sets $|\mathfrak{B}(\mathbb{K})|$ is substantially larger than $|\mathfrak{B}(\mathbb{K}_{\approx})|$, independently of the values of Frob and H%. Hence, BMF leads to a considerable loss of concepts. When comparing the conceptual and attribute scaling error to Frob and H%, we observe that the novel conceptual errors capture different aspects than the classical matrix norm error. For example, *Domestic* and *Chess* have similar values for H%, however, their error values with respect to attributes and concepts differ significantly. In detail, the ratio of $|CE|/|\mathfrak{B}(\mathbb{K}_{\approx})|$ is 0.98 for *Chess* and 0.46 for *Domestic*, and the ratio for $|AE|/|M_{\approx}|$ is 0.36 for *Chess* and .25 for *Domestic*.

While we do not know the number of concepts for *Airbnb-Berlin*, we do know that conceptual scaling error of the related $\mathbb{K}_{\approx}$ is 0 due to AE being 0 and Proposition 3. The factorization of the *UFC-Fights* produced an empty context $\mathbb{K}_{\approx}$. Therefore, all attribute derivations in $\mathbb{K}_{\approx}$ are the empty set, whose pre-image is an extent of $\mathbb{K}$, hence, AE is 0. We suspect that BMF is unable to cope with data sets that exhibit a very low density. It is noteworthy that we cannot elude this conclusion from the value of the Frob and H%. By investigating the binary factor $\mathbb{S}$ using the conceptual scaling error and the attribute error, we are able to detect the occurrence of this phenomenon. In detail, we see that 44 out of 44 attributes are inconsistent.

We can take from our investigation that low H% and Frob values do not guaranty good factorizations with respect to preserving the conceptual structure of the original data set. In contrast, we claim that the proposed scaling errors are capable of capturing such error to some extent. On a final note, we may point out that the conceptual scaling errors enable a quantifiable comparison of a scaling $\mathbb{S}$ to the original data set $\mathbb{K}$, despite different dimensionality.

4.1 Qualitative Analysis

The *domestic* data set includes forty-one animals as objects and fifty-five purposes for their domestication as attributes, such as *pets, hunting, meat, etc.*. The resulting $\mathbb{K}$ has a total of 2255 incidences and the corresponding concept lattice has 292 formal concepts. We applied the BMF algorithm as before, which terminated after 69 iterations with the scale depicted in Fig. 4. The incidence of $\mathbb{K}_{\approx} := \mathbb{S} \cdot H$ has seventy-three wrong incidences, i.e., wrongfully present or absent pairs, which results in H% of 3.2. The corresponding concept lattice of $\mathbb{K}_{\approx}$ has 148 concepts, which is nearly half of $\mathfrak{B}(\mathbb{K})$. Furthermore, out of these 148 concepts there are only 80 correct, i.e., in Ext($\mathbb{K}$). This results in a conceptual scaling error of 68, which is in particular interesting in the light of the apparently low H% error.

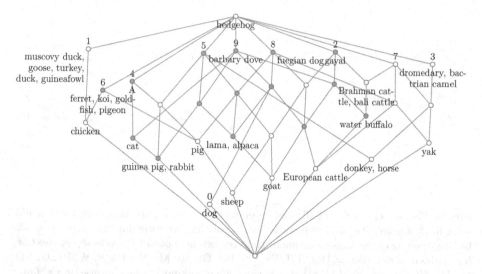

Fig. 5. Concept lattice of the *Domestic* scale context. $\mathcal{E}_{\sigma,\mathbb{S}}^{\mathbb{K}}$ is indicated in red. A={society finch, silkmoth, fancy mouse, mink, fancy rat, striped skunk, Guppy, canary, silver fox}

To pinpoint the particular errors, we employ i)–iii) from Sect. 3.1. The result of the first approach is visualized in Fig. 5 and displays the concept lattice of $\sigma^{-1}[\mathrm{Ext}(\mathbb{S})]$ in which the elements of $\mathcal{E}_{\sigma,\mathbb{S}}^{\mathbb{K}}$ are highlighted in red. First, we notice in the lattice diagram that the inconsistent extents $\mathcal{E}_{\sigma,\mathbb{S}}^{\mathbb{K}}$ are primarily in the upper part. Seven out of fifteen are derivations from attribute combinations of 9, 8, and 5. This indicates that the factorization was especially inaccurate for those attributes. The attribute extents of 6, 4, and 2 are in $\mathcal{E}_{\sigma,\mathbb{S}}^{\mathbb{K}}$, however, many of their combinations with other attributes result in extents of $\mathrm{Ext}(\mathbb{K})$.

The resulting lattices of applying approach ii) are depicted in Fig. 6, the consistent lattice of $\sigma^{-1}[\mathrm{Ext}(\mathbb{S})]|_{\mathrm{Ext}(\mathbb{K})}$ on the left and its join-complement on the right. The consistent part has nineteen concepts, all depicted attributes can considered in conjunctive normalform. The join-complement consists of twenty-two concepts of which the incorrect ones are marked in red.

Based on this representation, we can see that twenty out of the forty-one objects have no associated attributes. These include objects like *lama, alpaca* or *barbary dove*, which we have also indirectly identified by i) as derivations of 5, 8, 9. Furthermore, we see that thirteen out of the fifty-five attributes of $\mathbb{K}$ are not present in any conjunctive attributes. These attributes include domestication purposes like *tusk, fur,* or *hair*. Out of our expertise we suppose that these could form a meaningful cluster in the specific data realm. In the join-complement, we can identify the attributes 5,8,9 as being highly inconsistently scaled, as already observed in the paragraph above.

The third approach results in a scale $\mathbb{S}_O$ of four consistent attributes and a scale $\mathbb{S}_{\hat{O}}$ of six non-consistent attributes (Fig. 7). The scale $\mathbb{S}_O$ has seven concepts

116   T. Hanika and J. Hirth

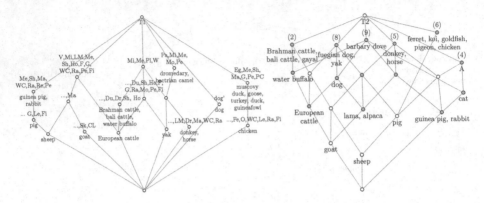

Fig. 6. The concept lattice of all valid extents of the scale $\mathbb{S}$ (left, in conjunctive normal-form in $\mathfrak{S}(\mathbb{K})$) and its join-complement (right) of the *Domestic* data set. Extents in the lattice drawing of the join-complement that are extents not in the *Domestic* context are highlighted in red. dog' = {Ed, TH, Pa, Gu, He, Dr, Sp, Me, Sh, Po, F, W, Re, G, ND, Le, Ra, Hu, Se, Th, Pe, PC, Fi} A={society finch, silkmoth, fancy mouse, mink, fancy rat, striped skunk, Guppy, canary, silver fox}, T1={fuegian dog, lama, ferret, alpaca, society finch, silkmoth, fancy mouse, koi, hedgehog, mink, fancy rat, striped skunk, goldfish, barbary dove, Guppy, canary, pigeon, silver fox, cat, gayal}, T2={dromedary, muscovy duck, bactrian camel, goose, turkey, hedgehog, duck, guineafowl} (Color figure online)

and the scale $\mathbb{S}_{\hat{O}}$ has twenty-two. We may note that the concept lattice of $\mathbb{S}_{\hat{O}}$ is identical to the join-complement of the previous approach. In general this is not the case, one cannot even assume isomorphy. While the concept lattice of $\mathbb{S}_O$ does miss some of the consistent extents of $\sigma^{-1}[\mathrm{Ext}(\mathbb{S})]|_{\mathrm{Ext}(\mathbb{K})}$, we claim that the combination of $\mathbb{S}_O$ and $\mathbb{S}_{\hat{O}}$ still provides a good overview of the factorization shortcomings.

5   Related Work

To cope with large data sets, a multitude of methods was introduced to reduce the dimensionality. One such method is the factorization of a data set $\mathbb{K}$ into two factors (scales) $\mathbb{S}, H$ whose product $\mathbb{S} \cdot H$ estimates $\mathbb{K}$. For binary data sets, a related problem is known as the *discrete basis problem* [11]: For a given $k \in \mathbb{N}$, compute two binary factors $\mathbb{S} \in \mathbb{B}^{n \times k}$ and $H \in \mathbb{B}^{k \times m}$ for which $\|K - SH\|$ is minimal. This problem is known to be NP-hard. This hardness result lead to the development of several approximation algorithms [1,15]. For example, one approach uses formal concepts as attributes of $\mathbb{S}$ [1] and objects of H. It is shown that a solution to the discrete basis problem can be given in terms of this representation. However, since the initial problem is still NP-hard, this approach is computationally intractable for large data sets.

The BMF approach [15] adapts a non-negative matrix factorization by using a penalty and thresholding function. This algorithm optimizes two initial matrices

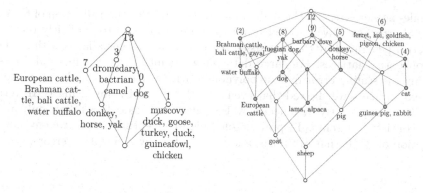

Fig. 7. The concept lattice of all valid (left) and invalid (right) attributes of the *Domestic* scale-measure. Extents in the lattice drawing of the invalid attributes that are not extents in the *Domesticated Animals* context are marked in red. A = {society finch, silkmoth, fancy mouse, mink, fancy rat, striped skunk, Guppy, canary, silver fox} T3 = {fuegian dog, lama, sheep, ferret, pig, alpaca, society finch, goat, silkmoth, fancy mouse, koi, guinea pig, rabbit, hedgehog, mink, fancy rat, striped skunk, goldfish, barbary dove, Guppy, canary, pigeon, silver fox, cat, gayal} T2 = {dromedary, muscovy duck, bactrian camel, goose, turkey, hedgehog, duck, guineafowl} (Color figure online)

to minimize the error $\|K - SH\|$. This procedure does compute an approximation to the solution of the discrete basis problem and has lower computational cost. An additional drawback of the BMF algorithm is that it may introduce closed objects sets in $S \cdot H$ that are not closed in the data set K. The main idea of the conceptual scaling error is the efficient computation and quantification of said closed sets.

Other evaluations of BMF, besides $\|K - S \cdot H\|$, have been considered [9]. They investigate the quality of implications in $S \cdot H$ for some classification task. Additionally, they use different measures [3], e.g., *fidelity* and *descriptive loss*. Other statistical approaches often find *euclidean loss, Kullback-Leibler* divergence, *Residual Sum of Squares*, adequate. All previously mentioned evaluation criteria do not account for the complete conceptual structure of the resulting data set. Moreover, they are not intrinsically able to pinpoint to the main error portions of the resulting scale data sets. Furthermore, approaches based on the computation of implications are infeasible for larger data set. An advantage of our approach is the polynomial estimation of the conceptual error in the size of S and K through the attribute scaling error.

6   Conclusion

With our work we have presented a new approach to evaluate dimension reduction methods in particular and data scaling methods in general. The proposed conceptual scaling error was derived from a natural notion of continuity, as used in scale-measures within the realm of FCA. Beyond the quantification of the conceptual error, we have succeeded in presenting a method to explicitly represent the error generated by the dimension reduction, and to visualize it with the help of conceptual lattices. For large data set we demonstrated a method for estimating the scaling error in time polynomial with respect to the data set size. In our experiments we showed that even though a factorization using BMF terminates with apparently high accuracy, the calculated scale does reflect only about 55% consistent extents. To prevent such high conceptual errors, we envision an adaption of BMF that optimizes additionally for low conceptual errors.

References

1. Belohlávek, R., Vychodil, V.: Discovery of optimal factors in binary data via a novel method of matrix decomposition. J. Comput. Syst. Sci. **76**(1), 3–20 (2010)
2. Czerniak, J., Zarzycki, H.: Application of rough sets in the presumptive diagnosis of urinary system diseases. In: Sołdek, J., Drobiazgiewicz, L. (eds.) Artificial Intelligence and Security in Computing Systems, vol. 752, pp. 41–51. Springer, Boston (2003). https://doi.org/10.1007/978-1-4419-9226-0_5. isbn: 978-1-4419-9226-0
3. Dias, S.M., Vieira, N.J.: Reducing the size of concept lattices: the JBOS approach (2010)
4. Dua, D., Graff, C.: UCI machine learning repository (2017)
5. Ganter, B., Wille, R.: Conceptual scaling. In: Roberts, F. (ed.) Applications of Combinatorics and Graph Theory to the Biological and Social Sciences, vol. 17, pp. 139–167. Springer, New York (1989). https://doi.org/10.1007/978-1-4684-6381-1_6
6. Ganter, B., Wille, R.: Formal Concept Analysis: Mathematical Foundations, p. x+284. Springer, Berlin (1999). https://doi.org/10.1007/978-3-642-59830-2
7. Ganter, B., Stahl, J. Wille, R.: Conceptual measurement and many-valued contexts. In: Gaul, W., Schader, M. (eds.) Classification as a Tool of Research, pp. 169–176. Amsterdam, North-Holland (1986)
8. Hanika, T., Hirth, J.: On the lattice of conceptual measurements. arXiv preprint arXiv:2012.05287 (2020)
9. Kumar, C.A., Dias, S.M., Vieira, N.J.: Knowledge reduction in formal contexts using non-negative matrix factorization. Math. Comput. Simul. **109**, 46–63 (2015)
10. Li, S.: Food.com recipes and interactions (2019). https://doi.org/10.34740/KAGGLE/DSV/783630
11. Miettinen, P., et al.: The discrete basis problem. IEEE Trans. Knowl. Data Eng. **20**(10), 1348–1362 (2008). https://doi.org/10.1109/TKDE.2008.53. issn: 1041-4347
12. Prediger, S., Stumme, G.: Theory-driven logical scaling: conceptual information systems meet description logics. In: Franconi, E., Kifer, M. (eds.) Proceedings of KRDB 1999, vol. 21, pp. 46–49. CEUR-WS.org (1999)
13. Rögnvaldsson, T., You, L., Garwicz, D.: State of the art prediction of HIV-1 protease cleavage sites. Bioinformatics **31**(8), 1204–1210 (2015)
14. Wille, R.: Restructuring lattice theory: an approach based on hierarchies of concepts. In: Rival, I. (ed.) Ordered Sets: Proceedings of the NATO Advanced Study Institute, vol. 83, pp. 445–470. Springer, Dordrecht (1982). https://doi.org/10.1007/978-94-009-7798-3_15. ISBN 978-94-009-7798-3
15. Zhang, Z., et al.: Binary matrix factorization with applications. In: 7th IEEE International Conference on Data Mining (ICDM 2007), pp. 391–400. IEEE (2007)
16. Zitnik, M., Zupan, B.: NIMFA: a python library for nonnegative matrix factorization. JMLR **13**, 849–853 (2012)

Conceptual Relevance Index for Identifying Actionable Formal Concepts

Mohamed-Hamza Ibrahim[1,3]([✉]), Rokia Missaoui[1], and Jean Vaillancourt[2]

[1] Département d'informatique et d'ingénierie, Université du Québec en Outaouais,
Gatineau, QC, Canada
`mohamed.ibrahim@polymtl.ca`, `rokia.missaoui@uqo.ca`
[2] Department of Decision Sciences, HEC Montreal, Montreal, QC, Canada
`jean.vaillancourt@hec.ca`
[3] Department of Mathematics, Faculty of Science, Zagazig University, Zagazig, Egypt

Abstract. Discovering meaningful conceptual structures is a substantial task in data mining and knowledge discovery applications. While off-the-shelf interestingness indices defined in Formal Concept Analysis may provide an effective relevance evaluation in several situations, they frequently give inadequate results when faced with massive formal contexts (and concept lattices), and in the presence of irrelevant concepts. In this paper, we introduce the *Conceptual Relevance* ($\mathcal{CR}$) score, a new scalable interestingness measure for the identification of relevant concepts. From a conceptual perspective, minimal generators provide key information about their associated concept intent. Furthermore, the relevant attributes of a concept are those that maintain the satisfaction of its closure condition. Thus, $\mathcal{CR}$ exploits the fact that minimal generators and relevant attributes can be efficiently used to assess concept relevance. As such, the $\mathcal{CR}$ index quantifies both the amount of conceptually relevant attributes and the number of the minimal generators per concept intent. Our experiments on synthetic and real-world datasets show the efficiency of this measure over the well-known stability index.

Keywords: Formal concept analysis · Pattern selection and relevance

1 Introduction

A wide range of crucial problems in different sub-disciplines including data mining, social network analysis, and machine learning can be formulated as a pattern mining task. Inspired by the mathematical power of Formal concept Analysis (FCA) [5], the lattice formalization is always rich with substantial local conceptual structures that are important to data mining tasks. Unfortunately, it could contain a large amount of irrelevant local structures. The irrelevant objects emerge due to a number of reasons, such as the imprecise collection of the data. On the flip side of the coin, the irrelevant attributes are redundant and frequently appear due to the completeness property of the lattice. In general, whether it is

© Springer Nature Switzerland AG 2021
T. Braun et al. (Eds.): ICCS 2021, LNAI 12879, pp. 119–126, 2021.
https://doi.org/10.1007/978-3-030-86982-3_9

an irrelevant attribute or object inside a formal concept, it does not sufficiently contribute to the actionability of patterns to help perform an action or take a decision. So, its removal from the concept has no impact on its conceptual structure and significantly purifies domain description and semantics. Traditionally, the concept selection strategy has been used to mine interesting patterns in a concept lattice [8]. In the FCA literature, several selection measures (see [8] for a detailed survey) have been proposed such as concept probability, separation [6] among others. On the basis of the Galois connection between the set of objects and the set of attributes, the closure and derivation conditions of formal concepts are often decisive properties for measuring the importance of these patterns. As such, the stability index, which depends primarily on these two properties, has recently been introduced as the most prominent index for assessing the concept quality [8]. However, it is known that computing stability is #P-complete [7], which often requires an exponential time complexity in the size of the intent (or extent), i.e., $O(2^{|Intent|})$. Furthermore, stability is dependent on generators, and it is widely known that using generators causes an overestimation of concept quality, resulting in redundant association rules.

In this paper, to improve the stability, we introduce the *Conceptual Relevance* (*CR*) index. The overall approach to the *CR* index consists of the following basic elements. First, we exploit the fact that using the minimal generators rather than all the generators of a concept frequently results in less redundant patterns (e.g., association rules). Second, we define and exploit relevant attributes. More precisely, these attributes are often essential for maintaining stable conceptual structures. As a result, we design the Conceptual Relevance of a concept to concurrently quantify the amounts of minimal generators and relevant attributes in its intent, packed in one measure.

The paper is organized as follows. Section 2 recalls basic definitions of FCA and stability index. Section 3 explains our proposed Conceptual Relevance index. In Sect. 4 we conduct the experimental study with a detailed discussion. Finally, Sect. 5 presents our conclusion and directions for future work.

2   Background

Here, we briefly recall the Formal concept analysis (FCA) terminology [5]. Given a *formal context* $\mathbb{K} = (\mathcal{G}, \mathcal{M}, \mathcal{I})$, where $\mathcal{G}$ is the set of objects, $\mathcal{M}$ is the set of attributes, and $\mathcal{I}$ is a binary relation between $\mathcal{G}$ and $\mathcal{M}$ with $\mathcal{I} \subseteq \mathcal{G} \times \mathcal{M}$. For $g \in \mathcal{G}, m \in \mathcal{M}, (g, m) \in \mathcal{I}$ holds iff the object g has the attribute m. Given arbitrary subsets $A \subseteq \mathcal{G}$ and $B \subseteq \mathcal{M}$, the following derivation operators are defined: $A' = \{m \in \mathcal{M} \mid \forall g \in A, (g, m) \in \mathcal{I}\}$ and $B' = \{g \in \mathcal{G} \mid \forall m \in B, (g, m) \in \mathcal{I}\}$, where A' is the set of attributes common to all objects of A and B' is the set of objects sharing all attributes from B. The closure operator $()''$ implies the double application of $()'$. The pair $c = (A, B)$ is called a *formal concept* of $\mathbb{K}$ with *extent* A and *intent* B iff $A'' = A$ and $B'' = B$. A partial order exists between two concepts $c_1 = (A_1, B_1) \preceq$ and $c_2 = (A_2, B_2)$ if $A_1 \subseteq A_2 \iff B_1 \supseteq B_2$. The set $\mathcal{C}$ of all concepts together with the partial order form a concept lattice. For two formal concepts $c_1 = (A_1, B_1) \preceq c_2 = (A_2, B_2)$, if $\nexists c3 = (A_3, B_3)$ s.t. $A_1 \subseteq$

$A_3 \subseteq A_2$, then c_1 is a *lower cover* of c_2, and c_2 is an *upper cover* of c_1, denoted by $c_1 \prec c_2$ and $c_2 \succ c_1$ respectively. The *intentional face* $f_{\text{int}}(c, c_u)$ of a concept $c = (A, B)$ w.r.t. its u-th upper cover concept, $c_u = (A_u, B_u) \in \mathcal{U}(c)$, is the difference between the intent sets [11], *i.e.*, $f_{\text{int}}(c, c_u) = B \setminus B_u$, where $\mathcal{U}(c)$ is the set of the upper covers of c. Given the family of faces $\Gamma(c)$, the set Z is said to be a *blocker* [12] of $\Gamma(c)$ if $\forall f_i \in \Gamma(c)$, $f_i \cap Z \neq \emptyset$, and the blocker Z is said to be *minimal* if $\nexists Z_j \subset Z$, $\forall f_i \in \Gamma(c)$, $f_i \cap Z_j \neq \emptyset$. Given a concept $c = (A, B)$ in a formal context $\mathbb{K} = (\mathcal{G}, \mathcal{M}, \mathcal{I})$, a subset $h_i \subseteq B$ is called a *generator* [14] of the concept intent iff $h_i'' = B$, and it is a *minimal generator* when $\nexists h_j \subseteq h_i$ such that $h_j'' = B$. We will use $\mathcal{H}_c$ to denote the minimal generator set of the intent associated with concept c.

Interestingness measures of a formal concept $c = (A, B)$ are widely used to assess its *relevancy*. In this context, the stability index $\sigma(c)$ of c has been found to be prominent for selecting relevant concepts [8]. The *intentional stability* $\sigma_{\text{in}}(c)$ [7] of a concept $c = (A, B)$ in $\mathbb{K}$ is:

$$\sigma_{\text{in}}(c) = \frac{|\{e \in \mathcal{P}(A) | e' = B\}|}{2^{|A|}} = \frac{|\{e \in \mathcal{P}(A) | e'' = A\}|}{2^{|A|}} \tag{1}$$

where $\mathcal{P}(A)$ is the power set of A. In Eq. (1), the intentional stability $\sigma_{\text{in}}(c)$ measures the dependency strength between the intent B and the objects in A.

3   Conceptual Relevance ($\mathcal{CR}$) Index

To set the stage for how the $\mathcal{CR}$ quantifies the relevance of a formal concept, the first thing we do is to define relevant attributes through the lens of FCA.

Definition 1 (Conceptually Relevant Attribute). *For a formal concept $c = (A, B)$, an attribute $m \in B$ is conceptually relevant if $(B \setminus \{m\})' \neq A$.*

That is, the concept c does not preserve its local conceptual structure after removing m from its intent. From a statistical perspective, this means that the attribute m has a significant statistical influence, and mainly depends on the distribution of the concept's intent parameter. Intuitively, this implies that the attribute m contains certain relevant information in c. Thus, taking it off from the concept intent results in the loss of essential conceptual information (which clearly appears through the expansion of its extent). Since the derivation operation on attribute subset can be simply done, the conceptually relevant attributes are easily identified. Furthermore, the minimal generator set $\mathcal{H}_c$ of a concept c can serve as a non-redundant generator set.

Definition 2 (Conceptual Relevance Index $\mathcal{CR}(c)$). *The intentional Conceptual Relevance of a concept $c = (A, B)$ with $A \neq \emptyset$ in the context $\mathbb{K} = (\mathcal{G}, \mathcal{M}, \mathcal{T})$ is:*

$$\mathcal{CR}_{in}(c) = \mathcal{F}(\alpha_{in}(c), \beta_{in}(c)) \tag{2}$$

where

$$\alpha_{in}(c) = \begin{cases} \frac{|\{m \in B | (B \setminus \{m\})' \neq A\}|}{|B|} & \text{if } B \neq \emptyset \\ 0 & \text{Otherwise.} \end{cases} \tag{3}$$

and

$$\beta_{in}(c) = \begin{cases} \frac{|\mathcal{H}_c|}{2^{|B|-2}} & \text{if } |\mathcal{H}_c| > 1 \text{ \& } |B| > 1 \\ 0 & \text{Otherwise.} \end{cases} \tag{4}$$

In Eq. 2, $\mathcal{CR}$ computes the activation function $\mathcal{F}$ of α_{in} and β_{in} relevance terms. $\mathcal{F}$ can be any function applied to squash additive, multiplicative, logarithmic or other linear or non-linear relationships between the two terms. For instance, it can simply be the arithmetic average that calculates the linear additive relationship of the two relevance terms. For the α_{in} term in Eq. (3), we iterate through the attributes of the intent B to count the number of the conceptually relevant ones that satisfy the derivation condition. From a conceptual perspective, the α_{in} term quantifies the ratio of the relevant attributes that exist in the concept intent B. For the β_{in} term in Eq. (4), we calculate the set of minimal generators of c as in [14]. We then count the number of minimal generators out of all potential generators in B. Note that the goal behind taking minus 2 in the denominator of Eq. (4) is to exclude the trivial empty set and the whole intent. From a pattern mining perspective, the β_{in} term quantifies the number of potential local relevant substructures inside the concept intent B. Since the attributes outside the scope of a given concept intent do not have any influence on its conceptual structure, only the attributes of the concept intent should be used to normalize its $\mathcal{CR}(c)$ terms. As a result, the size $|B|$ of the intent and the value of $2^{|B|}$ serve as normalization factors to scale the components α_{in} and β_{in} respectively.

The $\mathcal{CR}$ index requires a time and space complexity of $O(|B| \times |\mathcal{G}| \times |\mathcal{M}|)$.

4   Experimental Evaluation

The objective of our empirical evaluation is to address these two key questions: **Q1**: Is the $\mathcal{CR}$ index empirically accurate compared to the state-of-the-art indices for assessing the relevance of formal concepts? and **Q2**: Is the $\mathcal{CR}$ index faster than the state-of-the-art interestingness indices?

In order to obtain robust answers to Questions Q1 and Q2, we first select the following (synthetic[‡] and real-life[*]) datasets[1]: (1) [‡]**Dirichlet** [3] ($|\mathcal{G}| = 2000$, $|\mathcal{M}| = 15$, $|L| = 18166$ and $n = 2903$) is a random formal context generated using the Dirichlet model generator; (2) [‡]**CoinToss** [4] ($|\mathcal{G}| = 793$, $|\mathcal{M}| = 10$, $|L| = 913$ and $n = 645$) is a random formal context generated by indirect Coin-Toss model generator; (3)[*]**LinkedIn** [13] ($|\mathcal{G}| = 1269$, $|\mathcal{M}| = 34$, $|L| = 4847$ and $n = 1473$); (4) [*]**Diagnosis** [2] ($|\mathcal{G}| = 120$, $|\mathcal{M}| = 17$, $|L| = 88$ and $n = 81$); (5) [*]**PediaLanguages** [10] ($|\mathcal{G}| = 316$, $|\mathcal{M}| = 169$, $|L| = 188$ and $n = 22$); and (6) [*]**Bottlenose Dolphins** [9] ($|\mathcal{G}| = 62$, $|\mathcal{M}| = 62$, $|L| = 282$ and $n = 16$).

---

[1]   Available: https://github.com/tomhanika/conexp-clj/tree/dev/testing-data.
   A dataset description is given between parenthesis, where $|\mathcal{G}|$ (resp. $|\mathcal{M}|$) is the number of objects (resp. attributes). $|L|$ and n are the lattice size and the number of shared concepts respectively.

Subsequently, we compared the results of $\mathcal{CR}(c)$ using *the arithmetic average* as the activation $\mathcal{F}$ against the *intentional Stability* [8], which is currently the state-of-the-art interestingness index. We then consider the traditional approach [1] to validate the two relevance measures. That is, we apply the following scheme: 1) Divide the dataset $\mathbb{K} = (\mathcal{G}, \mathcal{M}, \mathcal{I})$ horizontally into two disjoint subsets $\mathbb{K}_R = (\mathcal{G}_1, \mathcal{M}, \mathcal{I}_1)$ and $\mathbb{K}_T = (\mathcal{G}_2, \mathcal{M}, \mathcal{I}_2)$ such that $\mathcal{G} = \mathcal{G}_1 \cup \mathcal{G}_2$. 2) Extract the two sets $\mathcal{S}_r$ and $\mathcal{S}_t$ of the shared formal concepts from $\mathbb{K}_R$ and $\mathbb{K}_T$, respectively. Note that a concept $c_r = (A_r, B_r) \in \mathcal{S}_r$ and its corresponding one $c_t = (A_t, B_t) \in \mathcal{S}_t$ are shared if they have the same intent but not necessarily the same extent. 3) Use $\mathbb{K}_R$ as a reference dataset to calculate the underlying relevance indices of the shared concepts in $\mathcal{S}_r$ while using $\mathbb{K}_T$ as a test dataset to evaluate the relevance index values of the corresponding shared concepts in $\mathcal{S}_t$. It is obvious that $n = |\mathcal{S}_r| = |\mathcal{S}_t|$. 4) Record the score list $\{(x_i, y_i)\}_{i=1}^n$, where x_i and y_i are the relevant measures of the i-th concept in $\mathcal{S}_r$ and its corresponding concept in $\mathcal{S}_t$, respectively. 5) Draw each pair (x_i, y_i) as a point in a 2D-plot so that the best case is $y_i = x_i$. We therefore consider the underlying interestingness measure to be accurate if its relevance values for the shared formal concepts of the reference set $\mathcal{S}_r$ are close/equal to the relevance values of the corresponding formal concepts in $\mathcal{S}_t$. Based on this scheme, we consider the following two metrics to assess the accuracy and the performance of the results: (1) The Pearson correlation coefficient (and its scatter plot): $\xi = \dfrac{\sum_{i=1}^n x_i y_i - n\bar{x}\bar{y}}{\sqrt{(\sum_{i=1}^n x_i^2 - n\bar{x}^2)}\sqrt{(\sum_{i=1}^n y_i^2 - n\bar{y}^2)}}$, where $\bar{x} = \frac{1}{n}\sum_{i=1}^n x_i$ and $\bar{y} = \frac{1}{n}\sum_{i=1}^n y_i$ are the mean values of $\{x_i\}_{i=1}^{|\mathcal{S}_r|}$ and $\{y_i\}_{i=1}^{|\mathcal{S}_t|}$ respectively. We recall that $n = |\mathcal{S}_r| = |\mathcal{S}_t|$ is the number of the shared concepts.

(2) The average elapsed time: $\tau = \frac{1}{2}\left[\dfrac{\sum_{c_i \in \mathcal{S}_r} t_i}{|\mathcal{S}_r|} + \dfrac{\sum_{c_j \in \mathcal{S}_t} t_j}{|\mathcal{S}_t|}\right]$, where t_i and t_j are the elapsed times for computing the underlying index of the concept $c_i \in \mathcal{S}_r$ and its corresponding one $c_j \in \mathcal{S}_t$ respectively.

We conduct our preliminary empirical study through two experiments.

Experiment I. The first experiment is dedicated to answering Q1. In line with the scheme explained above, we first divide each one of the six underlying datasets into reference $\mathbb{K}_R$ and tested $\mathbb{K}_T$ subsets. Two relevance indices, namely *Conceptual Relevance* and *stability*, are then computed on the extracted sets of shared concepts. On that basis, we calculate their Pearson correlation coefficients using their recorded score lists. Figure 1 displays the Pearson correlation scatter plot of reference $\mathbb{K}_R$ vs test $\mathbb{K}_T$ on the shared concepts. Overall, Conceptual Relevance is the most accurate of the two compared indices, achieving the best Pearson correlation coefficients on the six datasets. Stability comes close behind the Conceptual Relevance on Dirichlet, CoinToss and Diagnosis datasets, but considerably further behind it for the other datasets. $\mathcal{CR}(c)$ is at least 14% (33% and 16% resp.) more accurate than stability on LinkedIn (Pedia-Languages and Dolphins resp.) dataset.

Experiment II. This experiment is performed to answer Q2. We are interested here in assessing the performance of the indices. That is, we rerun Experiment I while reporting their computational times using the metric τ. Figure 2 shows the average elapsed time τ of the two relevance indices, namely the $\mathcal{CR}(c)$ and stability, on the shared concepts of the six underlying datasets. $\mathcal{CR}(c)$ outperforms stability on all datasets tested. It performs four times faster than the stability on the LinkedIn dataset, three times faster on the Pedia-Languages and at least twice as fast as stability on the other four datasets.

Discussion. In terms of accuracy, the results of Experiment I suggest that the Conceptual relevance index outperforms the stability index. It improves the assessment of the concept quality in two ways. First, rather than relying on generators as in stability which may result in redundant patterns, the Conceptual relevance precisely quantifies the amount of both actionable minimal generators

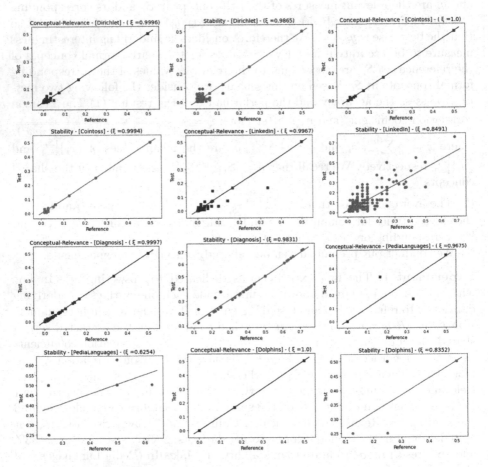

Fig. 1. The Pearson correlation scatter plot of reference $\mathbb{K}_R$ vs test $\mathbb{K}_T$ of the two relevancy measures: (arithmetic) Conceptual relevance (*in blue*), and Stability (*in red*). (Color figure online)

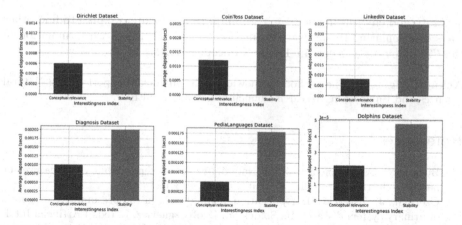

Fig. 2. The average elapsed time τ of the two relevancy measures: Conceptual relevance (arithmetic) and stability on the shared concepts of the six underlying datasets.

and relevant attributes in the concept intent, with the ability to encapsulate that in a single measurement and in a variety of ways using potential activation functions. Second, and unlike the stability index, $\mathcal{CR}(c)$ produces robust relevance scores to effectively discriminate between small and neighbour concepts (i.e., those with an immediate link) because the latter cannot have the same set of minimal generators, and hence may have distinct $\mathcal{CR}(c)$ values. The results of Experiment II about the performance of the two indices show that the arithmetic $\mathcal{CR}(c)$ considerably prevails over stability. This is due to the fact that it addresses the limitation of the stability index explained earlier by counting the number of relevant attributes in the intent and calculating the minimal generators. $\mathcal{CR}(c)$ requires polynomial time and space complexity that does not depend on the size of the intent power set.

5   Conclusion

The present paper targeted the vital challenge of extracting interesting concepts from a concept lattice using a new relevance score. That is, we proposed Conceptual Relevance index, an efficient interestingness index to assess the quality of the concept. The novelty of the $\mathcal{CR}$ index is twofold: (i) first, it identifies the relevant attributes in a concept that maintain its conceptual structure, and (ii) second, it leverages the strength of minimal generators to quantify the most relevant local substructures of the intent, taking advantage of the fact that minimal generators frequently lead to more relevant (with less redundancy) patterns than non minimal ones. $\mathcal{CR}$ requires only a polynomial time and space complexity in the number of the concept upper covers and minimal generators. In addition, its formula is flexible and can be easily adjusted with several variants of its activation function. The thorough empirical study on several synthetic and real-life concept lattices shows that $\mathcal{CR}$ can assess the quality of concepts in a more accurate and efficient manner than stability. In the future, we plan to find other ways of calculating the activation function in Eq. (2). Finally, a formulation of the $\mathcal{CR}$ index for concepts in Triadic Concept Analysis will be derived.

Acknowledgment. The authors acknowledge the financial support of the Natural Sciences and Engineering Research Council of Canada (NSERC).

References

1. Buzmakov, A., Kuznetsov, S.O., Napoli, A.: Is concept stability a measure for pattern selection? Procedia Comput. Sci. **31**, 918–927 (2014)
2. Czerniak, J., Zarzycki, H.: Application of rough sets in the presumptive diagnosis of urinary system diseases. In: Sołdek, J., Drobiazgiewicz, L. (eds.) Artificial Intelligence and Security in Computing Systems. SECS, vol. 752, pp. 41–51. Springer, Heidelberg (2003). https://doi.org/10.1007/978-1-4419-9226-0_5
3. Felde, M., Hanika, T.: Formal context generation using Dirichlet distributions. In: Endres, D., Alam, M., Şotropa, D. (eds.) ICCS 2019. LNCS (LNAI), vol. 11530, pp. 57–71. Springer, Cham (2019). https://doi.org/10.1007/978-3-030-23182-8_5
4. Felde, M., Hanika, T., Stumme, G.: Null models for formal contexts. Information **11**(3), 135 (2020)
5. Ganter, B., Wille, R.: Formal Concept Analysis: Mathematical Foundations. Springer, New York (1999). https://doi.org/10.1007/978-3-642-59830-2 Translator-C. Franzke
6. Klimushkin, M., Obiedkov, S., Roth, C.: Approaches to the selection of relevant concepts in the case of noisy data. In: Kwuida, L., Sertkaya, B. (eds.) ICFCA 2010. LNCS (LNAI), vol. 5986, pp. 255–266. Springer, Heidelberg (2010). https://doi.org/10.1007/978-3-642-11928-6_18
7. Kuznetsov, S.O.: On stability of a formal concept. Ann. Math. Artif. Intell. **49**(1), 101–115 (2007). https://doi.org/10.1007/s10472-007-9053-6
8. Kuznetsov, S.O., Makhalova, T.: On interestingness measures of formal concepts. Inf. Sci. **442**, 202–219 (2018)
9. Lusseau, D., Schneider, K., Boisseau, O.J., Haase, P., Slooten, E., Dawson, S.M.: The bottlenose dolphin community of doubtful sound features a large proportion of long-lasting associations. Behav. Ecol. Sociobiol. **54**(4), 396–405 (2003). https://doi.org/10.1007/s00265-003-0651-y
10. Morsey, M., Lehmann, J., Auer, S., Stadler, C., Hellmann, S.: Dbpedia and the live extraction of structured data from wikipedia. Program **46**(2), 157–181 (2012)
11. Pfaltz, J.L., Taylor, C.M.: Closed set mining of biological data. In: BIOKDD: Workshop on Data Mining in Bioinformatics, pp. 43–48 (2002)
12. Pfaltz, J.L., Taylor, C.M.: Scientific knowledge discovery through iterative transformation of concept lattices. In: SIAM Workshop on Discrete Mathematics and Data Mining, Arlington, VA, USA, pp. 1–10 (2002)
13. Rossi, R.A., Ahmed, N.K.: The network data repository with interactive graph analytics and visualization. In: AAAI (2015). http://networkrepository.com
14. Szathmary, L., Valtchev, P., Napoli, A., Godin, R., Boc, A., Makarenkov, V.: A fast compound algorithm for mining generators, closed itemsets, and computing links between equivalence classes. Ann. Math. Artif. Intell. **70**(1), 81–105 (2014). https://doi.org/10.1007/s10472-013-9372-8

Attribute Selection Using Contranominal Scales

Dominik Dürrschnabel[1,2](✉) (iD), Maren Koyda[1,2](✉) (iD), and Gerd Stumme[1,2] (iD)

[1] Knowledge and Data Engineering Group, University of Kassel, Kassel, Germany
{duerrschnabel,koyda,stumme}@cs.uni-kassel.de
[2] Interdisciplinary Research Center for Information System Design,
University of Kassel, Kassel, Germany

Abstract. Formal Concept Analysis (FCA) allows to analyze binary
data by deriving concepts and ordering them in lattices. One of the main
goals of FCA is to enable humans to comprehend the information that
is encapsulated in the data; however, the large size of concept lattices
is a limiting factor for the feasibility of understanding the underlying
structural properties. The size of such a lattice depends on the number
of subcontexts in the corresponding formal context that are isomorphic
to a contranominal scale of high dimension. In this work, we propose
the algorithm `ContraFinder` that enables the computation of all contranominal scales of a given formal context. Leveraging this algorithm,
we introduce δ-`adjusting`, a novel approach in order to decrease the
number of contranominal scales in a formal context by the selection of
an appropriate attribute subset. We demonstrate that δ-`adjusting` a
context reduces the size of the hereby emerging sub-semilattice and that
the implication set is restricted to meaningful implications. This is evaluated with respect to its associated knowledge by means of a classification
task. Hence, our proposed technique strongly improves understandability
while preserving important conceptual structures.

Keywords: Formal Concept Analysis · Contranominal scales ·
Concept lattices · Attribute selection · Feature selection · Implications

1 Introduction

One of the main objectives of Formal Concept Analysis (FCA) is to present data
in a comprehensible way. For this, the data is clustered into concepts which are
then ordered in a lattice structure. Relationships between the features are represented as implications. However, the complexity of the corresponding concept
lattice can increase exponentially in the size of the input data. Beyond that, the
size of the implication set is also exponential in the worst case, even when it
is restricted to a minimal base. As humans tend to comprehend connections in
smaller chunks of data, the understandability is decreased by this exponential
nature even in medium sized datasets. That is why reducing large and complex data to meaningful substructures by eliminating redundant information

© Springer Nature Switzerland AG 2021
T. Braun et al. (Eds.): ICCS 2021, LNAI 12879, pp. 127–141, 2021.
https://doi.org/10.1007/978-3-030-86982-3_10

enhances the application of Formal Concept Analysis. Nested line diagrams [26] and drawing algorithms [8] can improve the readability of concept lattices by optimizing their presentation. However, neither of them compresses the size of the datasets and thus grasping relationships in large concept lattices remains hard. Therefore, our research question is: **How can one reduce the lattice size as much as possible by reducing the data as little as possible?** There are different ways of reducing the data. In this paper, we focus on the removal of attributes. The size of the concept lattice is heavily influenced by the number of its Boolean suborders. A lattice contains such an k-dimensional Boolean suborder if and only if the corresponding formal context contains an k-dimensional contranominal scale [1,16]. Thus, to reduce the size of the concept lattice it is reasonable to eliminate those. However, deciding on the largest contranominal scale of a formal context is an $\mathcal{NP}$-complete problem. Therefore, choosing sensible substructures of formal contexts which can be augmented in order to reduce the number of large contranominal scales is a challenging task.

In this work, we propose the algorithm `ContraFinder` that is more efficient then prior approaches in computing all contranominal scales in real world datasets. This enables us to present our novel approach δ-`adjusting` which focuses on the selection of an appropriate attribute subset of a formal context. To this end, we measure the influence of each attribute with respect to the number of contranominal scales. Hereby, a sub-semilattice is computed that preserves the meet-operation. This provides the advantage to not only maintain all implications between the selected attributes but also does not produce false implications and thus retains underlying structure. We conduct experiments to demonstrate that the subcontexts that arise by δ-`adjusting` decrease the size of the concept lattice and the implication set while preserving underlying knowledge. We evaluate the remaining knowledge by training a classification task. This results in a more understandable depiction of the encapsulated data for the human mind.

Due to space constraints, this work only briefly sketches proofs. A version containing all proofs is released on arxiv.org[1].

2 Foundations

We start this section by recalling notions from FCA [10]. A *formal context* is a triple $\mathbb{K} := (G, M, I)$, consisting of an *object set* G, an *attribute set* M and a binary *incidence relation* $I \subseteq G \times M$. In this work, G and M are assumed to be finite. The *complementary formal context* is given by $\mathbb{K}^C := (G, M, (G \times M) \setminus I)$. The maps $\cdot' \colon \mathcal{P}(G) \to \mathcal{P}(M)$, $A \mapsto A' := \{m \in M \mid \forall g \in A \colon (g, m) \in I\}$ and $\cdot' \colon \mathcal{P}(M) \to \mathcal{P}(G)$, $B \mapsto B' := \{g \in G \mid \forall m \in B \colon (g, m) \in I\}$ are called *derivations*. A pair $c = (A, B)$ with $A \subseteq G$ and $B \subseteq M$ such that $A' = B$ and $B' = A$ is called a *formal concept* of the context (G, M, I). The set of all formal concepts of $\mathbb{K}$ is denoted by $\mathfrak{B}(\mathbb{K})$. The pair consisting of $\mathfrak{B}(\mathbb{K})$ and the order $\leq \subset (\mathfrak{B}(\mathbb{K}) \times \mathfrak{B}(\mathbb{K}))$ with $(A_1, B_1) \leq (A_2, B_2)$ iff $A_1 \subseteq A_2$ defines the

---

[1] https://arxiv.org/abs/2106.10978.

concept lattice $\mathfrak{B}(\mathbb{K})$. In every lattice and thus every concept lattice each subset U has a unique infimum and supremum which are denoted by $\bigwedge U$ and $\bigvee U$. The *contranominal scale* of *dimension* k is $\mathbb{N}_k^c := (\{1, 2, ..., k\}, \{1, 2, ..., k\}, \neq)$. Its concept lattice is the *Boolean lattices of dimension* k and consists of 2^k concepts. Let $\mathbb{K} = (G, M, I)$. We call an attribute m *clarifiable* if there is an attribute $n \neq m$ with $n' = m'$. In addition we call it *reducible* if there is a set $X \subseteq M$ with $m \not\subseteq X$ and $m' = X'$. Otherwise, we call m *irreducible*. $\mathbb{K}$ is called *attribute clarified* (*attribute reduced*) if it does not contain clarifiable (reducible) attributes. The definitions for the object set are analogous. If $\mathbb{K}$ is attribute clarified and object clarified (attribute reduced and object reduced), we say $\mathbb{K}$ is *clarified* (*reduced*). This contexts are unique up to isomorphisms. Their concept lattices are isomorphic to $\mathfrak{B}(\mathbb{K})$. A *subcontext* $\mathbb{S} = (H, N, J)$ of $\mathbb{K} = (G, M, I)$ is a formal context with $H \subseteq G$, $N \subseteq M$ and $J = I \cap (H \times N)$. We denote this by $\mathbb{S} \leq \mathbb{K}$ and use the notion $\mathbb{K}[H, N] := (H, N, I \cap (H \times N))$. If $\mathbb{S} \leq \mathbb{K}$ with $\mathbb{S} \cong \mathbb{N}_k^c$ we call $\mathbb{S}$ a *contranominal scale in* $\mathbb{K}$. For a (concept) lattice $(L, \leq)$ and a subset $S \subseteq L$, $(S, \leq_{S \times S})$ is called *suborder* of $(L, \leq)$ A suborder S of a lattice is called a *sub-meet-semilattice* if $(a, b \in S \Rightarrow (a \wedge b) \in S)$ holds. In a formal context $\mathbb{K} = (G, M, I)$ with $X, Y \subseteq M$ define an *implication* as $X \rightarrow Y$ with *premise* X and *conclusion* Y. An implication is *valid in* $\mathbb{K}$ if $X' \subset Y'$. In this case, we call $X \rightarrow Y$ an *implication of* $\mathbb{K}$. The set of all implications of a formal context $\mathbb{K}$ is denoted by $Imp(\mathbb{K})$. A minimal set $\mathcal{L}(\mathbb{K}) \leq Imp(\mathbb{K})$ defines an *implication base* if every implication of $\mathbb{K}$ follows from $\mathcal{L}(\mathbb{K})$ by composition. An implication base of minimal size is called *canonical base* of $\mathbb{K}$ and is denoted by $\mathcal{C}(\mathbb{K})$.

Now recall some notions from graph theory. A *graph* is a pair (V, E) with a set of *vertices* V and a set of *edges* $E \subset \binom{V}{2}$. Two vertices u, v are called *adjacent* if $\{u, v\} \in E$. The adjacent vertices of a vertex are called its *neighbors*. In this work graphs are undirected and have no multiple edges or loops. A graph with two sets S and T with $S \cup T = V$ and $S \cap T = \emptyset$ such that there is no edge with both vertices in S or both vertices in T is called *bipartite* and denoted by (S, T, E). A *matching* in a graph is a subset of the edges such that no two edges share a vertex. It is called *induced* if no two edges share vertices with some edge not in the matching. For a formal context (G, M, I) the *associated bipartite graph* is the graph where S and T correspond to G and M and the set of edges to I.

3   Related Work

In the field of Formal Concept Analysis numerous approaches deal with simplifying the structure of large datasets. Large research interest was dedicated to altering the incidence relation together with the objects and attributes in order to achieve smaller contexts. A procedure based on a random projection is introduced in [18]. Dias and Vierira [5] investigate the replacement of similar objects by a single representative. They evaluate this strategy by measuring the appearance of false implications on the new object set. In the attribute case a similar approach is explored by Kuitche et al. [17]. Similar to our method, many common prior approaches are based on the selection of subcontexts. For example,

Hanika et al. [12] rate attributes based on the distribution of the objects in the concepts and select a small relevant subset of them. A different approach is to select a subset of concepts from the concept lattice. While it is possible to sample concepts randomly [2], the selection of concepts by using measures is well investigated. To this end, a structural approach is given in [7] through dismantling where a sublattice is chosen by the iterative elimination of all doubly irreducible concepts. Kuznetsov [20] proposes a stability measure for formal concepts based on the sizes of the concepts. The support measure is used by Stumme et al. [25] to generate iceberg lattices. Our approach follows up on this, as we also preserve sub-semilattices of the original concept lattice. However, we are not restricted to the selection of iceberg lattices. Compared to many other approaches we do not alter the incidence or the objects and thus do not introduce false implications.

4 Computing Contranominal Scales

In this section, we examine the complexity of computing all contranominals and provide the recursive backtracking algorithm `ContraFinder` to solve this task.

4.1 Computing Contranominals Is Hard

The problem of computing contranominal scales is closely related to the problem of computing cliques in graphs and induced maximum matchings in bipartite graphs.

The relationship between the induced matching problem and the contranominal scale problem follows directly from their respective definitions.

Lemma 1. *Let (S, T, E) be a bipartite graph, $\mathbb{K} := (S, T, (S \times T) \backslash E)$ a formal context and $H \subset S, N \subset T$. The edges between H and N are an induced matching of size k in (S, T, E) iff $\mathbb{K}[H, N]$ is a contranominal scale of dimension k.*

The lemma follows directly from the definition of induced matchings and contranominal scales. To investigate the connection between the clique problem and the contranominal scale problem, define the conflict graph as follows:

Definition 1. *Let $\mathbb{K} := (G, M, I)$ be a formal context. Define the* conflict graph *of $\mathbb{K}$ as the graph $cg(\mathbb{K}) := (V, E)$ with the vertex set $V = (G \times M) \backslash I$ and the edge set $E = \{\{(g, m), (h, n)\} \in \binom{V}{2} \mid (g, n) \in I, (h, m) \in I\}$.*

The relationship between the cliques in the conflict graph and the contranominal scales in the formal context is given through the following lemma.

Lemma 2. *Let $\mathbb{K} = (G, M, I)$ be a formal context, $cg(\mathbb{K})$ its conflict graph and $H \subset G, N \subset M$. Then $\mathbb{K}[H, N]$ is a contranominal scale of dimension k iff $(H \times N) \backslash I$ is a clique of size k in $cg(\mathbb{K})$.*

The lemma follows from the definition of the conflict graph. Furthermore, all three problems are in the same computational class as the clique problem is NP-complete [15] and Lozin [21] shows the similar result for the induced matching problem in the bipartite case. Thus, Lemma 1 provides the following:

Proposition 1. *Deciding the CONTRANOMINAL PROBLEM is NP-complete.*

4.2   Baseline Algorithms

Building on Lemma 2 the set of all contranominal scales can be computed using algorithms for iterating all cliques in the conflict graph. The set of all cliques then corresponds to the set of all contranominal scales in the formal context. An algorithm to iterate all cliques in a graph is proposed by Bron and Kerbosch [3].

An alternative approach is to use branch and search algorithms such as [27]. Those exploit the fact that for each maximum matching and each vertex there is either an adjacent edge to this vertex in the matching or each of its neighboring vertices has an adjacent edge in the matching. Branching on these vertices the size of the graph is iteratively decreased. Note, that this idea, in contrast to our approach described below, does not exploit bipartiteness of the graph.

4.3   ContraFinder: An Algorithm to Compute Contranominal Scales

In this section we introduce the recursive backtracking algorithm ContraFinder to compute all contranominal scales. Due to Proposition 1, it has exponential runtime, thus two speedup techniques are proposed in the subsequent section.

The main idea behind ContraFinder is the following. In each recursion step a set of tuples corresponding to an attribute set is investigated:

Definition 2. *Let* $\mathbb{K} = (G, M, I)$ *be a formal context and* $N \subset M$*. Define* $C(N) := \{(g, m) \notin I \mid g \in G, m \in N \text{ and } \forall x \in N \setminus \{m\} : (g, x) \in I\}$ *as the set of* characterizing tuples *of* N*. We call* N *the* generator *of* $C(N)$*.*

The characterizing tuples encodes all contranominal scales for this attributes:

Lemma 3. *Let* $\mathbb{K} = (G, M, I)$*,* $N \subseteq M$ *and* $H(m) := \{g \in G \mid (g, m) \in C(N)\}$*. Then* $\mathbb{K}[O, N]$ *is a contranominal scale iff* O *contains exactly one element of each* $H(m)$ *with* $m \in N$*.*

The proof follows from the fact, that the non-incident pairs of each contranominal scale are represented by the combinations of characterizing tuples with different attributes. Lemma 3 implies that such contranominal scales can exist only if no $H(m)$ is empty and $|N| = |O|$. Both this sets can be reconstructed from a set of characterizing tuples corresponding to N. This is done in unpack_contranominals in Algorithm 1. Therefore, N does not have to be memorized in ContraFinder. The algorithm exploits the fact that for each set of characterizing tuples $C(N)$ the attributes N can be ordered and iterated in lexicographical order, similar to NextClosure [10, sec. 2.1].

Definition 3. *Let* $(M, \leq)$ *be a linearly ordered set. The* lexicographical order *on* $\mathcal{P}(M)$ *is a linear order. Let* $A = a_1, \dots, a_n$ *and* $B = b_1, \dots, b_m$ *with* $a_i < a_{i+1}$ *and* $b_i < b_{i+1}$*.* $A < B$ *in case* $n < m$ *if* $(a_1, \dots, a_n) = (b_1, \dots, b_n)$ *and in case* $n = m$ *if* $\exists i : \forall j \leq i : a_j = b_j$ *and* $a_i < b_i$*.*

Algorithm 1. ContraFinder

Input: Formal Context $\mathbb{K} = (G, M, I)$
Output: Set of all Contranominal Scales

```
def compute_contranominal_scales(G, M, I):
  characterizing_tuples(∅, M, ∅, I)

def characterizing_tuples(C_N, M̃, F, I):
  for m in M̃ in lexicographical order:
    M̃ = M̃ \ {m}
    cand_C_N = {(g, n) ∈ C_N | (g, m) ∈ I}
    cand_m = {(g, m) | (g, m) ∉ I, g ∉ F, ∄n : (g, n) ∈ C_N}
    if |{g | (g, n) ∈ C_N}| = |{g | (g, n) ∈ cand_C_N}| and |cand_m| > 0:
      unpack_contranominals(cand_C_N ∪ cand_m)
      C_Nnew = cand_C_N ∪ cand_m
      Fnew = F ∪ {g ∈ G | (g, m) ∉ I}
      characterizing_tuples(C_Nnew, M̃, Fnew, I)

def unpack_contranominals(C_N):
  N = {m | (g, m) ∈ C_N}
  for O in {{g_{m_1}, ..., g_{m_{|N|}}} | m_i ∈ N, g_{m_i} ∈ {g ∈ G | (g, m_i) ∈ C_N}}
    report (O, N) as contranominal scale
```

Similar to Titanic, our algorithm utilises the following anti-monotonic property. Each contranominal scale of dimension k has a contranominal scale of dimension $k - 1$ as subcontext. Thus, only attribute combinations N have to be considered if $\forall N' \subset N : C(N') \neq \emptyset$. The algorithm removes in each recursion step the attributes in $M̃$ in lexicographical order to guarantee that all attribute combinations of the formal context with contranominal scales are investigated.

In each step the set of forbidden objects F increases, since each contranominal scale contains exactly one non-incidence in each contained object.

Theorem 1. *The algorithm reports every contranominal scale exactly once.*

To proof this theorem, one has to show that the lexicographical order and the anti-monotonic property are respected. ContraFinder, combined with Lemma 1, can also be used to compute all maximum induced matchings in bipartite graphs.

4.4   Speedup Techniques

Clarifying and Reducing. In the following, we consider clarified and reduced formal contexts with regards to reconstructing the contranominal scales in the original context from the contranominal scales of the augmented one. This allows to use clarifying and reducing as a speedup technique.

In the clarified context, each pair of objects or attributes is merged if equality of their derivations holds. To deduce the original formal context from the clarified one the previously merged attributes and objects can be duplicated. Thus, contranominal scales containing merged objects or attributes are duplicated.

Now, we demonstrate how to reconstruct the contranominal scales from attribute reduced contexts. Thereby, for each eliminated attribute m we have to memorize the irreducible attribute set that has the same derivation as m.

Definition 4. *Let* $\mathbb{K} = (G, M, I)$ *be a formal context and* $R(\mathbb{K})$ *the set of all attributes that are reducible in* $\mathbb{K}$*. Define the map* $\omega: R(\mathbb{K}) \rightarrow \mathcal{P}(M \setminus R(\mathbb{K}))$ *with* $x \mapsto (N \subset M \setminus (R(\mathbb{K}) \cup \{x\}))$ *such that* $N' = x'$ *and* N *of greatest cardinality. For a fixed object set* $H \subseteq G$*, let* $\omega_H: R(\mathbb{K}) \rightarrow \mathcal{P}(M \setminus R(\mathbb{K}))$ *be the map with* $x \mapsto \{y \mid y \in \omega(x), \forall h \in H : (h, x) \notin I \Rightarrow (h, y) \notin I\}$.

Note, that the map ω is well defined as the uniqueness follows directly from the maximality of N. The following lemma provides a way to reconstruct the contranominal scales in the original context from the ones in the reduced one.

Lemma 4. *Let* $\mathbb{K} = (G, M, I)$ *be a formal context with* $\mathbb{K}_r$ *its attribute-reduced subcontext and* $\mathcal{K}$ *the set containing all contranominal scales of* $\mathbb{K}_r$*. Then the set* $\tilde{\mathcal{K}} = \{\mathbb{K}[H, \tilde{N}] \mid \mathbb{K}[H, N = \{n_1, \ldots, n_l\}] \in \mathcal{K}, \tilde{N} = \{\tilde{n}_i \mid n_i = \tilde{n}_i \vee n_i \in \omega_H(\tilde{n}_i)\}\}$ *contains exactly all contranominal scales of* $\mathbb{K}$.

This follows from the definition of reducibility. Thus, to reconstruct contranominal scales, for each $x \in R(\mathbb{K})$ all $y \in \omega(x)$ are considered. $U \cup x$ is a candidate for the attribute set of a contranominal scale in $\mathbb{K}$, if there is a $U \subset M \setminus \omega(x)$ with $U \cup y$ attribute set of a contranominal scale $\mathbb{S}_y$ for all y. This candidate forms the contranominal scale $\mathbb{K}[H, U \cup x]$, if and only if all contranominal scales $\mathbb{S}_y$ share the same object set H. The object reducible case can be done dually.

Knowledge-Cores. The notion of (p, q)-cores is introduced to FCA by Hanika and Hirth in [11]. Thereby, dense subcontexts are defined as follows:

Definition 5 (Hanika and Hirth [11]**).** *Let* $\mathbb{K} = (G, M, I)$ *and* $\mathbb{S} = \mathbb{K}[H, N]$ *be formal contexts.* $\mathbb{S}$ *is called a* (p, q)-core *of* $\mathbb{K}$ *for* $p, q \in \mathbb{N}$*, if* $\forall g \in H : |g'| \geq p$ *and* $\forall m \in N : |m'| \geq q$ *and* $\mathbb{S}$ *is maximal under this condition.*

Every formal context with fixed p and q has a unique (p, q)-core. Computing knowledge cores provides a way to reduce the number of attributes and objects in a formal context without removing large contranominal scales.

Lemma 5. *Let* $\mathbb{K}$ *be a formal context,* $k \in \mathbb{N}$*, and* $\mathbb{S} \leq \mathbb{K}$ *its* $(k - 1, k - 1)$-core*. Then for every contranominal scale* $\mathbb{C} \leq \mathbb{K}$ *of dimension* k *it holds* $\mathbb{C} \leq \mathbb{S}$.

The lemma follows from the maximality of (p, q)-cores. Thus, to compute all contranominal scales of dimension at least k it is possible to compute them in the $(k - 1, k - 1)$-core. Note that in this case however, smaller contranominal scales might get eliminated. Therefore, if the goal is to compute contranominal scales of smaller sizes the $(k - 1, k - 1)$-cores should not be computed.

5   Attribute Selection

In this section we propose δ-adjusting, a method to select attributes based on measuring their influence for contranominal scales as follows:

Definition 6. *Let* $\mathbb{K} = (G, M, I)$ *be a formal context and* $k \in \mathbb{N}$. *Call* $N \subset M$ *k-cubic if* $\exists H \subset G$ *with* $\mathbb{K}[H, N]$ *being a contranominal scale of dimension* k *and* $\nexists \tilde{N} \supseteq N$ *such that* $\tilde{N}$ *is* $(k+1)$-*cubic. Define the* contranominal-influence *of* $m \in M$ *in* $\mathbb{K}$ *as* $\zeta(m) := \sum_{k=1}^{\infty} \left(|\{N \subset M \mid m \in N, N \text{ is } k\text{-cubic}\}| \cdot \frac{2^k}{k} \right)$.

Subcontexts that are k-cubic are directly influencing the concept lattice, as those dominates the structure as the following shows.

Proposition 2. *An attribute set is* k-*cubic, iff the sub-meet-semilattice that is generated by its attribute concepts is a Boolean lattice of dimension* k *that has no Boolean superlattice in the original concept lattice.*

The contranominal influence thus measures the impact of an attribute on the lattice structure. In this, only the maximal contranominal scales are considered since the smaller non maximal-ones have no additional structural impact. As each contranominal scale of dimension k corresponds to 2^k concepts, we scale the number of attribute combinations with this factor. To distribute the impact of a contranominal scale evenly over all involved attributes, the measure is scaled by $\frac{1}{k}$. With this measure we now define the notions of δ-adjusting.

Definition 7. *Let* $\mathbb{K} = (G, M, I)$ *be a formal context and* $\delta \in [0, 1]$. *Let* $N \subset M$ *minimal such that* $\frac{|N|}{|M|} \geq \delta$, $\zeta(n) < \zeta(m)$ *for all* $n \in N, m \in M \setminus N$. *We call* $\mathbb{A}_\delta(\mathbb{K}) := \mathbb{K}[G, N]$ *the* δ-*adjusted subcontext of* $\mathbb{K}$ *and* $\underline{\mathfrak{B}}(\mathbb{A}_\delta(\mathbb{K}))$ *the* δ-*adjusted sublattice of* $\underline{\mathfrak{B}}(\mathbb{K})$.

Note, that δ-adjusting always results in unique contexts. Moreover, every δ-adjusted sublattice is a sub-meet-semilattice of the original one [10, Prop 31]. For every context $\mathbb{K} = (G, M, I)$ it holds that $\mathbb{A}_1 = \mathbb{K}$ and $\mathbb{A}_0 = \mathbb{K}[G, \emptyset]$. A context from a medical diagnosis dataset with measured contranominal influence and computed $\frac{1}{2}$-adjusted subcontext can be retraced in Fig. 1.

It is important to observe that for a context $\mathbb{K}$ and its reduced context $\mathbb{K}_r$ a different attribute set can remain if they are δ-adjusted, as can be seen in Fig. 2. Therefore, the resulting concept lattices for $\mathbb{K}$ and $\mathbb{K}_r$ can differ. To preserve structural integrity between δ-adjusted formal contexts and their concept lattices we thus recommend to only consider clarified and reduced formal contexts. In the rest of this work, these steps are therefore performed prior to δ-adjusting. Note, that since no attributes are generated no new contranominal scales can arise by δ-adjusting. Furthermore, removing attributes can not turn another attribute from irreducible to reducible. On the other hand however, objects can become reducible as can be seen again in Fig. 2. While 6 is irreducible in the original context, it is reducible in $\mathbb{A}_{\frac{3}{5}}(\mathbb{K})$.

	a	b	c	d	e	f	g	h	i	j	k	l	m	n	o
111			×	×	×		×	×		×					×
119	×			×	×	×	×			×	×				×
31			×	×	×	×			×	×	×		×		
32	×		×		×		×	×	×						×
17		×		×	×	×		×	×	×		×			
27			×	×	×	×		×	×	×			×		
105	×	×				×	×			×	×	×			
58		×		×	×	×		×	×			×	×		
65	×				×	×		×			×	×	×	×	
103	×		×				×			×	×				×
56		×	×	×	×				×	×		×	×		
98	×	×	×				×			×	×	×			
43		×	×	×	×			×		×			×	×	
50	×		×		×		×		×					×	×

Attribute Name	2	3	4	ζ
a: Lumbar pain y	1	22	6	84.7
b: Bladder inflammation y	1	29	0	79.3
c: Burning n	1	31	9	120.7
d: Lumbar pain n	2	19	0	54.7
e: Nausea n	0	16	3	54.7
f: Burning y	1	31	0	84.7
g: Temp. ∈ [40.0, 42.0]	2	24	5	88.0
h: Micturition pains n	1	18	5	70.0
i: Temp. ∈ [35.0, 37.5]	3	16	0	48.7
j: Pelvis nephritis n	1	19	1	56.7
k: Micturition pains y	1	33	0	90.0
l: Pelvis nephritis y	3	17	0	51.3
m: Urine pushing y	0	21	7	84.0
n: Temp. ∈ [37.5, 40.0]	2	23	3	77.3
o: Bladder inflammation n	1	26	1	75.3

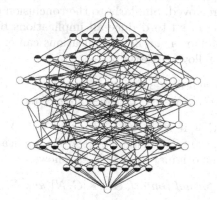
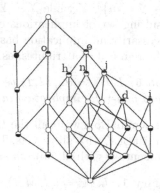

Fig. 1. Top: reduced and clarified medical diagnosis dataset [4]. The $\frac{1}{2}$-adjusted subcontext is highlighted. The objects are patient numbers. The attributes are described in the figure together with the count of k-cubic subcontexts and their contranominal influence ζ. Bottom: lattice of the original (left) and the $\frac{1}{2}$-adjusted (right) dataset. (Color figure online)

5.1   Properties of Implications

In this section we investigate δ-adjusting with respect to the influence on implications. Let $\mathbb{K} = (G, M, I)$ be a formal context, $m \in M$ and $X \to Y$ an implication in $\mathbb{K}$. If m is part of the implication; i.e., $m \in X$ or $m \in Y$, this implication vanishes. Therefore the removal of m in an implication $X \to Y$ of some implication base $\mathcal{C}(\mathbb{K})$ is of interest. If m is neither part of a premise nor a conclusion of an implication $X \to Y \in \mathcal{C}(\mathbb{K})$ its removal has no impact on this implication base. In case $m \in Y$, its elimination changes all implications $X \to Y$ to $X \to Y \setminus \{m\}$. Note that, even though all implications can still be deduced

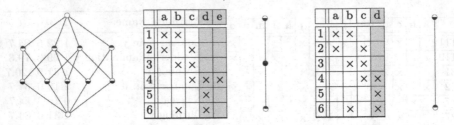

	a	b	c	d	e
1	×	×			
2	×		×		
3		×	×		
4			×	×	×
5				×	
6		×		×	

	a	b	c	d
1	×	×		
2	×		×	
3		×	×	
4			×	×
5				×
6		×		×

Fig. 2. A concept lattice together with two of its contexts $\mathbb{K}$ and $\mathbb{K}_r$ whereby $\mathbb{K}_r$ is attribute reduced while $\mathbb{K}$ contains the reducible element e. In both contexts the $\frac{3}{5}$-adjusted subcontext is highlighted. Their lattices (right to each context) differ. (Color figure online)

from $\mathcal{C}' = \{X \rightarrow Y : X \rightarrow Y \cup \{m\} \in \mathcal{C}(\mathbb{K})\}$ this set is not necessarily minimal and in this case is not a base. Especially if $\{m\} = Y$ the resulting $X \rightarrow \emptyset$ is never part of an implication base. In case $m \in X$, every $Z \rightarrow X$ in the base is changed to $Z \rightarrow X \setminus \{m\} \cup Y$ while $X \rightarrow Y$ is removed. Similarly to the conclusion case, the resulting set of implications can be used to deduce all implications but is not necessarily an implication base. Moreover, no new implications can emerge from the removal of attributes, as the following shows.

Lemma 6. *Let* $\mathbb{K} = (G, M, I)$ *be a formal context,* $N \subset M$ *and* $X, Y \subseteq N$ *with* $X \rightarrow Y$ *a non-valid implication in* $\mathbb{K}$. *Then* $X \rightarrow Y$ *is also non-valid in* $\mathbb{K}[G, N]$.

The lemma follows from the fact that if $X' \subset Y'$ in $\mathbb{K}$, then $X' \subset Y'$ in a subcontext of $\mathbb{K}$ with all objects. Thus, the relationship between the implications of a subcontext with all objects and the original context is as follows:

Corollary 1. *Let* $\mathbb{K} = (G, M, I)$ *be a formal context,* $\mathbb{S} = \mathbb{K}[G, N]$ *and* $N \subset M$. *Then* $Imp(\mathbb{S}) \subseteq Imp(\mathbb{K})$.

This influences the size of the base of a δ-adjusted subcontext as follows:

Lemma 7. *Let* $\mathbb{K} = (G, M, I)$ *a formal context, and* $\mathbb{S} = \mathbb{K}[G, N]$ *and* $N \subset M$. *Then* $|\mathcal{C}(\mathbb{S})| \leq |\mathcal{C}(\mathbb{K})|$.

To prove this lemma, one can construct an implication set of size at most $|\mathcal{C}(\mathbb{K})|$ that generates all implications. Revisiting the context in Fig. 1 together with its $\frac{1}{2}$-adjusted subcontext the selection of nearly 50% of the attributes (8 out of 15) results in a sub-meet-semilattice containing only 33% of the concepts (29 out of 88). Moreover, the implication base of the original context includes 40 implications. After the alteration its size is decreased to 11 implications.

6   Evaluation and Discussion

In this section we evaluate the algorithm ContraFinder and the process of δ-adjusting using real-world datasets.

6.1 Datasets

Table 1 provides descriptive properties of the datasets used in this work. The zoo [6,22] and mushroom [6,23] datasets are classical examples often used in FCA based research such as the TITANIC algorithm. The Wikipedia [19] dataset depicts the edit relation between authors and articles while the Wiki44k dataset is a dense part of the Wikidata knowledge graph. The original Wiki44k dataset was taken from [14], in this work we conduct our experiments on an adapted version by [13]. Finally, the Students dataset [24] depicts grades of students together with properties such as parental level of education. All experiments are conducted on the reduced and clarified versions of the contexts. For reproducibility the adjusted versions of all datasets are published in [9].

Table 1. Datasets used for the evaluation of ContraFinder and δ-adjusting.

	Zoo	Students	Wikipedia	Wiki44k	Mushroom
Objects	101	1000	11273	45021	8124
Attributes	43	32	102	101	119
Density	0.40	0.28	0.015	0.045	0.19
Number of concepts	4579	17603	14171	21923	238710
Mean objects per concept	18.48	16.73	20.06	109.47	91.89
Mean attributes per concept	7.32	5.97	5.88	7.013	16.69
Size of canonical base	401	2826	4575	7040	2323

6.2 Runtime of ContraFinder

ContraFinder is a recursive backtracking algorithm that iterates over all attribute sets containing contranominal scales. Thus, the worst case runtime is given by $O(n^k)$ where n is the number of attributes of the formal context and k the maximum dimension of a contranominal scale in it. The Branch-And-Search algorithm from [27] has a runtime of $O(1.3752^n)$ where n is the sum of attributes and objects. Finally the Bron-Kerbosch algorithm has a worst-case runtime of $O(3^{n/3})$ with n being the number of non-incident object-attribute pairs.

   To compare the practical runtime of the algorithms we test them on the previously introduced real world datasets. We report the runtimes in Table 2, together with the dimension of the larges contranominal scale and the total number of contranominal scales. Note, that for larger datasets we are not able to compute the number of all contranominal scales using Bron-Kerbosch (from Students) and the Branch-And-Search algorithm (Mushroom) below 24 h due to their exponential nature and thus stopped the computations. All experiments are conducted on an Intel Core i5-8250U processor with 16 GB of RAM.

Table 2. Experimental runtimes of the different algorithms on all datasets.

	Zoo	Students	Wikipedia	Wiki44k	Mushroom
ContraFinder	2.43	7.36	17.15	35.65	1961.0
Bron Kerbosch searching cliques	138.70	>86400	>86400	>86400	>86400
Branch and search algorithm	14.40	12005.82	1532.17	16783.58	>86400
Dim. of max. contranominal scale	7	8	9	11	10
Number of contranominal scales	$4.1 \cdot 10^7$	$7.8 \cdot 10^9$	$9.9 \cdot 10^8$	$2.0 \cdot 10^{14}$	$1.2 \cdot 10^{19}$

Table 3. Evaluation of k-adjusted contexts. The standard deviation is given in parenthesis. "Acc of DT" is the abbreviation for "Accuracy of the Decision Tree".

		Zoo	Students	Wikipedia	Wiki44k	Mushroom
$|\mathfrak{B}(\mathbb{K})|$	$\frac{1}{2}$-adjusted	**90**	**312**	**65**	323	**426**
	Sampling	496 (205)	1036 (327)	833 (517)	1397 (627)	8563 (4532)
	Hanika et al.	95	341	67	**254**	561
$|\mathcal{C}(\mathbb{K})|$	$\frac{1}{2}$-adjusted	98	**105**	626	**1003**	**339**
	Sampling	**95** (17)	156 (35)	758 (101)	1360 (135)	574 (93)
	Hanika et al.	100	**105**	**553**	1091	490
Acc of DT	$\frac{1}{2}$-adjusted	0.88 (0.08)	0.88 (0.06)	**0.99** (0.01)	**0.98** (0.03)	**0.98** (0.02)
	Sampling	**0.89** (0.15)	0.81 (0.15)	0.9 (0.14)	0.95 (0.06)	0.92 (0.13)
	Hanika et al.	0.88 (0.09)	**0.89** (0.06)	**0.99** (0.01)	**0.98** (0.16)	0.97 (0.03)

6.3 Structural Effects of δ-Adjusting

We measure the number of formal concepts generated by the formal context as well as the size of the canonical base. To demonstrate the effects of δ-adjusting we focus on $\delta = \frac{1}{2}$. Our two baselines are selecting the same number of attributes using random sampling and choosing the attributes of highest relative relevance as described in [12]. It can be observed, that in all three cases the number of concepts heavily decrease. However, this effect is considerably stronger for $\frac{1}{2}$-adjusting and the approach of Hanika et al. compared to sampling. Hereby, $\frac{1}{2}$-adjusting yields smaller concept lattices on four datasets. A similar effect can be observed for the sizes of the canonical bases where our method yields three times in the smallest cardinality.

6.4 Knowledge in the δ-Adjusted Context

To measure the degree of encapsulated knowledge in δ-adjusted formal contexts we conduct the following experiment using once again sampling and the relative relevant attributes of Hanika et al. as baselines. In order to measure if the remaining subcontexts still encapsulates knowledge we train a decision tree classifier on them predicting an attribute that is removed beforehand. This attribute is sampled randomly in each step. To prevent a random outlier from distorting the result we repeat this same experiment 1000 times for each context and method and report the mean value as well as the standard-deviation in Table 3. The experiment is conducted using a 0.5-split on the train and test data. For all five datasets, the results of the decision tree on the $\frac{1}{2}$-adjusted context are consistently high, however $\frac{1}{2}$-adjusting and the Hanika et al. approach outperform the sampling approach. Both this methods achieve the highest score on four contexts, in two of this cases the highest result is shared. The single highest score of sampling is just slightly above the other two approaches.

6.5   Discussion

The theoretical runtime of `ContraFinder` is polynomial in the dimension of the maximum contranominal. Therefore, compared to the baseline algorithms it performs better, the smaller the maximum contranominal scale in a dataset. Furthermore, the runtime of Bron-Kerbosch is worse, the sparser a formal context, as the number of pairs that are non-incident increases and thus more vertices have to be iterated. Finally, the Branch-And-Search algorithm is best in the case that the dimension of the maximum contranominal scale is not bounded. To evaluate, how this theoretical properties translate to real world data, we compute the set of all contranominal scales with the three algorithms on the previously described datasets. Only `ContraFinder` can compute the set of all contranominal scales on the larger datasets on our hardware under 24 h. The runtime of `ContraFinder` is thus superior to the other two on real-world datasets.

To evaluate the impact on the understandability of the δ-`adjusted` formal contexts, we conduct the experiments measuring the sizes of the concept lattices and the canonical bases. All three evaluated methods heavily decrease the size of the concept lattice as well as the canonical base. Compared to the random sampling $\frac{1}{2}$-`adjusting` and the method of Hanika et al. influence the size of this structural components much stronger. Among those two, $\frac{1}{2}$-`adjusting` seems to slightly outperform the method of Hanika et al. and is thus more suited to select attributes from a large dataset in order to be analyzed by a human.

To evaluate to what extent knowledge in the formal context of reduced size is encapsulated we conduct the experiment with the decision trees. This experiment demonstrates that the selected formal subcontext can be used in order to deduce relationships of the remaining attributes in the context. While meaningful implications are preserved and the implication set is downsized, $\frac{1}{2}$-`adjusted` lattices seem to be suitable to preserve large amounts of data from the original dataset. Similar good results can be achieved with the method of Hanika et al.; however, our algorithm combines this with producing smaller concept lattices and canonical bases and is thus more suitable for the task to prepare data for a human analyst by reducing sizes of structural constructs.

We conclude from these experiments that δ-`adjusting` is a solution to the problem to make information more feasible for manual analysis while retaining important parts of the data. In particular, if large formal contexts are investigated this method provides a way to extract relevant subcontexts.

7 Conclusion

In this work, we proposed the algorithm `ContraFinder` in order to enable the computation of the set of all contranominal scales in a formal context. Using this, we defined the contranominal-influence of an attribute. This measure allows us to select a subset of attributes in order to reduce a formal context to its δ-`adjusted` subcontext. The size of its lattice is significantly reduced compared to the original lattice and thus enables researchers to analyze and understand much larger datasets using Formal Concept Analysis. Furthermore, the size of the canonical base, which can be used in order to derive relationships of the remaining attributes shrinks significantly. Still, remaining data can be used to deduce relationships between attributes, as our classification experiment shows. This approach therefore identifies subcontexts whose sub-meet-semilattice is a restriction of the original lattice of a formal context to a small meaningful part.

Further work in this area could leverage `ContraFinder` in order to compute the contranominal-relevance of attributes more efficiently to handle even larger datasets. Moreover, a similar measure for objects could be introduced. However, one should keep in mind that hereby false implications can arise.

References

1. Albano, A., Chornomaz, B.: Why concept lattices are large - extremal theory for the number of minimal generators and formal concepts. In: 12th International Conference on Concept Lattices and Their Applications (CLA 2016). CEUR Workshop Proceedings, vol. 1466, pp. 73–86. CEUR-WS.org (2015)
2. Boley, M., Gärtner, T., Grosskreutz, H.: Formal concept sampling for counting and threshold-free local pattern mining. In: SIAM International Conference on Data Mining (SDM 2010), pp. 177–188. SIAM (2010)
3. Bron, C., Kerbosch, J.: Finding all cliques of an undirected graph (algorithm 457). Commun. ACM **16**(9), 575–576 (1973)
4. Czerniak, J., Zarzycki, H.: Application of rough sets in the presumptive diagnosis of urinary system diseases. In: Sołdek, J., Drobiazgiewicz, L. (eds.) Artificial Intelligence and Security in Computing Systems. The Springer International Series in Engineering and Computer Science, vol. 752, pp. 41–51. Springer, Boston (2002). https://doi.org/10.1007/978-1-4419-9226-0_5
5. Dias, S., Vieira, N.: Reducing the size of concept lattices: the JBOS approach. In: 7th International Conference on Concept Lattices and Their Applications (CLA 2010). CEUR Workshop Proceedings, vol. 672, pp. 80–91. CEUR-WS.org (2010)
6. Dua, D., Graff, C.: UCI machine learning repository (2017). http://archive.ics.uci.edu/ml
7. Duffus, D., Rival, I.: Crowns in dismantlable partially ordered sets. In: 5th Hungarian Combinatorial Colloquium, vol. I, pp. 271–292 (1978)
8. Dürrschnabel, D., Hanika, T., Stumme, G.: Drawing order diagrams through two-dimension extension. CoRR arXiv:1906.06208 (2019)
9. Dürrschnabel, D., Koyda, M., Stumme, G.: Attribute selection using contranominal scales [dataset], April 2021. https://doi.org/10.5281/zenodo.4945088
10. Ganter, B., Wille, R.: Formal Concept Analysis - Mathematical Foundations. Springer, Heidelberg (1999). https://doi.org/10.1007/978-3-642-59830-2

11. Hanika, T., Hirth, J.: Knowledge cores in large formal contexts. CoRR arXiv:2002.11776 (2020)
12. Hanika, T., Koyda, M., Stumme, G.: Relevant attributes in formal contexts. In: Endres, D., Alam, M., Şotropa, D. (eds.) ICCS 2019. LNCS (LNAI), vol. 11530, pp. 102–116. Springer, Cham (2019). https://doi.org/10.1007/978-3-030-23182-8_8
13. Hanika, T., Marx, M., Stumme, G.: Discovering implicational knowledge in wikidata. In: Cristea, D., Le Ber, F., Sertkaya, B. (eds.) ICFCA 2019. LNCS (LNAI), vol. 11511, pp. 315–323. Springer, Cham (2019). https://doi.org/10.1007/978-3-030-21462-3_21
14. Ho, V.T., Stepanova, D., Gad-Elrab, M.H., Kharlamov, E., Weikum, G.: Rule learning from knowledge graphs guided by embedding models. In: Vrandečić, D., et al. (eds.) ISWC 2018. LNCS, vol. 11136, pp. 72–90. Springer, Cham (2018). https://doi.org/10.1007/978-3-030-00671-6_5
15. Karp, R.: Reducibility among combinatorial problems. In: Proceedings of a Symposium on the Complexity of Computer Computations. The IBM Research Symposia Series, pp. 85–103. Plenum Press, New York (1972)
16. Koyda, M., Stumme, G.: Boolean substructures in formal concept analysis. CoRR arXiv:2104.07159 (2021)
17. Kuitché, R., Temgoua, R., Kwuida, L.: A similarity measure to generalize attributes. In: 14th International Conference on Concept Lattices and Their Applications (CLA 2018). CEUR Workshop Proceedings, vol. 2123, pp. 141–152. CEUR-WS.org (2018)
18. Kumar, C.: Knowledge discovery in data using formal concept analysis and random projections. Int. J. Appl. Math. Comput. Sci. 21(4), 745–756 (2011)
19. Kunegis, J.: KONECT: the Koblenz network collection. In: Proceedings of the 22nd International Conference on World Wide Web, pp. 1343–1350 (2013)
20. Kuznetsov, S.: Stability as an estimate of the degree of substantiation of hypotheses derived on the basis of operational similarity. Nauchno-Tekhnicheskaya Informatsiya, Seriya 2 24, 21–29 (1990)
21. Lozin, V.: On maximum induced matchings in bipartite graphs. Inf. Process. Lett. 81(1), 7–11 (2002)
22. Rowley, D.: PC/BEAGLE. Expert. Syst. 7(1), 58–62 (1990)
23. Schlimmer, J.: Mushroom Records Drawn from the Audubon Society Field Guide to North American Mushrooms. GH Lincoff (Pres), New York (1981)
24. Seshapanpu, J.: Students performance in exams, November 2018. https://www.kaggle.com/spscientist/students-performance-in-exams
25. Stumme, G., Taouil, R., Bastide, Y., Pasquier, N., Lakhal, L.: Computing iceberg concept lattices with titanic. Data Knowl. Eng. 42(2), 189–222 (2002)
26. Wille, R.: Lattices in data analysis: how to draw them with a computer. In: Rival, I. (ed.) Algorithms and Order. NATO ASI Series (Series C: Mathematical and Physical Sciences), vol. 255, pp. 33–58. Springer, Dordrecht (1989). https://doi.org/10.1007/978-94-009-2639-4_2
27. Xiao, M., Tan, H.: Exact algorithms for maximum induced matching. Inf. Comput. 256, 196–211 (2017)

Packing Problems, Dimensions and the Tensor Product of Complete Lattices

Christian Jäkel[✉] and Stefan E. Schmidt

Technische Universität Dresden, 01062 Dresden, Germany
christian.jaekel@tu-dresden.de

Abstract. This article treats the determination of the largest powerset lattice that can be order embedded into a complete lattice $\mathbb{L}$. That's a complexity measure for $\mathbb{L}$ and can be seen as an inner dimension. We show that this embedding problem translates to a set packing problem on the level of formal contexts. From this point of view, similarities to graph theoretic parameters emerge, which lead to a lattice theoretical interpretation of the clique number of simple graphs, in terms of an inner dimension of complete ortholattices. Furthermore, behaviour of the tensor product of complete (ortho)lattices is studied w.r.t. these inner dimensions.

Keywords: Formal concept analysis · Order two dimension · Packing problem · Cardinal product · Tensor product · Complete ortholattice · VC-dimension

1 Introduction

The *order 2-dimension* of a complete lattice $\mathbb{L} := (L, \leq)$, $\dim_2(\mathbb{L})$, is the smallest n such that an order embedding, that is an order preserving and reflecting map, from $\mathbb{L}$ to the powerset lattice of an n-element set $2^n := (2^n, \subseteq)$ exists.

This article treats the "opposite" problem, that is we are looking for the largest m such that 2^m can still be order embedded into $\mathbb{L}$. To distinguish these problems, we refer to the latter one as the *inner order 2-dimension*, $\mathrm{idim}_2(\mathbb{L})$, and denote the order 2-dimension as *outer order 2-dimension*, $\mathrm{odim}_2(\mathbb{L})$. This naming convention underlines the obviously involved duality. Since the inner order 2-dimension is equal to other lattice parameters, we dedicate Sect. 5 to summarize these equivalences.

In [8], the outer order 2-dimension and its behaviour under the tensor product of complete lattices was investigated. That's a minimization problem which is equivalent to a set cover problem w.r.t. formal contexts, and for the tensor product of complete lattices it holds that $\mathrm{odim}_2(\mathbb{L}_1 \otimes \mathbb{L}_2) \leq \mathrm{odim}_2(\mathbb{L}_1)\,\mathrm{odim}_2(\mathbb{L}_2)$. Furthermore, the equivalent set cover problem on formal contexts leads to a sufficient condition for multiplicativity of odim_2 w.r.t. the tensor product.

Section 3 treats the inner order 2-dimension and shows its equivalence to a set packing problem on the level of formal contexts. This fact adds nicely

© Springer Nature Switzerland AG 2021
T. Braun et al. (Eds.): ICCS 2021, LNAI 12879, pp. 142–151, 2021.
https://doi.org/10.1007/978-3-030-86982-3_11

to the observed duality between inner- and outer order 2-dimension, since the latter one is equivalent to a set cover problem. For the tensor product, we proof that $\mathrm{idim}_2(\mathbb{L}_1)\,\mathrm{idim}_2(\mathbb{L}_2) \leq \mathrm{idim}_2(\mathbb{L}_1 \otimes \mathbb{L}_2)$, and provide a sufficient criterion when multiplicativity of the inner order 2-dimension w.r.t. the tensor product of complete lattices holds (Sect. 6).

The other important aspect of this paper is the analysis of a specialized inner dimension of complete ortholattices and their tensor product. Since the respective formal contexts can always be interpreted as simple graphs, we are able to relate well known graph theoretic parameters to this inner dimension. Thereby, we extend the link between lattice theory and graph theory, as for example established in [4] and [13].

2 Basics of Formal Concept Analysis

In this section, we provide the facts from Formal Concept Analysis that we use in the sequel. Further extensive introduction can be found in [5].

A *(formal) context* is a triple $\mathbb{K} = (G, M, I)$, where the *incidence* $I \subseteq G \times M$ is a binary relation. For $A \subseteq G$ and $B \subseteq M$, we define two derivation operators:

$$A' := \{m \in M \mid \forall(a \in A) : (a, m) \in I\} \text{ and } B' := \{g \in G \mid \forall(b \in B) : (g, b) \in I\}.$$

If $A' = B$ and $B' = A$, the pair (A, B) is called a *formal concept* and for non empty A and B the cartesian product $A \times B$ is a *maximal rectangle* of $\mathbb{K}$. We denote the set of all maximal rectangles by $\mathrm{Rec}(\mathbb{K})$. Furthermore, for a formal concept (A, B), the set A is called *extent* and B *intent*. Let $\mathrm{Ext}(\mathbb{K})$ denote the set of all extents and $\mathrm{Int}(\mathbb{K})$ the one of all intents. The set of all formal concepts of $\mathbb{K}$ is denoted by $\underline{\mathfrak{B}}(\mathbb{K})$ and defines the *concept lattice* $\underline{\mathfrak{B}}(\mathbb{K})$, via the order $(A_1, B_1) \leq (A_2, B_2) :\Longleftrightarrow A_1 \subseteq A_2$. The *complementary context* is given as $\mathbb{K}^c = (G, M, I^c) := (G, M, (G \times M) - I)$.

For tow contexts $\mathbb{K}_1 = (G_1, M_1, I_1)$ and $\mathbb{K}_2 = (G_2, M_2, I_2)$, we introduce the *direct [cardinal] product* $\mathbb{K}_1 \,\check{\times}[\hat{\times}]\, \mathbb{K}_2 := (G_1 \times G_2, M_1 \times M_2, I_1 \,\check{\times}[\hat{\times}]\, I_2)$:

$$((g, h), (m, n)) \in I_1 \,\check{\times}[\hat{\times}]\, I_2 :\Longleftrightarrow (g, m) \in I_1 \text{ or } [\text{and}] \ (h, n) \in I_2.$$

They fulfil De Morgan laws $(\mathbb{K}_1 \,\check{\times}\, \mathbb{K}_2)^c = \mathbb{K}_1^c \,\hat{\times}\, \mathbb{K}_2^c$ and $(\mathbb{K}_1 \,\hat{\times}\, \mathbb{K}_2)^c = \mathbb{K}_1^c \,\check{\times}\, \mathbb{K}_2^c$.

For two complete lattices $\mathbb{L}_1$ and $\mathbb{L}_2$, the *tensor product* $\mathbb{L}_1 \otimes \mathbb{L}_2$, firstly defined in [14], is the concept lattice $\underline{\mathfrak{B}}(\mathbb{L}_1 \,\check{\times}\, \mathbb{L}_2)$, where $\mathbb{L}_1$ and $\mathbb{L}_2$ are considered as formal contexts with respect to their order relation. The concept lattice of the direct product is isomorphic to the tensor product of the factors concept lattices:

$$\underline{\mathfrak{B}}(\mathbb{K}_1 \,\check{\times}\, \mathbb{K}_2) \cong \underline{\mathfrak{B}}(\mathbb{K}_1) \otimes \underline{\mathfrak{B}}(\mathbb{K}_2). \tag{1}$$

Next, following the presentation in [3], we define a *context morphism*, between $\mathbb{K}_1 = (G_1, M_1, I_1)$ and $\mathbb{K}_2 = (G_2, M_2, I_2)$, as a pair of maps (α, β) with $\alpha \colon G_1 \to G_2$ and $\beta \colon M_1 \to M_2$. We say that a context morphism is *injective, surjective,* or *bijective* if the components α and β have this property, and that it is a *quasi-embedding* if for all $g \in G_1$ and $m \in M_1$ it holds that $g I_1 m \Leftrightarrow \alpha(g) I_2 \beta(m)$.

An injective quasi-embedding is called an *embedding* and a surjective embedding *isomorphism*. A context $\tilde{\mathbb{K}} = (\tilde{G}, \tilde{M}, \tilde{I})$ with $\tilde{G} \subseteq G_1$, $\tilde{M} \subseteq M_1$ and $\tilde{I} \subseteq I_1$ is called a *subcontext* of $\mathbb{K}_1$ if the canonical inclusion maps from $\tilde{G}$ to G_1 and $\tilde{M}$ to M_1 define an embedding. Note that this definition of a subcontext is equivalent to the standard definition $\tilde{I} = I \cap (\tilde{G} \times \tilde{M})$. Since we use context morphisms in our proofs, we prefer to define subcontexts through them.

The following proposition states that every quasi-embedding between formal contexts induces an order embedding between the respective concept lattices.

Proposition 1 (Proposition 1.1. from [3]). *For a quasi-embedding* (α, β) *from context* $\mathbb{K}_1$ *into* $\mathbb{K}_2$, *the maps* φ_α *with* $\varphi_\alpha(A, B) := (\alpha[A]'', \alpha[A]')$ *and* φ_β *with* $\varphi_\beta(A, B) := (\beta[B]', \beta[B]'')$ *are order embeddings from* $\mathfrak{B}(\mathbb{K}_1)$ *to* $\mathfrak{B}(\mathbb{K}_2)$.

The last part of this section introduces results from [8]. Firstly, the *rectangle cover number* is the minimal number of maximal rectangles which are necessary to cover the incidence relation of a formal context. A formal definition is:

$$\mathrm{rc}(\mathbb{K}) := \min\{\#\mathcal{R} \mid \mathcal{R} \subseteq \mathrm{Rec}(\mathbb{K}), \ I = \bigcup_{R \in \mathcal{R}} R\}.$$

This minimization problem can be translated to the outer order 2-dimension of the complementary context's concept lattice: $\mathrm{rc}(\mathbb{K}) = \mathrm{odim}_2(\mathfrak{B}(\mathbb{K}^c))$.

Secondly, a lower bound for the rectangle cover number is the *rectangle isolation number*, *i.e.*, the maximal number of elements from I, such that every maximal rectangle contains at most one of them:

$$\mathrm{ri}(\mathbb{K}) := \max\{\#\mathcal{I} \mid \mathcal{I} \subseteq I, \ \forall (R \in \mathrm{Rec}(\mathbb{K})) : \#(\mathcal{I} \cap R) \leq 1\}.$$

It holds that $\mathrm{ri}(\mathbb{K}) \leq \mathrm{rc}(\mathbb{K})$, and in case of equality the outer order 2-dimension is multiplicative w.r.t. the tensor product of the complementary context's concept lattices: $\mathrm{odim}_2(\mathfrak{B}(\mathbb{K}_1^c) \otimes \mathfrak{B}(\mathbb{K}_2^c)) = \mathrm{odim}_2(\mathfrak{B}(\mathbb{K}_1^c)) \, \mathrm{odim}_2(\mathfrak{B}(\mathbb{K}_2^c))$.

3   The Inner Order 2-Dimension

In this section, we translate the determination of the inner order 2-dimension to a set packing problem w.r.t. the complementary context. This will be achieved by a context embedding as an intermediate step. Therefore, we introduce for every $m \in \mathbb{N}$ two formal contexts: $\mathbb{U}_m := (\underline{m}, \underline{m}, \neq)$ and $\mathbb{E}_m := (\underline{m}, \underline{m}, =)$. The symbol $\mathbb{U}$ is inspired by the unequal relation and $\mathbb{E}$ by the equality relation. For every $m \in \mathbb{N}$ it holds that $\mathfrak{B}(\mathbb{U}_m) \cong 2^m$, $\mathbb{U}_m^c = \mathbb{E}_m$, and there exists an embedding from $\mathbb{U}_m$ into a context $\mathbb{K}$ iff there exists an embedding from $\mathbb{E}_m$ into $\mathbb{K}^c$.

Proposition 2. *For every* $m \in \mathbb{N}$, *there exists an order embedding from* 2^m *into a concept lattice* $\mathfrak{B}(\mathbb{K})$ *iff there exists an embedding from the context* $\mathbb{U}_m$ *into* $\mathbb{K}$.

Proof. "$\Rightarrow$": That is the content of Proposition 1 of [1].

"$\Leftarrow$": Since an embedding is a quasi-embedding, Proposition 1 implies the existence of an order embedding from 2^m into $\underline{\mathfrak{B}}(\mathbb{K})$.

Next, we translate the existence of a context embedding of $\mathbb{E}_m$ into a context $\mathbb{K}$ to a packing problem. Therefore, we introduce the notion of a neighbourhood.

Definition 1. *Let $\mathbb{K} = (G, M, I)$ be a formal context. For every $(g, m) \in I$, we define the* row *$(g, \cdot) := \{(g, m) \mid gIm\}$ and the* column *$(\cdot, m) := \{(g, m) \mid gIm\}$. The* neighbourhood *of (g, m) is given as $N(g, m) := (g, \cdot) \cup (\cdot, m)$. Furthermore, the set of $\mathbb{K}$'s neighbourhoods is denoted by $\mathcal{N}(\mathbb{K}) := \{N(g, m) \mid (g, m) \in I\}$ and gives rise to the* neighbourhood packing number, *which is defined as the largest number of $\mathbb{K}$'s pairwise disjoint neighbourhoods $\mathrm{np}(\mathbb{K}) := \max\{\#\tilde{\mathcal{N}} \mid \tilde{\mathcal{N}} \subseteq \mathcal{N}(\mathbb{K}), \forall N_1, N_2 \in \tilde{\mathcal{N}} : N_1 \cap N_2 = \emptyset\}$.*

Proposition 3. *For every $m \in \mathbb{N}$, there exists an embedding from the context $\mathbb{E}_m$ into a context $\mathbb{K} = (G, M, I)$ iff $\mathrm{np}(\mathbb{K}) \geq m$.*

Proof.

"$\Rightarrow$": Let $\alpha: \underline{m} \to G$ and $\beta: \underline{m} \to M$ be an embedding from $\mathbb{E}_m$ into $\mathbb{K}$. We define $\tilde{\mathcal{N}} := \{N(\alpha(i), \beta(j)) \mid i = j\} \subseteq \mathcal{N}(\mathbb{K})$. Since, (α, β) is an embedding, it holds that $\tilde{\mathcal{N}}$ contains m elements. Furthermore, the condition $i = j \Leftrightarrow \alpha(i)I\beta(j)$ implies that the neighbourhoods of $\tilde{\mathcal{N}}$ are pairwise disjoint (see Fig. 1).

"$\Leftarrow$": Let $\tilde{\mathcal{N}} \subseteq \mathcal{N}(\mathbb{K})$ contain m pairwise disjoint elements. We define an arbitrary enumeration $\iota: \underline{m} \hookrightarrow \tilde{\mathcal{N}}$, as well as the maps:

$$\tilde{\alpha}: \tilde{\mathcal{N}} \to G \text{ with } N(g, n) \mapsto g,$$

$$\tilde{\beta}: \tilde{\mathcal{N}} \to M \text{ with } N(g, n) \mapsto n.$$

I	n_1	$\cdots$	n_i	$\cdots$	n_m	$\cdots$
g_1	1	0	0	0	0	$\cdots$
$\vdots$	0	$\ddots$	0	0	0	$\cdots$
g_i	0	0	1	0	0	$\cdots$
$\vdots$	0	0	0	$\ddots$	0	$\cdots$
g_m	0	0	0	0	1	$\cdots$
$\vdots$	$\vdots$	$\vdots$	$\vdots$	$\vdots$	$\vdots$	$\ddots$

Fig. 1. A visualization of the incidence relation I. After permuting rows and columns, the diagonal with m elements is in the upper left corner. This makes it obvious that the neighbourhoods induced by this diagonal are disjoint.

An embedding $\mathbb{E}_m \hookrightarrow \mathbb{K}$ is given by $(\alpha, \beta) := (\tilde{\alpha} \circ \iota, \tilde{\beta} \circ \iota)$:
$$i = j \iff \iota(i) = \iota(j) \iff \alpha(i)I\beta(j).$$

The following theorem summarizes the conclusions from above and allows us to translate the determination of the inner order 2-dimension to a set packing problem w.r.t. the complementary context.

Theorem 1. *Let $\mathbb{K}$ be a formal context. It holds that the inner order 2-dimension of $\underline{\mathfrak{B}}(\mathbb{K})$ equals $\mathbb{K}^c$'s neighbourhood packing number: $\mathrm{idim}_2(\underline{\mathfrak{B}}(\mathbb{K})) = \mathrm{np}(\mathbb{K}^c)$.*

We saw that determining the largest $m \in \mathbb{N}$ such that $\mathbb{U}_m$ embeds into $\mathbb{K}$ translates to a lattice embedding problem. The similarity to the famous problem from graph theory, of finding a maximal clique, is obvious. In the next section, we will transform the *maximal clique problem* to a special lattice embedding problem, and compare it to the more general formal context case.

4   The Inner Orthodimension

We consider a simple graph $\mathbb{G} = (V, E)$ and interpret it as the formal context $\mathbb{G} = (V, V, R)$, with an irreflexive and symmetric binary relation R. The properties and construction of the respective concept lattice go back to [2], and are mentioned in [5] as well. The relationship of the concept lattice to graph theory is for example treated in [4] and [13]. The latter paper uses the name *neighborhood ortholattice* and establishes a connection between the *chromatic number* of graphs and certain lattice morphisms. That said, the concept lattice of a simple graph $\mathbb{G}$ can be characterized as a *complete ortholattice*. This is a complete bounded lattice $\mathbb{L} = (L, \leq, c)$ with an involutory antiautomorphism c, such that for all $x \in L$ it holds that $x \wedge x^c = 0$ and $x \vee x^c = 1$. An abstract *orthogonality relation* $\perp$ is defined through $x \perp y :\Longleftrightarrow x \leq y^c$. In the special case of concept lattices the *orthocomplement* is given via $(A, B)^c := (A', B') = (B, A)$. Also note that every complete ortholattice arises as the concept lattice of some simple graph.

For a simple graph $\mathbb{G}$, the *clique number*, $\omega(\mathbb{G})$, is defined as the number of vertices of the largest complete subgraph of $\mathbb{G}$ (see [10]). In our notation this translates to finding the largest $m \in \mathbb{N}$, such that a *symmetric context embedding* $(\alpha, \alpha) \colon \mathbb{U}_m \hookrightarrow \mathbb{G}$ exists. The following definition introduces a suitable notion of dimension for complete ortholattices, to translate the clique number to.

Definition 2. *An* orthoembedding, *between two complete ortholattices* $\mathbb{L}_1 = (L_1, \leq, c_1)$ *and* $\mathbb{L}_2 = (L_2, \leq, c_2)$, *is an order embedding* $\varphi \colon \mathbb{L}_1 \overset{\perp}{\hookrightarrow} \mathbb{L}_2$ *which additionally preserves and reflects orthogonality* $(x \perp y \Longleftrightarrow \varphi(x) \perp \varphi(y))$. *The* outer orthodimension *of a complete ortholattice* $\mathbb{L}$, *denoted by* $\mathrm{odim}_\perp(\mathbb{L})$, *is the smallest* n *such that an orthoembedding from* $\mathbb{L}$ *to* 2^n *exists. Contrary, the* inner orthodimension, *denoted by* $\mathrm{idim}_\perp(\mathbb{L})$, *is the largest* m *such that an orthoembedding from* 2^m *to* $\mathbb{L}$ *exists.*

Proposition 4. *Let* $\mathbb{G} = (V, V, R)$ *be a simple graph. It holds that there exists an orthoembedding* $\varphi \colon 2^m \overset{\perp}{\hookrightarrow} \mathfrak{B}(\mathbb{G})$ *iff there exists a symmetric context embedding* $(\alpha, \alpha) \colon \mathbb{U}_m \hookrightarrow \mathbb{G}$.

Proof. "$\Rightarrow$": For every $i \in \underline{m}$, let (A_i, B_i) denote the image of the atom $\{i\}$ under φ. Since $i \neq j \Longleftrightarrow \{i\} \perp \{j\}$, it holds that $i \neq j \Longleftrightarrow (A_i, B_i) \perp (A_j, B_j)$. This is equivalent to the following relationship:

$$i \neq j \Longleftrightarrow (A_i, B_i) \leq (A_j, B_j)^c = (B_j, A_j) \Longleftrightarrow A_i \subseteq B_j.$$

Consequently for every $i \in \underline{m}$, we can choose an element $v_i \in A_i \not\subseteq B_i$. That implies the property $(v_i, v_i) \notin R$. On the other hand, for every $j \neq i$, it must hold that $(v_j, v_i) \in R$ and by symmetry also $(v_i, v_j) \in R$. To sum it up, we have shown that $\mathbb{U}_m$ can symmetrically be embedded into $\mathbb{G}$.

"$\Leftarrow$": The map $\varphi_\alpha : 2^m \hookrightarrow \mathfrak{B}(\mathbb{G})$, with $\varphi_\alpha(A) := (\alpha[A]'', \alpha[A]')$, is an order embedding (Proposition 1). It additionally preserves and reflects orthogonality:

$$A \perp B \Longleftrightarrow A \subseteq B^c \Longleftrightarrow A \cap B = \emptyset \Longleftrightarrow \forall (a \in A), \forall (b \in B) : a \neq b$$
$$\Longleftrightarrow \forall (a \in A), \forall (b \in B) : \alpha(a) R \alpha(b) \Longleftrightarrow \alpha[A] \subseteq \alpha[B]'$$
$$\Longrightarrow \alpha[A]' \supseteq \alpha[B]'' \Longrightarrow \alpha[A]'' \subseteq \alpha[B]'$$
$$\Longleftrightarrow (\alpha[A]'', \alpha[A]') \leq (\alpha[B]', \alpha[B]'') = (\alpha[B]''', \alpha[B]'')$$
$$\Longleftrightarrow (\alpha[A]'', \alpha[A]') \leq (\alpha[B]'', \alpha[B]')^c \Longleftrightarrow \varphi_\alpha(A) \perp \varphi_\alpha(B).$$

In the lines with implications, we used the fact that $A \subseteq B \Rightarrow B' \subseteq A'$. These implications induce an equivalence too, since it holds that $\alpha[A]'' \subseteq \alpha[B]'$ implies $\alpha[A] \subseteq \alpha[A]'' \subseteq \alpha[B]'$.

Corollary 1. *For a simple graph* $\mathbb{G}$, *the clique number* $\omega(\mathbb{G})$ *is equal to the inner orthodimension* $\mathrm{idim}_\perp(\mathfrak{B}(\mathbb{G}))$.

Next, we introduce an equivalent packing problem w.r.t. the complementary context $\mathbb{G}^c = (V, V, R^c)$. Note that we take the full set theoretic complement of R which yields a reflexive and symmetric relation. This should not be confused with the complement from graph theory, where the diagonal is usually omitted.

Definition 3. *Let* $\mathbb{G}^c = (V, V, R^c)$ *be the complement of a simple graph. For every* $v \in V$, *we define the* symmetric neighbourhood $N(v) := N(v, v) = (v, \cdot) \cup (\cdot, v)$. *The set of all symmetric neighbourhoods of* $\mathbb{G}^c$ *is denoted by* $\mathcal{N}_s(\mathbb{G}^c) := \{N(v) \mid v \in V\} \subseteq \mathcal{N}(\mathbb{G}^c)$ *and gives rise to the* symmetric neighbourhood packing number, $\mathrm{snp}(\mathbb{G}^c) := \max\{\#\tilde{\mathcal{N}} \mid \tilde{\mathcal{N}} \subseteq \mathcal{N}_s(\mathbb{G}^c), \forall N_1, N_2 \in \tilde{\mathcal{N}} : N_1 \cap N_2 = \emptyset\}$.

Utilizing a symmetric version of Proposition 3, we get the following theorem:

Theorem 2. *Let* $\mathbb{G} = (V, V, R)$ *be a simple graph. It holds that the inner orthodimension of* $\mathbb{G}$*'s concept lattice is equal to* $\mathbb{G}^c$*'s symmetric neighbourhood packing number:* $\mathrm{idim}_\perp(\mathfrak{B}(\mathbb{G})) = \mathrm{snp}(\mathbb{G}^c)$.

Finally, in order to provide a holistic comparison to the inner- and outer order 2-dimension, we will cover some facts about the outer orthodimension as well. In [8], the outer orthodimension was treated (defined with a slightly different but equivalent notion of orthoembedding). For that, we consider again $\mathbb{G}^c = (V, V, R^c)$ together with a subset $S \subseteq V$. This subset defines a *square* if $S \times S \subseteq R^c$. Squares exist due to the reflexivity and symmetry of R^c. A *maximal square* is not contained in another square. Let $\mathrm{Sq}(\mathbb{G}^c)$ denote the set of $\mathbb{G}^c$'s maximal squares. The *square cover number*, $\mathrm{sc}(\mathbb{G}^c)$, is defined a s the minimal number of maximal squares necessary to cover R^c. It holds that $\mathrm{sc}(\mathbb{G}^c) = \mathrm{odim}_\perp(\mathfrak{B}(\mathbb{G}))$. Hence, we see that the duality between inner/outer orthodimension on one side and packing/cover problem on the other, holds for simple graphs and their concept lattices too.

5   Breadth, VC-Dimension and Graph Parameters

In this section, we relate the treated (ortho)lattice dimensions to other lattice-, context- and graph parameters. We start with the *breadth* of a lattice, which is the largest $m \in \mathbb{N}$ such that any join of elements $x_1, x_2, \ldots, x_{m+1}$ is already a join of a proper subset of these x_i's. In [11] it is stated that the breadth is equal to the inner order 2-dimension. On the other hand, we are not aware of a specialized notion of breadth for complete ortholattices, that equals the inner orthodimension.

To define another notion of dimension, let X be a set and $\mathcal{S} \subseteq 2^X$ a set system on X. A subset $Y \subseteq X$ is *shattered* by $\mathcal{S}$ if $\{\tilde{X} \cap Y \mid \tilde{X} \in \mathcal{S}\} = 2^Y$ and the *VC-dimension* (introduced in [12] by Vapnik and Chervonenkis) is the maximal cardinality of a set shattered by $\mathcal{S}$. It is shown in [1] that for a formal context $\mathbb{K}$ the VC-dimension of $\mathrm{Ext}(\mathbb{K})$ is equal to $\mathrm{idim}_2(\mathfrak{B}(\mathbb{K}))$. It can be argued whether the VC-dimension is a parameter of the set system $\mathrm{Ext}(\mathbb{K})$, the concept lattice $\mathfrak{B}(\mathbb{K})$ or the context $\mathbb{K}$. In case of a simple graph $\mathbb{G}$, various notions of VC-dimension associated with it exist. In [9] it is stated that by choosing the vertex sets of all cliques of $\mathbb{G}$ as the set system $\mathcal{S}$, the derived VC-dimension equals clique number $\omega(\mathbb{G})$ and hence also $\mathrm{idim}_\perp(\mathfrak{B}(\mathbb{G}))$.

Finally, we relate the inner- and outer orthodimension to graph theoretic parameters w.r.t. $\mathbb{G}^c$. Let $\mathbb{G}^c - \mathbb{E}_{\#V}$ denote the complement of a simple graph $\mathbb{G} = (V, V, R)$, without its diagonal. This means we consider the usual complement of simple graphs in terms of graph theory. The problem of finding the largest $m \in \mathbb{N}$ such that $\mathbb{E}_m$ symmetrically embeds into $\mathbb{G}^c$, is equivalent to determine the *independence number* α of $\mathbb{G}^c - \mathbb{E}_{\#V}$, i.e., the largest cardinality of a set of vertices that induces an *empty subgraph* (that is a subgraph without edges, see [6]). Hence, it holds that $\alpha(\mathbb{G}^c - \mathbb{E}_{\#V}) = \mathrm{snp}(\mathbb{G}^c) = \mathrm{idim}_\perp(\mathfrak{B}(\mathbb{G}))$. Another name for the independence number is *vertex packing number*, which emphasises the equivalence to a packing problem (see [7]).

Furthermore, we want to recall that in [8] it was shown that $\theta_e(\mathbb{G}^c - \mathbb{E}_{\#V}) = \mathrm{sc}(\mathbb{G}^c) = \mathrm{odim}_\perp(\mathfrak{B}(\mathbb{G}))$, where θ_e denotes the *edge clique cover number* of a simple graph.

6   Dimensions of the Tensor Product of Complete Lattices

In this section, we treat the inner order 2-dimension of the tensor product $\mathbb{L}_1 \otimes \mathbb{L}_2$ of complete lattices, as well as the inner orthodimension of the tensor product of two complete ortholattices. Since every complete lattice is isomorphic to a concept lattice (see [5]), it is sufficient to consider the tensor product $\mathfrak{B}(\mathbb{K}_1) \otimes \mathfrak{B}(\mathbb{K}_2)$. Due to the identity from Eq. 1, this tensor product is isomorphic to the concept lattice $\mathfrak{B}(\mathbb{K}_1 \tilde{\times} \mathbb{K}_2)$. Consequently, via Proposition 2 and 4, the determination of the inner lattice dimension translates to a context embedding problem into the direct product. As shown in Sect. 3 and 4, we end up with a neighbourhood packing problem w.r.t. the complementary context. And finally, De Morgan laws allow us to consider these packing problems in terms of the cardinal product.

In order to tackle the packing problems on the cardinal product, one can show that neighbourhoods of the cardinal product correspond to pairs of neighbourhoods with one component from each factor. Furthermore, the following definition introduces an optimization problem on neighbourhoods, that is dual to the packing problem, which will enable us to provide bounds for the packing number w.r.t. the cardinal product.

Definition 4. *Let* $\mathbb{K} = (G, M, I)$ *be a formal concept and* $\mathbb{G}^c = (V, V, R^c)$ *the complement of a simple graph. We define their* neighbourhood blocking number *and* symmetric neighbourhood blocking number *as:*

$$\mathrm{nb}(\mathbb{K}) = \min\{\#\tilde{I} \mid \tilde{I} \subseteq I, \forall N \in \mathcal{N}(\mathbb{K}), \exists (g, m) \in \tilde{I} \colon (g, m) \in N\},$$

$$\mathrm{snb}(\mathbb{G}^c) = \min\{\#\tilde{R} \mid \tilde{R} \subseteq R^c, \forall N \in \mathcal{N}_s(\mathbb{G}^c), \exists (v, w) \in \tilde{R} \colon (v, w) \in N\}.$$

Theorem 3. *Let* $\mathbb{K}_1, \mathbb{K}_2$ *be formal contexts and* $\mathbb{G}_1, \mathbb{G}_2$ *simple graphs. It holds:*

$$\mathrm{np}(\mathbb{K}_1)\,\mathrm{np}(\mathbb{K}_2) \leq \mathrm{np}(\mathbb{K}_1 \hat{\times} \mathbb{K}_2) \leq \min(\mathrm{np}(\mathbb{K}_1)\,\mathrm{nb}(\mathbb{K}_2), \mathrm{nb}(\mathbb{K}_1)\,\mathrm{np}(\mathbb{K}_2)),$$

$$\mathrm{snp}(\mathbb{G}_1^c)\,\mathrm{snp}(\mathbb{G}_2^c) \leq \mathrm{snp}(\mathbb{G}_1^c \hat{\times} \mathbb{G}_2^c) \leq \min(\mathrm{snp}(\mathbb{G}_1^c)\,\mathrm{snb}(\mathbb{G}_2^c), \mathrm{snb}(\mathbb{G}_1^c)\,\mathrm{snp}(\mathbb{G}_2^c)).$$

Proof. The lower and upper bound for the neighbourhood packing number will be proved. Bounds for the symmetric case can be shown analogously. Due to the observations above, we will make use of the fact that every neighbourhood $N \in \mathcal{N}(\mathbb{K}_1 \hat{\times} \mathbb{K}_2)$ can be expressed as a pair $(N_1, N_2) \in \mathcal{N}(\mathbb{K}_1) \times \mathcal{N}(\mathbb{K}_2)$.

For the lower bound, let $\tilde{\mathcal{N}}_1 \subseteq \mathcal{N}(\mathbb{K}_1)$ and $\tilde{\mathcal{N}}_2 \subseteq \mathcal{N}(\mathbb{K}_2)$ define maximal neighbourhood packings. Since every element of $\tilde{\mathcal{N}}_1 \times \tilde{\mathcal{N}}_2$ induces a neighbourhood in $\mathbb{K}_1 \hat{\times} \mathbb{K}_2$, and since these induced neighbourhoods are pairwise disjoint, the lower bound of $\mathrm{np}(\mathbb{K}_1 \hat{\times} \mathbb{K}_2)$ follows.

To prove the upper bound, let $\tilde{\mathcal{N}} \subseteq \mathcal{N}(\mathbb{K}_1 \hat{\times} \mathbb{K}_2)$ define a maximal neighbourhood packing and $\tilde{I} \subseteq I_1$ a minimal neighbourhood blocking. For $(g, m) \in \tilde{I}$, we define $\tilde{\mathcal{N}}_{g,m} := \{(N_1, N_2) \mid (N_1, N_2) \in \tilde{\mathcal{N}} \text{ and } (g, m) \in N_1\}$. Since $\forall (N_1 \in \mathcal{N}(\mathbb{K}_1)) \exists ((g, m) \in \tilde{I})$ with $(g, m) \in N_1$, it holds that $\tilde{\mathcal{N}} = \bigcup_{(g,m) \in \tilde{I}} \tilde{\mathcal{N}}_{g,m}$. Also for $(g, m) \in \tilde{I}$ the projection to the second component $\pi_2[\tilde{\mathcal{N}}_{g,m}]$ is a neighbourhood packing w.r.t. I_2. It implies that $\#\tilde{\mathcal{N}} = \#\bigcup_{(g,m) \in \tilde{I}} \tilde{\mathcal{N}}_{g,m} \leq \#\tilde{I}\,\mathrm{np}(\mathbb{K}_2) = \mathrm{nb}(\mathbb{K}_1)\,\mathrm{np}(\mathbb{K}_2)$. The upper bound's second part follows similarly. □

This, and the fact that the blocking number is an upper bound for the packing number, leads directly to the next theorem, which provides a sufficient condition for the multiplicativity of the inner dimensions w.r.t. the tensor product.

Theorem 4. *Let* $\mathbb{K}_1 = (G_1, M_1, I_1)$ *and* $\mathbb{K}_2 = (G_2, M_2, I_2)$ *be formal contexts and* $\mathbb{G}_1 = (V_1, V_1, R_1)$ *and* $\mathbb{G}_2 = (V_2, V_2, R_2)$ *simple graphs. It holds that:*

$$\mathrm{idim}_2(\mathfrak{B}(\mathbb{K}_1))\,\mathrm{idim}_2(\mathfrak{B}(\mathbb{K}_2)) \leq \mathrm{idim}_2(\mathfrak{B}(\mathbb{K}_1) \otimes \mathfrak{B}(\mathbb{K}_2)),$$

$$\mathrm{idim}_\perp(\mathfrak{B}(\mathbb{G}_1))\,\mathrm{idim}_\perp(\mathfrak{B}(\mathbb{G}_2)) \leq \mathrm{idim}_\perp(\mathfrak{B}(\mathbb{G}_1) \otimes \mathfrak{B}(\mathbb{G}_2)).$$

If it is true that $\mathrm{np}(\mathbb{K}_1^c) = \mathrm{nb}(\mathbb{K}_1^c)$ *or* $\mathrm{np}(\mathbb{K}_2^c) = \mathrm{nb}(\mathbb{K}_2^c)$, *or,* $\mathrm{snp}(\mathbb{G}_1^c) = \mathrm{snb}(\mathbb{G}_1^c)$ *or* $\mathrm{snp}(\mathbb{G}_2^c) = \mathrm{snb}(\mathbb{G}_2^c)$, *the respective inner lattice dimension is multiplicative w.r.t. the tensor product of complete (ortho)lattices.*

7   Conclusion

In this paper, we analysed the inner order 2-dimension and the inner orthodimension of complete (ortho)lattices. We showed that their determination is equivalent to a set packing problem with neighbourhoods in a formal context and symmetric neighbourhoods in the complement of a simple graph. In addition, the inner dimensions of the tensor product of complete (ortho)lattices were treated, which lead to a sufficient condition for their multiplicativity w.r.t. the tensor product.

From a more general perspective, this paper provides a holistic approach to the order 2-dimension of complete lattices. It is natural to divide it into an outer and inner dimension. The outer dimension is a minimization problem (which is equivalent to a cover problem) and the inner dimension a maximization problem (equivalent to a packing problem). Furthermore, the treatment of the orthodimension constitutes a bridge to graph theory, by translating the independence number of a simple graph to the inner orthodimension of complete ortholattices. Additionally, the neighbourhood packings generalize symmetric neighbourhood packings and thereby lift graph theoretic parameters to formal concept analysis and lattice theory.

References

1. Albano, A., Chornomaz, B.: Why concept lattices are large: extremal theory for generators, concepts, and VC-dimension. Int. J. Gen. Syst. **46**(5), 440–457 (2017)
2. Birkhoff, G.: Lattice Theory, 3rd edn. American Mathematical Society, Providence (1967)
3. Deiters, K., Erné, M.: Negations and contrapositions of complete lattices. Discrete Math. **181**(1–3), 91–111 (1998)
4. Dörfler, W.: A complete lattice in graph theory. Combinatorics **1** (1976)
5. Ganter, B., Wille, R.: Formal Concept Analysis: Mathematical Foundations. Springer, New York (1997)
6. Godsil, C., Royle, G.: Algebraic Graph Theory. Graduate Texts in Mathematics, Springer, New York (2001). https://doi.org/10.1007/978-1-4613-0163-9
7. Houck, D.J., Vemuganti, R.R.: An algorithm for the vertex packing problem. Oper. Res. **25**(5), 773–787 (1977)
8. Jäkel, C., Schmidt, S.E.: Cover problems, dimensions and the tensor product of complete lattices. In: 14th International Conference on Concept Lattice and Their Applications (2018)
9. Kranakis, E., Krizanc, D., Ruf, B., Urrutia, J., Woeginger, G.J.: VC-dimensions for graphs (extended abstract). In: Nagl, M. (ed.) WG 1995. LNCS, vol. 1017, pp. 1–13. Springer, Heidelberg (1995). https://doi.org/10.1007/3-540-60618-1_61
10. Pardalos, P.M., Xue, J.: The maximum clique problem. J. Global Optim. **4**, 301–328 (1994)
11. Stephan, J.: Varieties generated by lattices of breadth two. Order **10**, 133–142 (1993)
12. Vapnik, V.N., Chervonenkis, A.Y.: On the uniform convergence of relative frequencies of events to their probabilities. In: Vovk, V., Papadopoulos, H., Gammerman, A. (eds.) Measures of Complexity, pp. 11–30. Springer, Cham (2015). https://doi.org/10.1007/978-3-319-21852-6_3

13. Walker, J.W.: From graphs to ortholattices and equivariant maps. J. Comb. Theory B **35**, 171–192 (1983)
14. Wille, R.: Tensorial decomposition of concept lattices. Order **2**, 81–95 (1985)

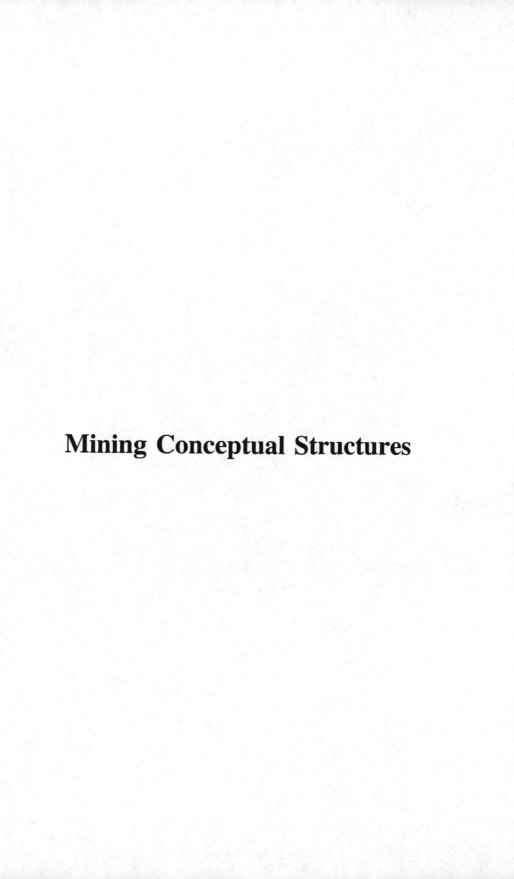

Mining Conceptual Structures

Random Generation of a Locally Consistent Spatio-Temporal Graph

Aurélie Leborgne$^{(\boxtimes)}$, Marija Kirandjiska, and Florence Le Ber

Université de Strasbourg, CNRS, ENGEES, ICube UMR 7357,
67000 Strasbourg, France
{aurelie.leborgne,florence.le-ber}@unistra.fr

Abstract. In this paper, an original approach, for the generation of locally coherent spatio-temporal graphs embeddding frequent inexact patterns, is presented. This approach is based on a work carried out previously, in which a configurable generator for spatio-temporal graphs has been implemented. These graphs contain spatial and spatio-temporal edges that are labelled with the RCC8 topological relations. The objective being to check the consistency of these relations during the construction of the graph, the path-consistency method, based on the composition of weak relation, has been implemented in the graph generator. The approach is precisely described and some experiences are detailed. Our final objective is to build a generator allowing to generate test bases that can be used to highlight the advantages and disadvantages of graph extraction methods.

Keywords: Spatio-temporal graph · RCC8 · Consistency · Graph generation

1 Introduction

The regular improvement of data collection tools and techniques leads more and more often to model and analyze data that have a spatial but also a temporal dimension. A natural way to model such data is to use spatio-temporal graphs (ST graphs), which can be used to represent different phenomena such as events in videos [19], movement of dunes on the seaside [9], or brain activity [12], *etc.*

In order to analyze the collected data, e.g. for extracting recurrent phenomena in time and/or space, it is necessary to develop algorithms to search for frequent patterns/subgraphs in ST graphs. However, to develop such algorithms, it is essential to have a test base of annotated ST graphs. Unfortunately, the annotation of such data is a very tedious task and even impossible to perform precisely given the amount of data we handle. The only solution to obtain a test base is therefore to develop a spatio-temporal graph generator in which we master the frequent patterns present in these ST graphs.

The generation of such graphs has been described in [11]. In this paper, we are interested in how to manage the coherence of graphs for the considered

© Springer Nature Switzerland AG 2021
T. Braun et al. (Eds.): ICCS 2021, LNAI 12879, pp. 155–169, 2021.
https://doi.org/10.1007/978-3-030-86982-3_12

set of relations, namely, the qualitative spatial relations of RCC8 theory [15]. These relations make it possible to model the evolution of land use on a territory. Figure 1, for example, represents the evolution of a set of neighboring plots (modeled by polygons) over time.

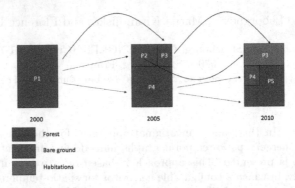

Fig. 1. Evolution of land use in a territory

This article is organized as follows. Section 2 describes the theoretical elements on which our approach is based, namely the spatio-temporal graph model, the RCC8 relations and then the qualitative constraint networks. Sections 3 and 4 present the generation algorithm and the experiments carried out. Finally, a conclusion closes the article.

2   Preliminaries

2.1   Graphs Simulation

Graph generation is an important issue in many fields, to simulate real graphs, to test algorithms or to analyze, visualize or transform data [3]. In most cases, the goal is to generate realistic graphs. Many models have been presented in this sense for the generation of complex graphs adapted to the representation of natural or human systems (semantic web, social networks). Most approaches are based on statistical distributions of graph properties (number of vertices, number of edges, degree of vertices, *etc.*). Barabási-Albert model [4,5] is one of the best known. In the Chung-Lu model [1] the probability of an edge is proportional to the product of the degrees of its two vertices. The Recursive MATrix method (R-MAT) [6] and Park and Kim model [13] are recursive models to generate synthetic graphs. The RDyn approach was recently designed [17] for generating temporal graphs representing the dynamics of network communities. In a context closer to ours, Kuramochi and Karypis [10] proposed an algorithm to generate random general graphs including known patterns to create synthetic datasets. Nevertheless, the consistency issue in the generated graph is not addressed, as edges have no semantics in these approaches.

In [11], we have developed an approach to generate, in a random way, semantic-temporal graphs, where the edges are endowed with semantics. We introduce below the model of such a graph, inspired by [9]. This is a spatio-temporal graph, defined as the union of three sub-graphs:

- **The graph of spatial relations**, that spatially characterizes the interactions between entities at a given time. It is composed of nodes (disks), and edges (in green) on Fig. 2.
- **The graph of spatio-temporal relations**, which is based on the same characteristics as the graph of spatial relations, but considering entities at different times. It is composed of nodes (disks), and edges (in red) on Fig. 2.
- **The graph of filiation relations**, defines the concept of identity. It allows to characterize the transmission of the identity through time. It is composed of nodes (disks), and edges (in blue) on Fig. 2.

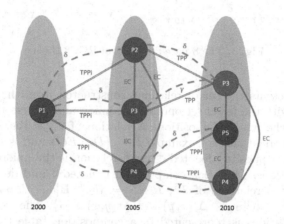

Fig. 2. ST graph modeling the evolution of the territory of Fig. 1 (Color figure online)

Formally, a ST graph is defined as follows. Let $\mathcal{T} = \{t_1, t_2, ...t_n\}$, a time domain, where t_i represents a time instance of a given granularity and $t_i < t_{i+1}$ for all $i \in [1,n]$. Let Δ a set of entities, $\{e_1, e_2, ..., e_m\}$. Let also Σ, a set of spatial relations, and Φ, a set of filiation relations.

A spatio-temporal graph $\mathcal{G}$ is a tuple (U, E_Σ, E_Φ), where U is the set of vertices $(e_l, t_i) \in \Delta \times \mathcal{T}$, E_Σ is the set of tuples $((e_i, t_i)T(e_j, t_j))$ where $(e_i, t_i), (e_j, t_j) \in U$, $t_i \leq t_j \leq t_{i+1}$, and $T \in \Sigma$, and E_Φ is the set of tuples $((e_i, t_i)\rho(e_j, t_{i+1}))$ where $(e_i, t_i), (e_j, t_{i+1}) \in U$, and $\rho \in \Phi$.

This graph model was initially introduced to represent the evolution of geographical entities [9]. Other filiation relations are studied in [8]. Besides, an algorithm has been proposed to check the consistency of this representation with regards to the specifications of a spatio-temporal database.

2.2 RCC8 Relations

The spatial and spatio-temporal relations we use are the base relations **B** of the RCC8 theory [15] on the spatial domain Δ. These relations define the position of two regions: $DC(x,y)$ regions x and y are disconnected; $EC(x,y)$ they are externally connected; $PO(x,y)$ they partially overlap; $TPP(x,y)$ x is a tangential proper part of y; $TPP_i(x,y)$ y is a tangential proper part of x; $NTPP(x,y)$ x is a non-tangential proper part of y; $NTPP_i(x,y)$ y is non-tangential proper part of x; $EQ(x,y)$ x and y are equal (see Fig. 3).

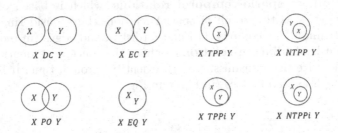

Fig. 3. The 8 base relations of RCC8 theory

Set $2^{\mathbf{B}}$ represents the set of relations constructed from the base relations. It is provided with the usual set operations, union and intersection, the inverse operation and the weak composition. A relation of $2^{\mathbf{B}}$ is therefore written as a union of basic relations, for example $R = \{DC, EC\}$ and is interpreted as a disjunction. The opposite (denoted $\smile$) of a relation is the union of the inverses of its base relations. The weak composition is noted $\diamond$ and defined as follows: Let R and S two relations of $2^{\mathbf{B}}$, $R \diamond S = \{b \in \mathbf{B}|b \cap (R \circ S) \neq \emptyset\}$ where $R \circ S = \{(x,z) \in \Delta^2|\exists y \in \Delta, (x,y) \in R \text{ et}(y,z) \in S\}$. The weak composition of the basic relations is represented in a composition table [14], as shown in Fig. 7. For example, suppose that three regions x, y, z are such as $TPP(x,y)$ and $EC(y,z)$ holds, then $\{DC, EC\}(x,z)$ holds (see Fig. 4).

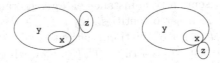

Fig. 4. Two possible configurations for x and z knowing $TPP(x,y)$ and $EC(y,z)$

2.3   Consistency

The notion of consistency of a set of spatial or temporal relations between regions has been studied in the framework of qualitative constraint networks [7]. A network of qualitative constraints is a couple $N = (V, C)$ where V is a set of variables on a continuous domain $\mathcal{D}$ and C an application that associates to each pair of variables (V_i, V_j) a set C_{ij} of base relations $\{r_1, ..., r_l\}$ taken from an algebra of relations. This set represents the disjunction of possible relations between the two entities represented by the variables V_i and V_j. A consistent instantiation of N is one where each variable V_i takes a value $e_i \in \mathcal{D}$ such that for any pair (V_i, V_j) the atomic relation verified by the variables V_i and V_j belongs to C_{ij}.

Checking the consistency of a network is an NP-complete problem in the general case [20]. Local methods have been proposed to check weaker forms of consistency, including path-consistency: a qualitative constraint network N is said to be path-consistent if for all variables $V_i, V_j, V_k \in V$, $C_{ij} \subseteq C_{ik} \circ C_{kj}$ [7].

The path-consistency method consists in performing the triangulation operation: $C_{ij} = C_{ij} \cap (C_{ik} \circ C_{kj})$ for any triplet until a fixed point is obtained. The final network is path-consistent and equivalent to the initial network. In the framework of RCC8, where we can't use the composition, but the weak composition $\diamond$, we will speak about algebraic closure [16].

Various algorithms have been proposed to check the path-consistency. Their computation time is related to the number of accesses to the composition table and thus to the size of the relation set $2^{\mathbf{B}}$ [2]. The authors of [18] present an algorithm for incrementally checking the consistency of a qualitative constraint network, which grows by adding spatial or temporal entities. The algorithm exploits a triangulated graph: when an entity is added at step t, it is linked to all the entities present at step $t-1$ (triangulation). The path-consistency method is then applied to the graph.

Our approach is different as our aim is to generate a graph where each relation is atomic, and where the issue is to assign to the current edge a relation which is consistent with the existing ones, as we detail below.

3 Generation of Locally Consistent ST Graphs

We present here an approach for generating locally consistent spatio-temporal graphs including frequent inexact patterns (subgraphs). We rely on the method presented in [11], which allows to generate such graphs, including patterns, but without dealing with the issue of consistency.

We briefly describe here the algorithm for generating spatio-temporal graphs and their embedded patterns, and then detail and justify the algorithm for checking the local consistency of the generated spatial and spatio-temporal relations. Let us note that these two types of relations are derived from the set $2^{\mathbf{B}}$ (see Sect. 2.2).

The algorithm described in [11] simulates spatio-temporal graphs containing patterns *drown* in a uniform stochastic generation of nodes and edges. It is a fully parameterizable algorithm, exploiting Poisson's law, in which it is possible to choose the size of the generated graph, the number of spatial, temporal and filiation relations per node, as well as the size of the source-patterns to be embedded and the number of their transformations. In this paper, we consider a modified algorithm to control the proportion of patterns, in number of nodes, in the total graph. The other parameters are listed in Table 1.

Table 1. Parameters for the generation of spatio-temporal graphs

Parameter	Description
λ_n	Expectation of the zero-truncated Poisson distribution for the total number of nodes in the graph
λ_r	Expectation of the zero-truncated Poisson distribution for the number of nodes per time instant
Λ_e	Triplet of Poisson law expectations for the number of spatial/spatio-temporal/filiation relations per node
$labels_n$	List of available labels for nodes
$labels_e$	Size 3 table of available label lists for each type of relation
$patterns$	A list of tuples where each tuple is composed of a time instant number and the pattern to insert at this time instant

This algorithm has three main steps. It first calculates the total number of nodes (parameter λ_n, Table 1) of the graph to be generated.

- **Step 1:** generation and transformation of source-patterns, according to specific parameters (see below); each pattern is assigned to a time instant of the graph, this information is stored in the parameter *patterns*.
- **Step 2:** random generation of nodes for each time instant in the graph (parameters λ_r and $labels_n$). The number of nodes is adjusted according to the number of nodes in the patterns assigned to the current time instant.
- **Step 3:** random generation of relations between nodes (parameters Λ_e and $labels_e$). The nodes of the current time instant are connected to each other and to the nodes of the previous time instant. The number of edges is adjusted for the nodes of the patterns (if they already have any). Each edge is labeled with an atomic relation.

In the first step, the pattern generation is based on the following parameters (Table 2): the number of inserted patterns depends on a proportion p (as a percentage of the number of nodes) that these patterns should represent in the total graph. The number of nodes in a source-pattern is randomly drawn in a range (*pnodes*). Parameters λ_r and λ_e have the same role as for the complete graph. Each source-pattern is repeated according to a value (support) randomly drawn in the interval *support*. Finally, each repetition gives rise to transformations (parameter λ_t) in order to introduce variations based on each source pattern.

The average theoretical complexity of this algorithm is $O(\lambda_n \times \lambda_r)$, each node of the graph being potentially linked to all nodes of the same time instant and of the preceding time instant. In the worst case, when the number of time instants decreases, the complexity tends to $O(\lambda_n^2)$ [11].

The objective of the work presented here is to generate a locally consistent graph based on the consistency model presented in Sect. 2.3. More precisely, it consists in generating spatial and spatio-temporal relations while making sure that they form spatial or temporal consistent triangles with the existing edges in the graph.

Table 2. Parameters for pattern generation

Parameter	Description
p	Proportion of nodes in the patterns/number in the graph
$pnodes$	Interval for the number of nodes in a source pattern
λ_r	Expectation of the zero-truncated Poisson distribution for the number of nodes per time instant
Λ_e	Triplet of Poisson law expectations for the number of spatial/spatial-temporal/filiation relations per node
$support$	Interval for the number of repetitions of a source-pattern
λ_t	Expectation of the Poisson law for the number of transformations to be performed on a source-pattern

Definition 1. *A **consistent triangle** is a clique of 3 vertices in which the three relations modeled by edges are consistent with each other, that is, e_i, e_j, e_k being the vertices of such a triangle, $R_{ik} \subseteq R_{ij} \diamond R_{jk}$ and $R_{ij} \subseteq R_{ik} \diamond R_{kj}$.*

Definition 2. *A subgraph consisting of three nodes that belong to the same time instant will be called a **spatial triangle**. The composition schemes of the 4 possible cases, depending on the direction of the edges xy and yz, are shown in Fig. 5a.*

Definition 3. *A subgraph consisting of three nodes that belong to two successive time instants will be called a **temporal triangle**. Composition schemes of the 4 possible cases, depending on the direction of the edges xy and yz, are presented in Fig. 5b.*

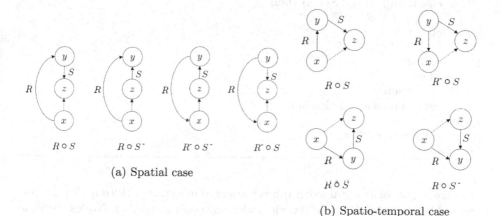

(a) Spatial case

(b) Spatio-temporal case

Fig. 5. Different configurations for the composition of edges connecting the nodes x and y on the one hand, and y and z on the other hand, in a triangle

Choosing to limit our approach to a local coherence (3-coherence) is linked to practical aspects: on the one hand, the embedded patterns are small (3–4 nodes per time instant, 2 or 3 time instants at most); on the other hand, the number of relations per node is generally low (even if experiments have been conducted with high densities, see Sect. 4). Finally, we seek to limit the complexity of ST graph generation.

Algorithm 1 describes this method. An initialization phase is necessary (l. 1). It allows to initialize a list L with all the relations of **B**. To determine a relation between nodes x and z, we search all the nodes y, that have a relation with both x and z (l. 2). The different configurations (Fig. 5) are considered. For each node, the list is updated by keeping only the possible relations among those already present in L (l. 4, 6, 8, 10). Finally, the relation between x and z is randomly assigned among the possible relations (present in L) (l. 14). In case the list is empty, no relation is assigned.

The theoretical complexity of Algorithm 1 is $O(\lambda_r)$ since, given a pair (x, z), it examines at most all nodes in the current and preceding time instants. In contrast, since all relations are atomic relations, only one access to the composition table is needed for processing a triangle.

Algorithm 1. Generation of a relation between two nodes with local consistency check

---

Input: nodes x, z
Output: relation between x and z
1: $L = \mathbf{B}$
2: **for each** node y such that (x,y) and (y,z) $\in E_\Sigma$ **do**
3:     **if** $R(x, y)$ and $S(y, z)$ **then**
4:        $L \leftarrow L \cap R \diamond S$
5:     **else if** $R(x, y)$ and $S(z, y)$ **then**
6:        $L \leftarrow L \cap R \diamond S^\smile$
7:     **else if** $R(y, x)$ and $S(z, y)$ **then**
8:        $L \leftarrow L \cap R^\smile \diamond S^\smile$
9:     **else**
10:       $L \leftarrow L \cap R^\smile \diamond S$
11:     **end if**
12: **end for**
13: **if** $L \neq \emptyset$ **then**
14:     **return** random relation in L
15: **else**
16:     **return** no relation
17: **end if**

An example of an obtained graph is presented in Fig. 6: pattern nodes are designated by the letter P, while generic nodes have only a number. Nodes with the same number have the same label. On this example, at time t_4, P2 is connected to P1 by a spatial edge $NTPP$, P2 is connected to P3 (t_5) by a spatio-temporal edge DC, P1 and P3 are connected to P6 (t_5) respectively by edges having labels

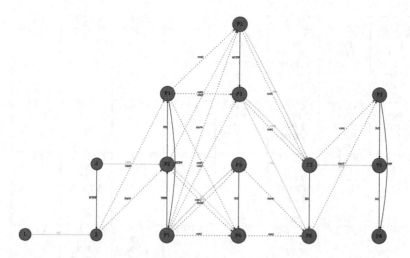

Fig. 6. A coherent spatio-temporal graph including patterns: spatial edges are represented in black, spatio-temporal edges in color, filiation edges in dashed lines (Color figure online)

PO and EC. To connect P1 and P3, the algorithm must successively examine triangles (P1, P2, P3) and (P1, P6, P3):

- For (P1, P2, P3), we have $NTPP^{\smile} \diamond DC = NTTP_i \diamond DC = \{DC, EC, PO, TPP_i, NTPP_i\}$, as shown in the blue box of the composition table (Fig. 7).
- For (P1, P6, P3), we have $PO \diamond EC^{\smile} = PO \diamond EC = \{DC, EC, PO, TPP_i, NTPP_i\}$, as shown in the yellow box of the composition table (Fig. 7).

Finally the relation between P1 and P3 must be chosen in the set $\{DC, EC, PO, TPP_i, NTPP_i\}$, here TPP_i has been selected.

4   Experimentations

In this experimental phase we studied the performance, in terms of computation time, of the generation algorithm by varying the different parameters (see Tables 1 and 2).

This set of tests was performed on an Ubuntu machine 18.04.4 LTS, 32 Go of RAM and 32 cores. However our algorithm only used one of these cores.

In order to observe the influence of the different parameters on the complexity of the generation of consistent spatio-temporal graphs, we varied these parameters one by one.

$\diamond$	DC	EC	PO	TPP	NTPP	TPP_i	$NTPP_i$	EQ
DC	DC, EC, PO, TPP, NTPP, TPP_i, $NTPP_i$, EQ	DC, EC, PO, TPP, NTPP	DC, EC, PO, TPP, NTPP	DC, EC, PO, TPP, NTPP	DC, EC, PO, TPP, NTPP	DC	DC	DC
EC	DC, EC, PO, TPP_i, $NTPP_i$	DC, EC, PO, TPP, TPP_i, EQ	DC, EC, PO, TPP, NTPP	EC, PO, TPP, NTPP	PO, TPP, NTPP	DC, EC	DC	EC
PO	DC, EC, PO, TPP_i, $NTPP_i$	DC, EC, PO, TPP_i, $NTPP_i$	DC, EC, PO, TPP, NTPP, TPP_i, $NTPP_i$, EQ	PO, TPP, NTPP	PO, TPP, NTPP	DC, EC, PO, TPP_i, $NTPP_i$	DC, EC, PO, TPP_i, $NTPP_i$	PO
TPP	DC	DC, EC	DC, EC, PO, TPP, NTPP	TPP, NTPP	NTPP	DC, EC, PO, TPP, TPP_i, EQ	DC, EC, PO, TPP_i, $NTPP_i$	TPP
NTPP	DC	DC	DC, EC, PO, TPP, NTPP	NTPP	NTPP	DC, EC, PO, TPP, NTPP	DC, EC, PO, TPP, NTPP, TPP_i, $NTPP_i$, EQ	NTPP
TPP_i	DC, EC, PO, TPP_i, $NTPP_i$	EC, PO, TPP_i, $NTPP_i$	PO, TPP_i, $NTPP_i$	EQ, PO, TPP, TPP_i	PO, TPP, NTPP	TPP_i, $NTPP_i$	$NTPP_i$	TPP_i
$NTPP_i$	DC, EC, PO, TPP_i, $NTPP_i$	PO, TPP_i, $NTPP_i$	PO, TPP_i, $NTPP_i$	PO, TPP_i, $NTPP_i$	PO, TPP, NTPP, EQ, TPP_i, $NTPP_i$	$NTPP_i$	$NTPP_i$	$NTPP_i$
EQ	DC	EC	PO	PO	NTPP	TPP_i	$NTPP_i$	EQ

Fig. 7. Composition table for the base relations of RCC8 theory (Color figure online)

4.1 Variation of the Node Number

In this first experiment, only the parameter λ_n varies, which determines the total number of nodes in the graph. Parameter λ_r is fixed so that the number of time instant does not change (the number of nodes per time instant varies proportionally to the total number of nodes, see Fig. 8(a)). Figure 8(b) shows that the generation time of the graphs grows exponentially with the total number of nodes and thus with the number of nodes per time instant. In fact, for each node created, the algorithm has to go through the nodes of the same time instance and of the previous one to establish the relations: as λ_r is the average number of nodes per time instant, so on average there are at most $2\lambda_r \times \lambda_n \approx \lambda_n^2$ operations.

In a second step, in order to examine the influence of the number of nodes per time, we fixed the total number of nodes and varied the number of nodes per time instance. This experiment shows that there is a linear relation between the

Parameter	Value
graph generation	
λ_n	varies from 10000 to 10^6
λ_r	λ_n / 100
Λ_e	[5,5,2]
Patterns generation	
p	30
$pnodes$	[5,15]
λ_r	2
Λ_e	[5,5,2]
$support$	[10,20]
λ_t	average pattern size / 2

(a)

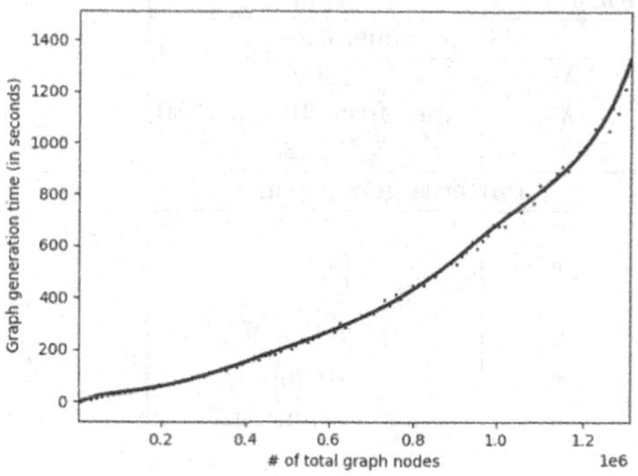

(b)

Fig. 8. Graph generation time as a function of the total number of nodes (a) Parameters (b) Resulting curve

generation time of the graphs and the number of nodes per time (see Fig. 9(b)), for a fixed total number of nodes. Everything being fixed, the only variation is due to the number of nodes to be visited to establish the relations in the current time instance and with the previous one. As above, the number of operations is on average $2\lambda_n \times \lambda_r$. Parameter λ_n being fixed, the calculation time is therefore proportional to λ_r.

4.2 Variation of the Edge Number

We are interested here in the influence of the generation of edges on the generation time of graphs. We varied therefore the number of relations per node. In this experiment, the total number of nodes and nodes per time instant are fixed. Figure 10 illustrates this experience. There is a linear relationship between the number of relations per node and the generation time of the complete graph until we reach a plateau with around 100 relations per node. The linear part can be explained in this way: for each node we have on average $\lambda_e = \Lambda_e[1] + \Lambda_e[2] + \Lambda_e[3]$ creation of edges and $\Lambda_e[1] + \Lambda_e[2]$ constraint checkings to be performed. For the whole graph, there are $\lambda_n \times \lambda_e$ operations, this value growing linearly with λ_e, λ_n being fixed. The constant part is due to the saturation of the graph, *i.e.* each node has reached its maximum number of edges. Indeed, in this experiment, a time instance contains an average of 100 nodes, each of which has at most one relation of each type with a node of the same or previous time instance. Note that the computational time associated with the consistency checking of relations is only related to the number of triplets to examine, since each edge carries only an atomic relation.

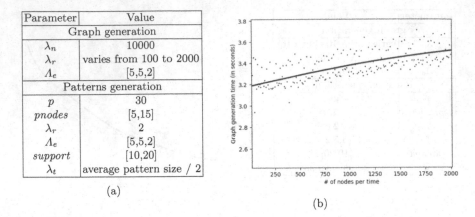

Parameter	Value
\multicolumn{2}{c}{Graph generation}	
λ_n	10000
λ_r	varies from 100 to 2000
Λ_e	[5,5,2]
\multicolumn{2}{c}{Patterns generation}	
p	30
$pnodes$	[5,15]
λ_r	2
Λ_e	[5,5,2]
$support$	[10,20]
λ_t	average pattern size / 2

(a)

(b)

Fig. 9. Generation time of a graph as a function of the number of nodes per time instant (a) Parameters (b) Resulting curve

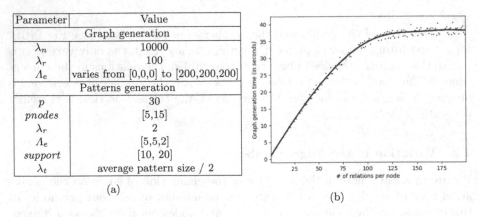

Parameter	Value
\multicolumn{2}{c}{Graph generation}	
λ_n	10000
λ_r	100
Λ_e	varies from [0,0,0] to [200,200,200]
\multicolumn{2}{c}{Patterns generation}	
p	30
$pnodes$	[5,15]
λ_r	2
Λ_e	[5,5,2]
$support$	[10, 20]
λ_t	average pattern size / 2

(a)

(b)

Fig. 10. Graph generation time as a function of the number of relations per node (a) Parameters (b) Resulting curve

4.3   Variation of the Pattern Number

In this last experiment, we vary the number of patterns inserted in the graphs (or more exactly the proportion of nodes coming from patterns, set by the parameter p, Fig. 11(a)), the graph size being constant. Figure 11(b) shows that by increasing this proportion, the generation time of the graphs increases linearly. This can be explained as follows: the generation and transformation time of the source patterns is constant (parameters $pnodes$, λ_r, Λ_e, $support$ and λ_t are fixed), the size of the patterns is constant (parameter $pnodes$), only the number of source-patterns to be generated to reach a given proportion of nodes wrt the total number of nodes in the graph varies.

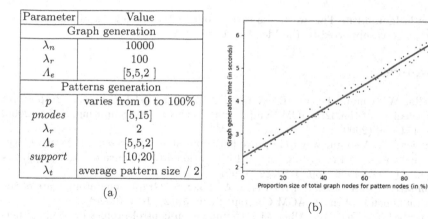

Parameter	Value
Graph generation	
λ_n	10000
λ_r	100
Λ_e	[5,5,2]
Patterns generation	
p	varies from 0 to 100%
$pnodes$	[5,15]
λ_r	2
Λ_e	[5,5,2]
$support$	[10,20]
λ_t	average pattern size / 2

(a)

(b)

Fig. 11. Graph generation time as a function of the proportion of inserted patterns (a) Parameters (b) Resulting curve

5   Conclusion

This paper presents a method to generate spatio-temporal graphs which spatial and spatio-temporal edges are locally consistent. To do so, we rely on an existing algorithm for generating random spatio-temporal graphs [11]. This algorithm has been modified in the sense that at each addition of an edge (spatial or spatio-temporal) between two nodes, the consistency of this edge with the pre-existing edges connecting these two nodes to the same nodes is checked. The path-consistency method is used for this purpose, in the framework of the RCC8 theory.

The particularity of the algorithm is to insert in the generated graph frequent inexact patterns. These patterns are generated and transformed, also including the local consistency checking.

In addition, complexity tests were performed in order to highlight the most costly steps in the generation of spatio-temporal graphs. These tests have confirmed that the added consistency checking step does not change the general complexity of the original algorithm.

Our general aim is to generate 'realistic' graphs, with respect to an application domain, here the evolution of farming territories. Generated graphs are 'realistic' if they are similar to graphs representing real spatio-temporal data. Spatial consistency is a characteristic of these real graphs. Other characteristics (e.g., node degree for the various relation types) will also be studied.

In the future, a more extensive path-consistency could be developed, following the work of [18] Furthermore, graphs generated by this approach will be used to test various frequent pattern mining methods in a spatio-temporal graph. Qualitative experiments will then be conducted to evaluate the quality of the frequent patterns that will be mined on the generated spatio-temporal graphs.

Acknowledgements. This work was carried out in the framework of the METEC-Graphe project, supported by the Idex Université de Strasbourg.

References

1. Aiello, W., Chung, F., Lu, L.: A random graph model for massive graphs. In: Proceedings of the 32th ACM Symposium on Theory of Computing, STOC 2000, pp. 171–180 (2000)
2. Bessière, C.: A simple way to improve path consistency processing in interval algebra networks. In: Proceedings of the 13th National Conference on Artificial Intelligence (AAAI-1996), pp. 375–380 (1996)
3. Bonifati, A., Holubová, I., Prat-Pérez, A., Sakr, S.: Graph generators: state of the art and open challenges. ACM Comput. Surv. **53**(2), 1–30 (2020)
4. Campbell, C., Shea, K., Albert, R.: Comment on control profiles of complex networks. Science **346**(6209), 561 (2014)
5. Ferrer i Cancho, R., Solé, R.: Optimization in complex networks. In: Pastor-Satorras, R., Rubi, M., Diaz-Guilera, A. (eds.) Statistical Mechanics of Complex Networks. Lecture Notes in Physics, vol. 625, pp. 114–126. Springer, Heidelberg (2003). https://doi.org/10.1007/978-3-540-44943-0_7
6. Chakrabarti, D., Zhan, Y., Faloutsos, C.: R-MAT: a recursive model for graph mining. In: Proceedings of the 2004 SIAM International Conference on Data Mining, pp. 442–446 (2004)
7. Condotta, J.F., Ligozat, G., Saade, M.: Empirical study of algorithms for qualitative temporal or spatial constraint networks. In: Proceedings of the 17th European Conference on Artificial Intelligence, Riva del Garda, Italy (2006)
8. Del Mondo, G., Rodríguez, M.A., Claramunt, C., Bravo, L., Thibaud, R.: Modeling consistency of spatio-temporal graphs. Data Knowl. Eng. **84**, 59–80 (2013)
9. Del Mondo, G., Stell, J.G., Claramunt, C., Thibaud, R.: A graph model for spatio-temporal evolution. J. Univ. Comput. Sci. **16**, 1452–1477 (2010)
10. Kuramochi, M., Karypis, G.: Frequent subgraph discovery. In: Proceedings 2001 IEEE International Conference on Data Mining, pp. 313–320 (2001)
11. Leborgne, A., Nuss, J., Le Ber, F., Marc-Zwecker, S.: An approach for generating random temporal semantic graphs with embedded patterns. In: Graph Embedding and Mining, ECML-PKDD 2020 Workshop Proceedings (2020)
12. Leborgne, A., Le Ber, F., Degiorgis, L., Harsan, L., Marc-Zwecker, S., Noblet, V.: Analysis of brain functional connectivity by frequent pattern mining in graphs. application to the characterization of murine models. In: Proceedings of the International Symposium on Biomedical Imaging, ISBI 2021, pp. 1–4 (2021)
13. Park, H., Kim, M.S.: TrillionG: a trillion-scale synthetic graph generator using a recursive vector model. In: Proceedings of the 2017 ACM International Conference on Management of Data, pp. 913–928 (2017)
14. Randell, D.A., Cohn, A.G., Cui, Z.: Computing transitivity tables: a challenge for automated theorem provers. In: Kapur, D. (ed.) CADE 1992. LNCS, vol. 607, pp. 786–790. Springer, Heidelberg (1992). https://doi.org/10.1007/3-540-55602-8_225
15. Randell, D.A., Cui, Z., Cohn, A.G.: A spatial logic based on regions and connection. In: Proceedings 3rd International Conference on Knowledge Representation and Reasoning, pp. 165–176. Morgan Kaufmann Publishers (1992)
16. Renz, J., Ligozat, G.: Weak composition for qualitative spatial and temporal reasoning. In: van Beek, P. (ed.) CP 2005. LNCS, vol. 3709, pp. 534–548. Springer, Heidelberg (2005). https://doi.org/10.1007/11564751_40

17. Rossetti, G.: RDYN: graph benchmark handling community dynamics. J. Complex Netw. **5**(6), 893–912 (2017)
18. Sioutis, M., Condotta, J.-F.: Incrementally building partially path consistent qualitative constraint networks. In: Agre, G., Hitzler, P., Krisnadhi, A.A., Kuznetsov, S.O. (eds.) AIMSA 2014. LNCS (LNAI), vol. 8722, pp. 104–116. Springer, Cham (2014). https://doi.org/10.1007/978-3-319-10554-3_10
19. Sridhar, M., Cohn, A.G., Hogg, D.C.: Relational graph mining for learning events from video. In: Stairs 2010: Proceedings of the Fifth Starting AI Researchers' Symposium, pp. 315–327 (2011)
20. Vilain, M., Kautz, H., Beek, P.V.: Constraint propagation algorithms for temporal reasoning: a revised report. In: Weld, D.S., De Kleer, J. (eds.) Readings on Qualitative Reasoning about Physical Systems, pp. 373–381. Morgan Kaufmann, Burlington (1989)

Mining Contextual Rules to Predict Asbestos in Buildings

Thamer Mecharnia[1,2(✉)], Nathalie Pernelle[3], Celine Rouveirol[3],
Fayçal Hamdi[4], and Lydia Chibout Khelifa[2]

[1] LISN, Université Paris Saclay, Gif-sur-Yvette, France
thamer@lri.fr
[2] Centre Scientifique et Technique du Bâtiment (CSTB), Champs sur Marne, France
chibout.khelifa@cstb.fr
[3] LIPN, Université Sorbonne Paris-Nord, CNRS, UMR 7030, Villetaneuse, France
{nathalie.pernelle,celine.rouveirol}@lipn.univ-paris13.fr
[4] CEDRIC,Conservatoire National des Arts et Métiers, Paris, France
faycal.hamdi@cnam.fr

Abstract. In the context of the work conducted at CSTB (French Scientific and Technical Center for Building), the need for a tool providing assistance in the identification of asbestos-containing materials in buildings was identified. To this end, we have developed an approach, named CRA-Miner, that mines logical rules from a knowledge graph that describes buildings and asbestos diagnoses. Since the specific product used is not defined, CRA-Miner considers temporal data, product types, and contextual information to find a set of candidate rules that maximizes the confidence. These rules can then be used to identify building elements that may contain asbestos and those that are asbestos-free. The experiments conducted on an RDF graph provided by the CSTB show that the proposed approach is promising and a satisfactory accuracy can be obtained.

Keywords: Rule mining · Knowledge graph · Temporal Data · Asbestos

1 Introduction

Asbestos[1] has been known to be harmful for quite a long time, nevertheless, the dangers associated with it have only been identified since the beginning of the 20th century. Breathing the air that contains asbestos fibers can lead to asbestos-related diseases, such as lung cancer and chest lining. However, for its fireproof qualities, many countries have extensively used asbestos in buildings, especially from 1950 to 1970. The use of asbestos is illegal today in many countries, but several thousand tons have already been used in the past and asbestos is still present in a considerable number of buildings. Thus, the identification of

---

[1] https://en.wikipedia.org/wiki/Asbestos.

© Springer Nature Switzerland AG 2021
T. Braun et al. (Eds.): ICCS 2021, LNAI 12879, pp. 170–184, 2021.
https://doi.org/10.1007/978-3-030-86982-3_13

building parts containing asbestos is a crucial task. As part of the PRDA[2], the CSTB[3] has been asked to develop an online tool assisting in the identification of asbestos-containing materials in buildings that aims to guide the tracking operator in the preparation of its tracking program (called the ORIGAMI Project). Professionals regularly inspect buildings and collect samples to detect the presence of asbestos in building components. However, information is needed to prioritize a large number of possible tests. The problem is related to the fact that the available building descriptions only contain the classes of used products without giving their accurate references or any other information about them (i.e., valued properties, providers, etc.). In [8], an ontology-based approach that estimates the probability of the existence of asbestos products in a building is defined. To generate this probability, this hybrid approach combines statistical and rule-based methods. However, it is not fully effective since it relies on the construction year of the building, and on reliable but incomplete external resources describing some product references that were used in that period of time. Considering expert feedbacks, we know that the context in which a product is used can also be relevant to predict the presence of asbestos in this product (i.e., the characteristics of the building, the nature of the building components in which the product appears, other products used in the same component, etc.). Recently, the CSTB has made available a set of diagnoses conducted on a large number of buildings. These data have been represented using the Asbestos Ontology proposed in [8] and can be used to learn prediction rules. Many rule mining approaches have been proposed that can learn to classify data based on RDF descriptions [5,6,10]. However, none of them use the ontology semantics, the part-of relations, and the numerical built-in predicates that are needed to represent the context and the temporal constraints.

In this paper, we propose an ontology-based approach to discover rules that can be used to detect the products that contain asbestos in a building or not. The proposed approach focuses on rule premises that describe the product, its context, and the temporal constraints expressed as open intervals. The potentially relevant predicates that can appear in the context are declared by the expert and heuristics are defined to limit the search space when multi-valued part-of relations are exploited. Furthermore, general knowledge about how the asbestos usage evolves through time is exploited to generate the temporal interval.

The rest of this paper is organized as follows. In Sect. 2, we present related works. In Sect. 3, we describe the Asbestos Ontology. Then, in Sect. 4, we present our predictive approach. Section 5 presents the results obtained on a real data set of diagnoses. Finally, Sect. 6 draws conclusions and outlines the future research directions.

---

[2] Asbestos Research and Development Plan launched by the Department of Housing, Town Planning and Landscapes (DHUP), attached to the General Directorate of Planning, Housing and Nature (Minister of Housing and Sustainable Habitat).

[3] French Scientific and Technical Center for Building. http://www.cstb.fr/en/.

2 Related Work

In the context of Knowledge Graphs (KG), rule mining can be used to enrich graphs (by means of link or type prediction, adding new axioms, entity linking), or to detect erroneous RDF triples. To have scalability properties, most of the recent approaches for link or type predictions are based on deep learning methods and embedding that allow translating high-dimensional vectors into relatively low-dimensional spaces [11]. Nevertheless, other applications that need interpretable rules to understand and maintain some domain knowledge, are still in awe of discovering logical rules. Many approaches have addressed the problem of discovering first-order logic (FOL) rules over relational data [4,12] or texts [14]. However, different approaches and hypotheses are needed to discover rules in knowledge graphs. Indeed, data is generally incomplete and counter-examples are not always available (i.e., due to the open-world assumption, it cannot be assumed that a fact that is not in a KG is false). Besides, ontology semantics can be exploited when available. Some unsupervised approaches aim to discover graph patterns in voluminous RDF graphs without taking into account the ontology [6,10]. [6] uses an optimized generate and test strategy while controlling the search space by limiting the number of atoms that appear in the rule. [10] allows to discover FOL rules that may involve SWRL[4] built-in predicates to compare numerical or string values, and negation to identify contradictions. However, these values must be defined in the KG and associated with two variables of the rule. So, the approach does not allow us to discover a reference constant like "*age (X, a), a ≥ 18 → adult (X)*", which is one of the goals in our application. Both approaches are based on a Partial Completeness Assumption (PCA) implying that when at least one object is represented for one entity and one property, all the objects are represented, and others can be considered as counter-examples. The classification approaches based on FOLDT (First-order logical decision tree) such as TILDE [1] (Top-down induction of logical decision trees) are based on decision trees in which nodes can share variables and involve numerical predicates with threshold values. However, these latter approaches do not use the semantics of ontology in the exploration of the search space. Other approaches such as [2] can be guided by the ontology semantics to avoid constructing semantically redundant rules. However, the author has shown that the exploitation of reasoning capabilities during the learning process does not allow mining rules on large KGs.

Some approaches have focused on learning DL concept descriptions such as DL-FOCL [13], an optimization of DL-FOIL [3], or CELOE [7]. Such approaches are generally based on a separate-and-conquer strategy that builds a disjunct of partial solutions, where partial solutions are specialized using refinement operators, so that the description correctly cover as many positive instances as possible while ruling out all the negative ones. To learn expressive DL descriptions, they exploit refinement operators that return a specialization expressed through the $\mathcal{ALCO}$ operators (i.e., universal and existential restrictions on roles, intersec-

---

[4] https://www.w3.org/Submission/SWRL/.

tion, complement, union, one-of enumerations and roles with concrete domains). However, they do not allow to take into account class instance properties that change over time. [8] discovers rules that can predict the presence of asbestos considering the construction year of the building, but this statistic and semantic hybrid approach is based on incomplete external web resources that describe how the presence of asbestos in frequently used marketed products has evolved during the last century.

In this work, we aim to discover interpretable classification rules from positive and negative examples described in the Asbestos knowledge graph provided by the CSTB. These horn-clause rules will be used to evaluate the presence of asbestos (negative or positive) in a product. Since the marketed products that have been used in the buildings are unknown, the rules exploit a product's context defined by domain experts to express those elements of this context have a potential impact on the presence of asbestos : (1) part-of properties to take into account the building components and the others used products, (2) the building's construction year. Since the building's construction year can have an important impact on the presence of asbestos, a rule can use SWRL comparison operators to compare a variable year to the reference year (ex. SWRL:lowerThanOrEqual(YEAR, ref_year)) which is the reference year that maximizes the quality of the rule. None of the previously mentioned approaches allow exploiting the ontology and such built-in numerical predicates in the resulting rules. These rules will be transformed in SWRL so that the expert can predict the presence of asbestos in buildings using an existing reasoner.

3 Asbestos Ontology

In this section, we briefly present the upper part of the Asbestos Ontology (see Fig. 1) that has been proposed in [8] based on the CSTB documentation resources, expert knowledge and the needs in terms of prediction. The main concepts of this ontology are:

- Building: a construction characterized by a code (CSTB internal code that corresponds to a given type of building: school, housing, etc.), the building type, the construction year, an address.
- Structure: building subspace (e.g. balcony, staircase, roof, etc.).
- Location: indicates a basic element that belongs to a building structure (e.g., door, window, wall, etc.).
- Product: describes a product that can be used in the composition of locations (e.g., glue, coating, etc.). A product is described by its name.
- Diagnostic Characteristic : specifies the results of the existence of asbestos test when it exists. The value of *has_diagnostic* is "positive" when the product contains asbestos and "negative" otherwise.
- Predicted Characteristic : can be used to store that it is predicted that a product is asbestos-free or not.

The Asbestos Ontology describes 8 subclasses of structure, 19 subclasses of location and 38 subclasses of product.

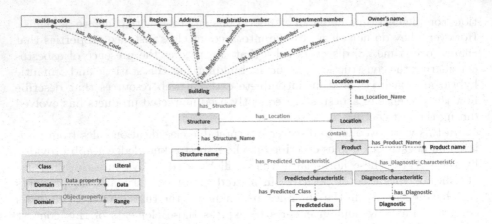

Fig. 1. Main concepts of the asbestos ontology

4   CRA-Miner Approach

In this section, we first describe the contextual rules for the asbestos prediction that we want to provide to experts to help them detect asbestos-containing materials in a building. We then present the CRA-Miner algorithm that generates these rules from the populated Asbestos Ontology.

4.1   Contextual Rules for Asbestos Prediction

A Contextual Rule for the prediction of Asbestos (CRA) is a conjunction of predicates that concludes on the presence or absence of Asbestos in a product P. We consider a context-free upper bound of the search space $\top$ that is defined as $product(P), has\_diagnostic\_characteristic(P, D) \rightarrow has\_diagnostic(D, Value)$. The set of contextual rules that can be constructed from $\top$ is defined using a conceptual context that is by default the whole ontology. However, a domain expert can delimit the context by choosing the classes and attributes that can impact the presence of asbestos. This selection can either be used to discard irrelevant ontology elements or to test new hypotheses. The chosen context, that corresponds to the language bias in Inductive Logic Programming (ILP) [9], will then be used to specialize a rule.

Definition 1. *(Conceptual context) A conceptual context CO is a sub-graph of the ontology, i.e. a subset of classes and properties, that specifies the ontology elements that can be used in the body of the rule.*

Example 1. Let's $CO = \{product, location, structure, contain, has\_location, has\_region, has\_year, has\_structure, has\_diagnostic\_characteristic\}$.

A contextual rule is based on the ontology vocabulary defined in the conceptual context and the specializations of the $SWRL : CompareTo$ predicate that can be added to introduce temporal constraints for the building year (i.e. open intervals):

Definition 2. *(Contextual rule) Let CO be a conceptual context, a contextual rule is a rule $\overrightarrow{B} \rightarrow h$, where $\overrightarrow{B} = \{B_1, B_2, ..., B_n\}$, and $\forall B_i \in \overrightarrow{B}, \exists B_j \in CO \cup \{SWRL : CompareTo\}$ s.t. $B_i \sqsubseteq B_j$ and h is the predicate has_diagnostic instanciated by the value "positive" or "negative".*

A contextual rule must be closed and connected as defined in rule mining approaches such as [6].

Example 2. A closed and connected rule that can be discovered using the context defined in Example 1 is:

$$glue(P),\ contain(L,\ P),\ has\_location(S,\ L),\ painting(P2),\ contain(L,\ P2),$$
$$has\_structure(B,\ S),\ has\_year(B,\ Y),\ has\_region(B,\ "Paris"),$$
$$lessThanOrEqual(Y,\ "1950"),\ has\_diagnostic\_characteristic(P,\ D)$$
$$\rightarrow has\_diagnostic(D,\ "positive")$$

This rule expresses that a glue that appears in a building located in Paris and constructed before 1950, when used in the same location as that of a painting, it contains asbestos.

Additional constraints are defined to reduce the search space complexity for multi-valued properties that describe part-of relations: *contain*, *has_location*, and *has_structure*.

First, the expert can define the maximum number of occurrences of co-located building components that can appear in the body of the rule : $maxSibS$ is used to define the maximum number of sibling structures, $maxSibL$ is the maximum number of sibling locations, and $maxSibP$ is the maximum number of sibling products.

Example 3. If the expert considers that the co-located structures cannot affect the presence of asbestos in P, then $maxSibS = 0$ and the approach will not build the following rule since the $S2$ structure should not be considered (sibling of $S1$ that contains the target product for the *has_structure* property):

$$Coating(P),\ contain(L,\ P),\ Location(L),\ has\_location(S1,\ L),$$
$$Vertical\_Separator(S1),\ has\_structure(B,\ S1),\ has\_structure(B,\ S2),\ Floor(S2)\ ,$$
$$has\_year(B,\ Y),\ has\_region(B,\ "Lyon"),\ SWRL:lessThanOrEqual(Y,\ "1963"),$$
$$has\_diagnostic\_characteristic(P,\ D)$$
$$\rightarrow has\_diagnostic(D,\ "positive")$$

Furthermore, the CSTB experts consider that only specific co-located components can affect the marketed product used for P and therefore the presence of asbestos. For instance, the presence of a coating in the same location than a target glue is not significant, while the presence of a floor coating can impact the marketed glue that has been used in this location. A similar hypothesis is assumed for locations and structures. Therefore, only the most specific classes can be added for sibling products, sibling locations or sibling structures involved in the considered part-of relations.

To evaluate the quality of a rule, we use the classical measures of *head coverage* [6] and *confidence* that has been defined in the relational setting.

The *head coverage* (*hc*) is the ratio between the support, i.e. the number of correct predictions $has\_diagnostic(D, \text{"positive"})$ (resp. $has\_diagnostic$ $(D, \text{"negative"})$) implied by the rule, and the number of diagnoses $has\_diagnostic$ $(D, \text{"positive"})$ (resp. $has\_diagnostic(D, \text{"negative"})$) that appear in the knowledge graph:

$$hc(\overrightarrow{B} \rightarrow has\_diagnostic(D, val)) = \frac{supp(\overrightarrow{B} \rightarrow has\_diagnostic(D, val))}{\#(D, val) : has\_diagnostic(D, val)}$$

The confidence (*conf*) is defined as the ratio between the support of the rule and the number of diagnoses that can participate to an instanciation of the body of the rule.

$$conf(\overrightarrow{B} \rightarrow has\_diagnostic(D, val)) = \frac{supp(\overrightarrow{B} \rightarrow has\_diagnostic(D, val))}{\#D : \exists X_1, ..., X_n : \overrightarrow{B}}$$

CRA-Miner aims to discover all the most general rules that conform with the defined language bias and such that $hc \geq minHc$ et $conf \geq minConf$.

4.2   Evolution of the Presence of Asbestos over Time

It has been shown in [8] that the number of marketed products that contain asbestos remains stable until 1972, and then decreases to zero in 1997 when its usage is prohibited in France. Indeed, these products have either become asbestos-free or their production has been discontinued. Thus even if the probability of asbestos varies depending on the class products, we know that this probability decreases over time. So if a contextual rule concludes on the absence of asbestos for a product used in a building constructed after a given year Y_1, the confidence can only increase for $Y_2 \geq Y_1$. This property is used to prune the search space when the predicate *greaterThanOrEqual* or *lessThanOrEqual* is generalized.

4.3   Algorithm CRA-Miner

The aim of the algorithm CRA-Miner is to generate from the positive and negative examples described in the KG all contextual rules such that $hc \geq minHc$ and $conf \geq minConf$. These rules will be used to predict the presence or absence of asbestos in products that have not been tested.

CRA-Miner is a top-down generate and test algorithm that specializes in the upper bound T of the search space by considering the hierarchy of product classes, and by adding temporal constraints, and constraints constructed using the conceptual context. The algorithm takes as input the knowledge graph, the language bias, the thresholds $minConf$ and $minHc$, and the thresholds $maxSibP$, $maxSibL$ and $maxSibS$ that are used to limit the number of co-located components that can be considered in the rule. The result is a set $\mathcal{CR}$ of contextual rules. The exploration of the search space is guided by the subsumption relations of the ontology (top-down exploration of the targeted products, their locations, and their structures) and the construction of the temporal constraints exploiting the fact that the number of products containing asbestos decreases over time.

At each specialization step, the generated rules that obtain a confidence value and a head coverage higher than the specified thresholds, and that improve the confidence value of the rule from which it is derived, are stored in $\mathcal{CR}$. For all the rules such that $conf = 1$ or $hc < minHc$, the specialization will stop.

We describe the algorithm's steps for the most general context that has been defined by the CSTB experts, in other words, the context CO defined in Example 1. In this context, the rule can predict the presence of asbestos in a product using the building's construction year, the region the building is located in, and all its types of components. The five specialization steps of the algorithm are as follows :

1- **Specialization of T with sub-classes of products**:
   During this step, we replace the class *product* by more specific classes (e.g. coating, glue, painting) to generate all the context-free rules that only depends on the type of product used. The top-down exploration stops when $hc < minHc$.

2- **Specialization with the temporal constraint**: For each context-free rule generated by the previous step, we add to the body of the rule the path of properties that is needed to reach the construction year from the target product P: $has\_location(S, L), contain(L, P), has\_structure(B, S), has\_year(B, Y)$. The predicate $SWRL:lowerThanOrEqual(Y, y)$ (for a rule that concludes on "positive") or $SWRL:greaterThanOrEqual(Y, y)$ (for "negative"), is also added to compare the construction year Y to a reference year y which maximizes the confidence and preserves $hc \geq minHc$.
   For example, if the rule R1 is generated in step 1:
   R1 : $coating(P), has\_diagnostic\_characteristic(P, D) \rightarrow has\_diagnostic(D, "positive")$. This rule can then be specialized as follows:
   R2 : $coating(P), has\_location(S, L), contain(L, P), has\_structure(B, S), has\_year(B, Y), SWRL:lowerThanOrEqual(Y, 1980), has\_diagnostic\_characteristic(P, D) \rightarrow has\_diagnostic(D, "positive")$
   To discover the best year value, CRA-Miner explores the possible values from the most recent year to the oldest one and considers the rules that conclude on "*negative*" and "*positive*" differently.
   In Fig. 2, we show how the confidence evolves between 1946 and 1997 for the rules that conclude on "*positive*" for a product class example. When the reference year decreases, hc decreases and the confidence increases. To cover the maximum number of diagnoses while maximizing the confidence, we stop the exploration when $hc < minHc$ (i.e. 1966 on the Fig. 2) and choose the previously explored year value such that $hc \geq minHc$ and the confidence

stays maximum (i.e. 1970 on the Fig. 2). A similar but symmetrical process is applied to choose y for the rules that conclude on *"negative"*.

3- **Specialization with location and/or structure subclasses** : The hierarchy of locations and structures is explored to specialize the rules generated with step 1 and 2 with specific building components that contains the target product P.

For example, the rule x can be specialized by specificying that the location is a *wall* and that the structure is a *balcony*:

R3 : *coating(P), wall(L), balcony(S), has_location(S, L), contain(L, P), has_structure(B, S), has_year(B, Y), SWRL:lowerThanOrEqual(Y, 1980), has_diagnostic_characteristic(P, D) → has_diagnostic(D, "positive")*

4- **Enrichment by the region** : All the generated rules are enriched by the datatype property 'has_region' which represents the region where the building is located.

5- **Specialization by co-located components**. During this step, new object properties are added that represents **sibling specific products, sibling specific locations or sibling specific structures** : $contain(L, P_i)$ and $C_p(P_i)$ where i varies from 0 to $maxSiblingP$ and C_p is a leaf of the product hierarchy, then $has\_location(S, L_j), C_l(L_j)$ where j varies from 0 to $maxSiblingL$ and C_L is a leaf of the product hierarchy), and $has\_structure(S, L_j), C_l(L_j)$ where j varies from 0 to $maxSiblingS$ and C_S .

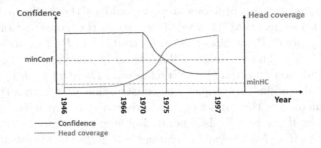

Fig. 2. Evolution of confidence and head coverage over time for the rules that conclude on "positive" for a class product example.

The number of generated and tested rules is mostly impacted by the temporal specialization (in the worst case the whole time interval will be tested) and the addition of co-located components (in the worst case all the possible combinations of co-located components will be checked). Despite this, CRA-Miner can be parallelized since each rule can be specialized independently from the others.

5   Experiments

We have evaluated our approach on a KG that has been populated using a set of diagnostic documents provided by the CSTB. This KG contains 51970 triples that describe 2998 product instances, 341 locations, 214 structures and 94 buildings. The construction year of those buildings varies between 1948 and 1997. We have 1525 products that contain asbestos and 1473 products are asbestos-free. All experiments were performed on a server with 80 physical processors (Intel Xeon E7-4830 2.20 GHz) and 528 GB of RAM.

The aim of the experimentation is (1) to learn rules on a subset of diagnostics and study the quality of the prediction that can be made on the remaining products (2) compare the results of our approach to a naive approach that only uses the product classes and the construction year (baseline) (3) compare the results of our approach with the two rule-mining approaches AMIE3 [6] and TILDE [1] (4) compare our results with an approach [8] that calculates asbestos probability using external resources (ANDEVA[5] and INRS[6]).

To evaluate our approach, we divided the KG data into 3 tiers, and we performed cross-validation. Since we have many different product classes, we set a low head-coverage threshold at $minHC = 0.001$ to observe as many rules as possible. Then we evaluated the results when $minConf$ varies from 0.6 to 0.9 using the classical precision, recall, F-Measure, and accuracy measures. The maximum number of siblings has been set at 0 for structures and at 3 for locations and products by the expert.

Table 1 shows that CRA-miner discovers 75 rules on average. The results show that co-located components are effectively exploited to predict the presence of asbestos: 29 rules involve at least a sibling product (maximum 2 sibling products) and 17 rules involve sibling locations (maximum 3 locations). Furthermore, the results shows that CRA-miner has discovered 14 rules that exploit a temporal constraint.

We have adhered to a pessimistic approach that chooses to classify a product as positive if at least one rule concludes that it contains asbestos.

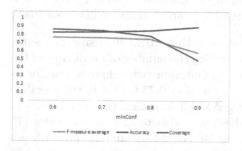

Fig. 3. CRA-Miner results according to $minConf$ threshold

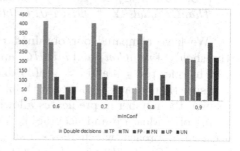

Fig. 4. Detailed CRA-Miner results according to $minConf$ thresholds

---

[5] National Association for the Defense of Asbestos Victims http://andeva.free.fr/ expositions/gt_expos_produits.htm.
[6] National Institute of Research and Security http://www.inrs.fr.

Figure 3 presents the average F-measure, accuracy, and coverage (i.e. ratio of products that can be classified in the testing set) when $minConf$ varies. These results suggest that when the $minConf$ threshold increases, the accuracy increases but the data coverage decreases. The best F-measure average 0.77 (average between the positive's and negative's F-measure) is obtained for a $minConf$ fixed to 0.6. With such a threshold, we can decide for 87% of the test samples. Figure 4 details results (TN, TP, FN, FP, unclassified negative: UN, unclassified positive: UP) as well as the number of products that have been classified as positive and negative by different rules (double decisions). More precisely, the true positives TP (resp. true negatives TN) are the products that contain asbestos classified by the discovered rules as positive (resp. negative). The false positives FP (resp. false negative FN) are the asbestos-free products classified by the rules as positives, while the unclassified products are either positives (UP) or asbestos-free (UN) in the KG. This figure shows that a threshold fixed to 0.6 leads to an average of only 82 contradictory decisions for test samples that describe a thousand products.

We have compared the contextual CRA-Miner approach with a non-contextual baseline that is only based on the product class to mine rules. This baseline allows us to estimate the benefits of taking into account the hierarchy of products and the context in which they have been used (i.e., the location type and other products used in the same location). Figure 5 shows that the F-measure and the coverage are lower for the baseline approach regardless of the $minConf$ threshold that is varying from 0.6 to 0.9. In particular, Table 1 shows that the baseline only classifies 46% of the test samples and obtains a F-measure average of 0.55. Indeed, CRA-miner allows to discover complex rules such as:

plaster_or_cement_based_coating(?P), has_location(?S, ?L), contain(?L, ?P), smoothing_bubbling_leveling_plasters(?P2), contain(?L, ?P2), has_structure (?B, ?S), has_year(?B, ?Y), has_diagnostic_characteristic(?P, ?D) , less-ThanOrEqual(?Y, "1991-01-01T00:00:00") → has_Diagnosis(?D, "positive")

We have compared our obtained results with AMIE3 [6] using the same thresholds of $minConf$ and $minHC$, and setting the number of predicates of the sought rules to $l = 4$ and $l = 6$ (cf. Table 1)[7]. Our approach achieves a better F-measure than what is obtained with [6] (0.77 against 0.73 for $l = 6$, the specified l being the number of predicates allowing AMIE3 to obtain the best results in terms of F-Measure and accuracy). AMIE3 was able to discover 91 rules (75 with our approach) which allows it to cover 99% of the test data (87% with our approach). On the other hand, it obtains a lower accuracy (0.74 compared to 0.83 with CRA-Miner). This important coverage is accompanied by numerous double decisions (277). The approach is pessimistic (i.e., if a product is associated with two different decisions, it considered the product as one containing asbestos), AMIE3 finds more TP (473 against 415 with CRA-Miner) but almost twice as much FP (226 against 121 with CRA-Miner), and TNs are also less numerous

---

[7] Despite the fact that AMIE3 is used to search only for conclusive rules on *has_Diagnosis*, a length > 6 does not yield results in less than three weeks.

(only 264 against 303 with CRA-Miner). Having a semantic context and being able to represent time intervals makes it possible to discover rules that involve more atoms while improving their readability for an expert in the field (more precisely, a rule can be defined for a time interval while AMIE3 can only generate rules involving a specific year).

Additionally, we tested our language bias using the TILDE system [1] that generates relational decision trees which allow representing complex language bias emulating similar target languages (relational context and maxSibling values) and handling (although not optimally) a hierarchy of types. The relational context used is slightly different, only imposing at least one instantiated type in the context (not necessarily the product). This top-down strategy obtains by definition a coverage of 100% without double decisions but leads to a lower precision for the positive and negative examples. Indeed, it gets more FP and FN since the last general rule classifies all the unclassified remaining individuals as positive or negative whatever its description is. CRA-Miner was not able to classify all examples (87%) but the obtained accuracy is higher (0.83 against 0.51 for TILDE). Given the strategy of TILDE, it was not possible to use the inequalities on years, because introducing this possibility yields the possibility to learn closed intervals on years and an overfitting that is difficult to control.

We have also compared CRA-Miner to the hybrid approach used in [8]. This approach uses two external resources that describe marketed products that contained asbestos during at least one period to compute a probability based on the product class and the construction year. Table 1 shows that [8] obtains a higher F-measure and accuracy in particular for positive products (0.94 against 0.79 for CRA-Miner). This can be explained by the additional information provided by the web resources that focus on positive products. However, CRA-Miner could cover more data samples (87% against 83% for the hybrid). Indeed, the hybrid approach could not decide on a product if its class was not mentioned in the external resources.

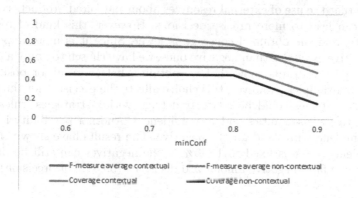

Fig. 5. Comparison between contextual and non-contextual approaches according to minConf thresholds

Table 1. Comparison between CRA-Miner, AMIE3 with $l = 4$ et $l = 6$ (minHC=0.001, minConf=0.6), TILDE, the baseline approach, and the hybrid approach

System classification	Rule mining systems					Systems based on external resources
System	CRA-Miner	AMIE3 $l = 4$	AMIE3 $l = 6$	TILDE	Baseline	Hybrid
# rules	75	45	91	34	24	/
Double decision	82	50	277	0	0	0
TP	415	381	473	424	146	465
TN	303	288	264	88	257	348
FP	121	146	226	359	30	16
FN	28	74	32	127	24	5
UP	66	54	3	0	338	38
UN	67	58	0	0	204	127
Pos. precision	**77%**	72%	68%	54%	83%	97%
Pos. recall	82%	75%	**93%**	77%	29%	92%
Pos. F-measure	**0,79**	0,73	**0,79**	0.63	0,43	0.94
Neg. precision	**92%**	80%	89%	41%	91%	99%
Neg. recall	**62%**	59%	54%	20%	52%	71%
Neg. F-measure	**0,74**	0,68	0,67	0.27	0,66	0.83
Avr. F-mesure	**0,77**	0,71	0,73	0.45	0,55	0.89
Accuracy	**0,83**	0,75	0,74	0.51	0,88	0.97
Coverage	87%	89%	**100%**	**100%**	46%	83%

These experiments have first shown that all the predicates of the context selected by the expert are relevant to classifying the product. Indeed, the baseline obtains a very low recall, and the results show that all the predicates have been used in at least one rule. The comparison with the other two available rule-mining systems illustrates that CRA-Miner obtains the best precision values, with a lower but still high value of coverage (87%). As expected, the experiments also show that the use of external resources about marketed products containing asbestos can lead to more precise decisions. However, this kind of resource is incomplete, and the obtained coverage is lower. Since it is more important to detect positive examples than negative ones, we have chosen to apply a pessimist strategy, and the results show that we obtain a better recall for positive than for negative examples. However, this choice affects the precision for the positives and other strategies could be considered (e.g., voting strategies, rules ordered according to their semantics and/or confidence). Another possibility is to use a higher confidence threshold for the negative. The results have shown that when the confidence value is fixed to 1, 43% of the negatives can still be discovered with only one false negative among 210 decisions (99.52% of precision).

6   Conclusion

In this paper, we presented the CRA-Miner rule discovery approach which can predict the presence of asbestos in products based on a semantic context, heuristics dedicated to part-of relations, and computed constraints on numerical values that represent temporal information. The experiments show that we can obtain a better precision and accuracy than two other rule-mining systems and better coverage than an approach based on external resources.

In the future, we plan to investigate the combination of CRA-Miner with the approach in [8] (that uses external resources) to enable decisions for the undefined individuals and improve the data coverage. Since results of our approach will be used by asbestos experts to select which products have the strongest priority to get tested, we also need to rank the positive, unclassified, and negative products according to the applied rules and define an interface that can present and explain this ranking to the experts. Besides, we plan to generalize CRA-Miner to fit different problems that involve part-of relations and temporal constraints (such as prediction of adverse events for treatments composed of several drugs in pharmacology). The idea is to follow the model of TILDE [1] where the language bias is declarative but the algorithm is generic (i.e., not ontology-based).

References

1. Blockeel, H., De Raedt, L.: Top-down induction of first-order logical decision trees. Artif. Intell. **101**(1–2), 285–297 (1998)
2. d'Amato, C., Tettamanzi, A.G.B., Minh, T.D.: Evolutionary discovery of multi-relational association rules from ontological knowledge bases. In: Blomqvist, E., Ciancarini, P., Poggi, F., Vitali, F. (eds.) EKAW 2016. LNCS (LNAI), vol. 10024, pp. 113–128. Springer, Cham (2016). https://doi.org/10.1007/978-3-319-49004-5_8
3. Fanizzi, N., d'Amato, C., Esposito, F.: DL-FOIL concept learning in description logics. In: Železný, F., Lavrač, N. (eds.) ILP 2008. LNCS (LNAI), vol. 5194, pp. 107–121. Springer, Heidelberg (2008). https://doi.org/10.1007/978-3-540-85928-4_12
4. Fürnkranz, J., Kliegr, T.: A brief overview of rule learning. In: Bassiliades, N., Gottlob, G., Sadri, F., Paschke, A., Roman, D. (eds.) RuleML 2015. LNCS, vol. 9202, pp. 54–69. Springer, Cham (2015). https://doi.org/10.1007/978-3-319-21542-6_4
5. Hamilton, W.L., Ying, R., Leskovec, J.: Representation learning on graphs: methods and applications. IEEE Data Eng. Bull. **40**(3), 52–74 (2017). http://sites.computer.org/debull/A17sept/p52.pdf
6. Lajus, J., Galárraga, L., Suchanek, F.: Fast and exact rule mining with AMIE 3. In: Harth, A., et al. (eds.) ESWC 2020. LNCS, vol. 12123, pp. 36–52. Springer, Cham (2020). https://doi.org/10.1007/978-3-030-49461-2_3
7. Lehmann, J., Auer, S., Bühmann, L., Tramp, S.: Class expression learning for ontology engineering. J. Web Semant. **9**(1), 71–81 (2011)
8. Mecharnia, T., Khelifa, L.C., Pernelle, N., Hamdi, F.: An approach toward a prediction of the presence of asbestos in buildings based on incomplete temporal descriptions of marketed products. In: Kejriwal, M., Szekely, P.A., Troncy, R. (eds.) K-CAP 2019, Marina Del Rey, CA, USA, 19–21 November 2019, pp. 239–242. ACM (2019)
9. Muggleton, S., Raedt, L.D.: Inductive logic programming: theory and methods. J. Log. Program. **19**(20), 629–679 (1994)
10. Ortona, S., Meduri, V.V., Papotti, P.: Robust discovery of positive and negative rules in knowledge bases. In: 2018 IEEE 34th International Conference on Data Engineering (ICDE), pp. 1168–1179 (2018)

11. Paulheim, H., Tresp, V., Liu, Z.: Representation learning for the semantic web. J. Web Semant. **61–62**, 100570 (2020)
12. Quinlan, J.R.: Learning logical definitions from relations. Mach. Learn. **5**, 239–266 (1990)
13. Rizzo, G., Fanizzi, N., d'Amato, C.: Class expression induction as concept space exploration: from dl-foil to dl-focl. Future Gener. Comput. Syst. **108**, 256–272 (2020)
14. Schoenmackers, S., Davis, J., Etzioni, O., Weld, D.S.: Learning first-order horn clauses from web text. In: Proceedings of the 2010 Conference on Empirical Methods in Natural Language Processing, EMNLP 2010, 9–11 October 2010, MIT Stata Center, Massachusetts, USA, A meeting of SIGDAT, a Special Interest Group of the ACL, pp. 1088–1098. ACL (2010)

Temporal Sequence Mining Using FCA and GALACTIC

Salah Eddine Boukhetta[✉], Christophe Demko, Karell Bertet,
Jérémy Richard, and Cécile Cayère

Laboratory L3i, La Rochelle University, La Rochelle, France
salah.boukhetta@univ-lr.fr

Abstract. In this paper, we are interested in temporal sequential data analysis using `GALACTIC`, a new framework based on Formal Concept Analysis (FCA) for calculating a concept lattice from heterogeneous and complex data. Inspired by pattern structure theory, `GALACTIC` mines data described by predicates and is composed of a system of plugins for an easy integration of new data characteristics and their descriptions. Here we use the `GALACTIC` library to analyse temporal sequential data, where each item x_i in the sequence has an associated timestamp t_i: $s = \langle (t_i, x_i) \rangle_{i \leq n}$. We introduce descriptions and strategies dedicated to temporal sequences, and new unsupervised measures. We show on some datasets that the distance constraint subsequence strategy allows to generate good concept lattices.

Keywords: Formal concept analysis · Lattice · Pattern structures · Temporal sequences · Maximal common subsequences · Distance constraint

1 Introduction

Sequences appear in many areas: sequences of words in a text, trajectories, surfing the internet, or buying products in a supermarket. A sequence is a succession $\langle x_i \rangle$ of symbols or sets. Sequence mining aims at finding frequent patterns in a dataset of sequences and is studied since the early stages of pattern mining.

GSP algorithm [35], one of the first algorithms, has been proposed several decades ago. Others algorithms have then been proposed to improve GSP, such as PrefixSpan [33], SPADE [42]. These algorithms take as input a dataset of sequences and a minimum support threshold, and generate all frequent sequential patterns. Closed patterns, that represent the same information in a reduced form, give raises to more efficient approaches to extract closed sequential patterns, that are maximal subsequences, such as CloSpan [40], BIDE [38]. Pattern constraints propose to extract the patterns verifying input constraints such as a maximal subsequence size, a regexp, a gap between items, a given sub-pattern [3,37]. Some heuristics for a non exhaustive exploration of the search space of patterns have also been proposed in order to reduce the number of patterns. CSSampling [13]

© Springer Nature Switzerland AG 2021
T. Braun et al. (Eds.): ICCS 2021, LNAI 12879, pp. 185–199, 2021.
https://doi.org/10.1007/978-3-030-86982-3_14

is a pattern sampling approach. Others approaches propose to better summarize the data using machine learning [30,36].

We are interested in temporal sequences $\langle (x_i, t_i) \rangle$ where the item x_i is associated with a timestamp t_i. The temporal information may improve the expressiveness of patterns, and the challenge is then to extract sequential patterns with temporal information. Timestamped patterns are not interesting since they are too reductive. This is why intervals are introduced, representing a gap or a delay between items. For example, $(a, [s, e], b)$ denotes a sequential pattern (a, b) that frequently occurs with a delay or a transition time in the interval $[s, e]$. Chronicles were introduced in [15], where the interval represents a delay between items, and the issue is to discover all possible time constraints. A chronicle can obviously be represented by a graph. In a recent and complete state of the art, Guyet [21] has identified two kinds of issue in temporal pattern mining. A first issue is a complete temporal relation discovery, as for example a complete discovery of chronicles [11,34]. The second issue aims to extract patterns where the temporal information is added to subsequence patterns extracted by classical sequence mining approaches, that correspond to "linear" chronicles, as in the FACE system [14] and in [24]. Let us also cite [19,41] that proposes to extract the representative values of transition using clustering methods. Guyet also propose NegPSpan [23] to extract negative sequential patterns and QTempIntMiner [22] to extract temporal information.

More recently, some sequence mining approaches are positioned in the Formal Concept Analysis (FCA) framework, based on the formalism of pattern structures [17,28]. FCA appears in 1982 [39], then in the Ganter and Wille's 1999 work [18], where the notion of concept, concept lattice and rules issued from binary data are formally defined and studied. FCA is a branch of applied lattice theory that appeared in the book of Barbut and Monjardet in 1970 [1], the closure operator is identified as a central notion to establish links between binary data, lattices and basis of rules [2]. The formalism of pattern structures [17] and abstract conceptual navigation [16] extends FCA to deal with non-binary data, where data is described by common patterns. In [9], the authors introduce Closed Partial Orders (CPO) as a graph for sequential data where each path in the graph represents a sequential pattern. Some approaches aim at discovering and building CPO patterns using FCA. Let us also cite RCA-Seq in [32] that extends RCA to mine sequential data. We can mention works for mining medical care trajectories [7], sequence mining to discover rare patterns [10], and studies on demographic sequences [20].

However, pattern lattices are huge, often intractable [27], and the need for approaches to drive the search towards the most relevant patterns is a current challenge. Indeed, with two decades of research on sequence mining and the increase of data and computational power, sequence mining algorithms are now more effective for processing huge databases of sequences. The problem turns from the deluge of data to the deluge of patterns, and recent studies are more focused on the mining of less but meaningful patterns.

Inspired by pattern structures, the NEXTPRIORITYCONCEPT algorithm, introduced in a recent article [12] proposes a user-driven pattern mining approach for heterogeneous and complex data as input with different strategies of exploration aiming at reducing the number of concepts while maintaining the lattice property. This algorithm allows a generic pattern computation through specific *descriptions* of objects by predicates. It also proposes to reduce a concept by the refinement of a concept into a fewer one through specific user exploration *strategies*, resulting in a reduction of the number of generated concepts in the whole lattice. In a recent work [5,6], authors proposed a new sequence mining approach using the NEXTPRIORITYCONCEPT algorithm, the *description* corresponds to maximal common subsequences, and several *strategies* are proposed, from the naive one generating all the possible patterns, to more specific strategies reducing the number of patterns.

In this article, we propose a new temporal sequence mining approach using the NEXTPRIORITYCONCEPT algorithm, with descriptions and strategies dedicated to temporal sequences. We extract closed patterns composed of maximal common distantial subsequences, that correspond to linear chronicles, with an interval representing a possible delay between two consecutive items. We also propose three strategies of pattern exploration, the naive, the step and the middle one. While the Naive strategy generates all the possible patterns, the Step and the Middle strategies aim to reduce the patterns in a pattern discovery approach. In order to evaluate the obtained pattern lattice, we introduce new unsupervised quality measures: the global logarithmic stability, the representability and the distinctiveness. Section 2 introduces basic definitions related to temporal and distantial sequences and a short description of the NEXTPRIORITYCONCEPT algorithm. Section 3 is dedicated to the definition of descriptions, strategies, and quality measures. Experimental results are presented in Sect. 4.

2   Preliminaries

2.1   Temporal Sequences

A **sequence** $s = \langle x_i \rangle_{i \leq n}$ is a succession of items x_i from an alphabet Σ, where $x_i \in \Sigma$. A **temporal sequence** $s = \langle (t_i, x_i) \rangle_{i \leq n}$, is a sequence where each item x_i is associated with a timestamp t_i. To avoid confusion when dealing with several sequences, we will introduce the notation, $s = \langle (t_i^s, x_i^s) \rangle_{i \leq n_s}$. A **distantial sequence** $d(s)$ of a temporal sequence s, is defined by $d(s) = \langle (x_i, \lfloor d_i \rceil), (x_n) \rangle_{i < n}$ with $d_i = t_{i+1} - t_i$. The example in Table 1 is a part of a dataset representing daily actions of individuals of the L3i laboratory[1], where the timestamp indicates an hour in the day and daily actions can be: $\Sigma = \{Wakeup(Wa), Breakfast(B), Work(Wo), Dinner(D), Coffee(C), Lunch(L), Sports(Sp), Read(R), Sleep(Sl)\}$. The distantial sequence of $s1$ is $d(s_1) = \langle (Wa, 1), (B, ?), (L, 6), (D) \rangle$ meaning that the individual 1, woke up, 1 h after he had his Breakfast, then after 2 h he had lunch, and after 6 h he takes his Dinner.

Maximal common subsequences are an immediate description of a set of sequences [5] issued from the subsequence relation, we extend it to distantial

---

[1] https://l3i.univ-larochelle.fr/.

Table 1. Daily actions examples

Id	Temporal sequences	Distantial subsequence
s_1	$\langle(\mathbf{11},\mathbf{Wa}),(\mathbf{12},\mathbf{B}),(\mathbf{14},\mathbf{L}),(\mathbf{20},\mathbf{D})\rangle$	$\langle(Wa,1),(B,2),(L,6),(D)\rangle$
s_2	$\langle(\mathbf{10},\mathbf{Wa}),(\mathbf{11},\mathbf{B}),(\mathbf{14},\mathbf{L}),(20,Sp),(21,R),(\mathbf{22},\mathbf{D})\rangle$	$\langle(Wa,1),(B,3),(L,8),(D)\rangle$
s_3	$\langle(\mathbf{8},\mathbf{Wa}),(9,Wo),(10,C),(\mathbf{11},\mathbf{B}),(\mathbf{13},\mathbf{L}),(14,Sp),(\mathbf{21},\mathbf{D})\rangle$	$\langle(Wa,3),(B,2),(L,8),(D)\rangle$
s_4	$\langle(\mathbf{7},\mathbf{Wa}),(\mathbf{8},\mathbf{B}),(9,Wo),(\mathbf{13},\mathbf{L}),(\mathbf{20},\mathbf{D}),(22,Sl)\rangle$	$\langle(Wa,1),(B,5),(L,7),(D)\rangle$
s_5	$\langle(\mathbf{8},\mathbf{Wa}),(\mathbf{9},\mathbf{B}),(\mathbf{14},\mathbf{L}),(18,Sp),(\mathbf{21},\mathbf{D}),(23,Sl)\rangle$	$\langle(Wa,1),(B,5),(L,7),(D)\rangle$

subsequences. A sequence $a = \langle x_i^a \rangle_{i \leq n_a}$ is **subsequence** of a sequence $b = \langle x_i^b \rangle_{i \leq n_b}$ if there are integers $1 \leq i_0 < \cdots < i_{n_a} \leq n_b$ such that $x_j^a = x_{i_j}^b$ for $j \leq n_a$, and we write $a \sqsubseteq_s b$. For two temporal sequences $a = \langle(t_i^a, x_i^a)\rangle_{i \leq n_a}$, and $b = \langle(t_i^b, x_i^b)\rangle_{i \leq n_b}$, the distantial sequence $d(a) = \langle(x_i^a, \lfloor d_i^a \rfloor),(x_{n_a}^a)\rangle_{i < n_a}$ is a **distantial subsequence** of $d(b) = \langle(x_i^b, \lfloor d_i^b \rfloor),(x_{n_b}^b)\rangle_{i < n_b}$, and we write $d(a) \sqsubseteq_d d(b)$ if $\langle x_j^a \rangle \sqsubseteq_s \langle x_i^b \rangle$ and $d_j^a = t_{i_{j+1}}^b - t_{i_j}^b$ with $j < n_a$. For example, $s_1' = \langle(9,Wa),(12,L),(18,D)\rangle$, with $d(s_1') = \langle(Wa,\lfloor 3 \rfloor),(L,\lfloor 6 \rfloor),(D)\rangle$ is a distantial subsequence of $d(s_1)$ in Table 1.

For a set of temporal sequences A, exact distantial subsequences may be rare because the elements of the subsequences must appear all after the same amount of time. To extend this to **Common Distantial Subsequences** $CDS(A)$, we introduce the interval $\lfloor d_i^{min}, d_i^{max} \rceil$ of possible distances between items:

$$CDS(A) = \{r = \langle(x_i^r, \lfloor d_i^{r,min}, d_i^{r,max} \rceil),(x_{n_r})\rangle_{i < n_r}\} \text{ where:} \tag{1}$$

- $r \sqsubseteq_s a \ \forall a \in A$
- $d_i^{r,min} = min(\{d_i^k : k \sqsubseteq_d a, \forall a \in A\})$
- $d_i^{r,max} = max(\{d_i^k : k \sqsubseteq_d a, \forall a \in A\})$

In Table 1, $r = \langle(Wa, \lfloor 1,3 \rceil),(B, \lfloor 2,5 \rceil),(L, \lfloor 6,8 \rceil),(D)\rangle$, is a common distantial subsequence of all the sequences, meaning that all people have Breakfast after 1 to 3 h from Wakeup, and after 2 to 5 h they have lunch.

2.2 The NextPriorityConcept Algorithm

The NextPriorityConcept algorithm [12] computes concepts for heterogeneous and complex data for a set of objects G. It is inspired by Bordat's algorithm [4], also found in Linding's work [31], that recursively computes the immediate predecessors of a concept, starting with the top concept $(G, \delta(G))$ containing the whole set of objects, until no more concepts can be generated. The use of a priority queue ensures that each concept is generated before its predecessors, and a mechanism of propagation of constraints ensures that meets will be computed. NextPriorityConcept computes a concept lattice and therefore is positioned in the FCA framework, its main characteristics are:

Descriptions as an application generating predicates The algorithm introduces the notion of *description* δ as an application to provide predicates describing a set of objects $A \subseteq G$. Each concept $(A, \delta(A))$ is composed of a subset of objects A and a set of predicates $\delta(A)$ describing them, corresponding to their pattern. Such generic use of predicates makes it possible to consider heterogeneous data as input, i.e., numerical, discrete or more complex data. A concept $(A, \delta(A))$ can be interpreted as a generalized convex hull, where each line corresponds to a predicate, and the elements inside the hull correspond to the objects A that verify all the predicates. Unlike classical pattern structures, predicates are not globally computed in a preprocessing step, but locally for each concept as the border lines of a convex hull.

Strategies as an application generating selectors The algorithm also introduces the notion of *strategy* σ to provide predicates called *selectors* describing candidates for an object reduction of a concept $(A, \delta(A))$ i.e., for predecessors of $(A, \delta(A))$ in the pattern lattice. A selector proposes a way to refine the description $\delta(A)$ for a reduced set $A' \subset A$ of objects. Several strategies are possible to generate predecessors of a concept, going from the naive strategy classically used in FCA that considers all the possible predecessors, to strategies allowing to obtain few predecessors and smaller lattices. Selectors are only used for the predecessors generation, they are not kept either in the description or in the final set of predicates. Therefore, choosing or testing several strategies at each iteration in a user-driven pattern discovery approach would be interesting.

The main result in [12] states that the NEXTPRIORITYCONCEPT algorithm computes the formal context $\langle G, P, I_P \rangle$ and its concept lattice (where P is the set of predicates describing the objects in G, and $I_P = \{(a, p),\ a \in G, p \in P\ :\ p(a)\}$ is the relation between objects and predicates) if description δ verifies $\delta(A) \sqsubseteq \delta(A')$ for $A' \subseteq A$. The run-time of the NEXTPRIORITYCONCEPT algorithm has a complexity $O(|\mathcal{B}|\,|G|\,|P|^2\,(c_\sigma + c_\delta))$ (where $\mathcal{B}$ is the number of concepts, c_σ is the cost of the strategy and c_δ is the cost of the description), and a space memory in $O(w\,|P|^2)$ (where w is the width of the concept lattice).

3 NEXTPRIORITYCONCEPT for Temporal Sequences

In order to mine temporal sequences using the NEXTPRIORITYCONCEPT algorithm, we have to define descriptions and strategies for a set G of temporal sequences as input whose size is smaller than n:

A description δ is a mapping $\delta : 2^G \to 2^P$ which defines a set of predicates $\delta(A)$ describing any subset $A \subseteq G$ of temporal sequences.

A strategy σ] is a mapping $\sigma : 2^G \to 2^P$ which defines a set of selectors $\sigma(A)$ to select strict subset $A' \subset A$ as predecessor candidates of any concept $(A, \delta(A))$ in the pattern lattice.

Predicates and selectors are computed using the subsequence relation in the form "*is a temporal subsequence of*". For better readability, the sets $\delta(A)$ and $\sigma(A)$ will be treated either as sets of predicates/selectors, or as sets of subsequences, they can reciprocally be deduced from each other.

3.1   Description for Temporal Sequences

The maximal common distance subsequences $CDS(A)$ of a set of temporal sequences A represents an obvious description $\delta_D(A)$. This description may then be parameterized with two constraints. A sliding `window` constraint, that is used to limit the search of subsequences to a specific part of temporal sequences. For example, if we want to analyse tourists data and get the essential activities per day, we could use a window of 24 h. And a maximal `gap` constraint defines the maximal distance allowed between two items in the subsequence. Formally, a distantial description is defined for a set of temporal sequences $A \subseteq G$ by:

Distantial description

$$\delta_D(A) = \{p = \langle (x_i^p, \lfloor d_i^{p,min}, d_i^{p,max} \rceil), (x_n^p) \rangle_{i<n_p} : p \in CDS(A), p \text{ maximal}\} \tag{2}$$

Window constraint. For $A \subseteq G$ and a window w:

$$\delta_{Dw}(A, w) = \{p \quad : \quad p \in \delta_D(A) \text{ and } \sum_{i=0}^{n-1} d_i^{p,max} \leq w\} \tag{3}$$

Gap constraint. For $A \subseteq G$ and a gap g:

$$\delta_{Dg}(A, g) = \{p \quad : \quad p \in \delta_D(A) \text{ and } d_i^{p,max} \leq g, \text{ for } 0 \leq i < n\} \tag{4}$$

To compute the description of a set A of temporal sequences, we iterate on the sequences of A, and update the resulting subsequences of $\delta_D(A)$ with the common parts. Therefore the complexity of the description is $c_{\delta_D} = O(s|A|\, log(|A|)) \leq O(s|G|\, log(|G|))$ where s is the maximal size of the computed subsequences. To ensure that the NEXTPRIORITYCONCEPT algorithm generates a concept lattice, any descriptions must verify $\delta(A) \sqsubseteq \delta(A')$ for $A' \subseteq A$:

Proposition 1. *For $A' \subseteq A \subseteq G$, we have $\delta_D(A) \sqsubseteq \delta_D(A')$*

Proof: Let A and A' be two subsets of sequences such that $A' \subseteq A$. Let $c \in \delta_D(A)$, i.e., c is a maximal common distantial domain subsequence of A. From $A' \subseteq A$ we can deduce that c is also a subsequence of sequences in A', but c is not necessarily a maximal distantial subsequence for A'. If c is a maximal subsequence in A' then $c \in \delta_D(A')$. Otherwise, there exists $c' \in \delta_D(A')$ such that c is a subsequence of c'. In these two cases, we can deduce that, $\delta_D(A) \sqsubseteq \delta_D(A')$.   □

3.2   Strategies and Selectors for Temporal Sequences

Strategies are used by the NEXTPRIORITYCONCEPT algorithm to refine each concept $(A, \delta(A))$ into concepts with fewer objects (sequences) and more specific descriptions. It may generate subsequences with more elements as for classical sequences or with shorter distances between elements exploiting the distance information. We define three strategies: The STEP strategy generates subsequences by subtracting a step distance from distances between elements. The NAIVE strategy generates all possible distantial subsequences. The MIDDLE strategy generates subsequences by dividing the distances by two.

Step Distance Strategy. For $A \subseteq G$ and a step st:

$$\sigma_{\mathrm{SDS}}(A, st) = X \cup Y \cup Z \text{ where} \tag{5}$$

$$X = \{s : \langle x_i^s \rangle = \langle x_i^p \rangle, \forall p \in \delta_{\mathrm{D}}(A) \text{ and } d_i^{s,min} = d_i^{p,min} + st\} \tag{6}$$

$$Y = \{s : \langle x_i^s \rangle = \langle x_i^p \rangle, \forall p \in \delta_{\mathrm{D}}(A) \text{ and } d_i^{s,max} = d_i^{p,max} - st\} \tag{7}$$

$$Z = \{s' : s' = p + x : x \in \Sigma\} \tag{8}$$

The STEP strategy reduces the distance between elements. By changing the step we subtract more from distances to get less predecessors. The greater the step is, the fewer selectors, and thus less predecessors will be generated.

Naive Distance Strategy. The NAIVE strategy is defined for a step $st = 1$.

$$\sigma_{\mathrm{NDS}}(A) = \sigma_{\mathrm{SDS}}(A, 1) \tag{9}$$

Middle Distance Strategy. The step is the middle of the distances:

$$\sigma_{\mathrm{MDS}}(A) = \{s : s \in \sigma_{\mathrm{SDS}}(A, M), M = (d_i^{s,max} - d_i^{s,min})/2\} \tag{10}$$

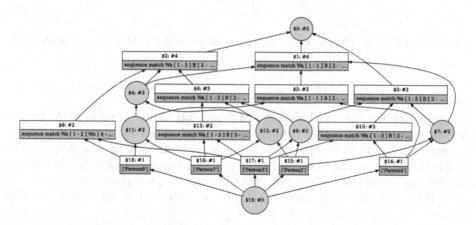

Fig. 1. Reduced concept lattice for NAIVE strategy and the DISTANTIAL description.

Figure 1 shows the reduced concept lattice generated with the NAIVE strategy $\sigma_{\mathrm{NDS}}(A)$ and the distantial description $\delta_{\mathrm{D}}(A)$ for our example. Each concept $(A, \delta_{\mathrm{D}}(A))$ is composed of a set A of sequences, together with their maximal common distantial subsequences $\delta_{\mathrm{D}}(A)$. The lattice contains 20 concepts. The concept \$1 has concepts \$4, \$5 and \$7 as predecessors, that share the same subsequence $\langle Wa, B, L, D \rangle$ with different distances between elements (see Table 2).

The NAIVE strategy generates all possible subsequences. Figure 2 shows the lattice obtained with the MIDDLE strategy and the distantial description. The lattice is composed of 10 concepts. Concept \$1, is a direct predecessor of the top concept, it contains the description: *sequence match* $Wa[1 - 3]B[2 - 5]L[1 - 6]S[2 - 7]D$, while the same description was generated in concept 6 with the NAIVE strategy.

Table 2. Some concepts of the lattice generated using σ_{NDS} and δ_{D}

Id concept	Description
$1	sequence match $\langle Wa[1-1]B[2-5]L[6-8]D\rangle$
$4	sequence match $\langle Wa[1-1]B[3-5]L[6-8]D\rangle$
$5	sequence match $\langle Wa[1-1]B[2-5]L[6-7]D\rangle$
$7	sequence match $\langle Wa[1-1]B[2-3]L[6-8]D\rangle$

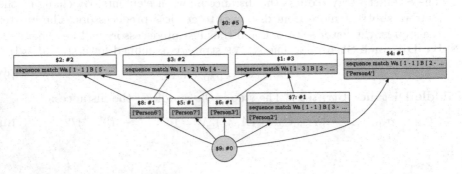

Fig. 2. Reduced concept lattice for MIDDLE strategy and the DISTANTIAL description.

3.3   Measures

There are few unsupervised measures of the quality of concepts. In FCA the well known stability measure [29] computes how much a concept is stable, i.e., how a concept depends on its objects, to preserve the same description. A concept is stable if its description does not depend much on particular objects. *As the idea behind stability is that a stable concept is likely to have a real world interpretation even if the description of some its objects (i.e., elements in the extent) is noisy* [25].

$$Stab((A, \delta(A))) = \frac{\kappa(A)}{2^{|A|}} \text{ where } \kappa(A) = \left| \left\{ \tilde{A} \subseteq A : \delta\left(\tilde{A}\right) = \delta(A) \right\} \right| \quad (11)$$

The major drawback of this definition is the difficulty of comparing concepts with high support since the stability tends to 1. This issue was discussed in [8,25] and the logarithmic stability for a concept $(A, \delta(A))$ has been introduced:

$$LStab((A, \delta(A))) = -\log_2(1 - Stab((A, \delta(A)))) = |A| - \log_2(2^{|A|} - \kappa(A)) \quad (12)$$

We extend the logarithmic stability of a concept to the **normalized logarithmic stability** $\lambda((A, \delta(A)))$ where values are between 0 and 1.

$$\lambda\lambda((A, \delta(A))) = \frac{-\log_2(1 - Stab((A, \delta(A))) + \frac{1}{2^{|A|}})}{|A|} = 1 - \frac{\log_2(2^{|A|} - \kappa(A) + 1)}{|A|}$$

$$\tag{13}$$

$$\lambda((\emptyset, \delta(\emptyset))) = 1 \text{ by convention} \tag{14}$$

We extend the stability of a concept to the **Global normalized logarithmic stability** of a concept lattice:

$$\lambda(L) = \sum_{(A, \delta(A)) \in L} p((A, \delta(A)))\lambda((A, \delta(A))) \tag{15}$$

where $p((A, \delta(A))) = \frac{\kappa(A)}{2^{|G|}}$ is the probability that a concept $(A, \delta(A))$ will be generated. This measure can naturally be extended to classical FCA for a concept (A, B) with $\beta(A)$ instead of $\delta(A)$.

The **representability** and the **distinctiveness** are unsupervised measures of quality to measure the ability to distinguish the different objects with sufficiant number of predicates. Let us observe that objects correspond to join irreducible $j(L)$ and meet irreducible $m(L)$ of a lattice L. The representability $R(L)$ shows how much we can preserve more information represented by the generated predicates (meet irreducible). The distinctiveness $D(L)$ is a measure of separation of a concept lattice, that indicates how much we distinguish objects.

$$R(L) = \frac{m(L)}{|L|} \qquad (16) \qquad\qquad D(L) = \frac{j(L)}{|L|} \qquad (17)$$

4 Experiments

In this section, we experimentally evaluate our descriptions and strategies for mining temporal sequences. We use GALACTIC[2] (**GA**lois **LA**ttices, **C**oncept **T**heory, **I**mplicational systems and **C**losures), a development platform of the NEXTPRIORITYCONCEPT algorithm, which, mixed with a system of plugins, makes it possible easy integration of new kinds of data with specific descriptions and strategies. We have implemented our description and strategy plugins for temporal sequences, and the global logarithmic stability as new measure. Experiments were performed on an Intel Core i7 2.20 GHz machine with 32 GB main memory. We have run our experiments on two datasets of sequences:

Wine-City dataset is issued from the museum "La Cité du Vin" in Bordeaux, France[3], gathered from the visits over a period of one year. The museum is a large "open-space", where visitors are free to explore the museum the way they want. The dataset contains 10000 sequences, with an average sequence size of 9.

---

[2] https://galactic.univ-lr.fr.
[3] https://www.laciteduvin.com/en.

Catch-me-if-you-can dataset (Catch-me for short) composed of sequences of user navigation on web pages available in KAGGLE website[4] [26]. The dataset contains 82797 sequences, with an average sequence size of 6.4.

In our experiments, we vary the size of the dataset (number of sequences) using a random function, then each experiment is performed ten times, and we compute the mean of each measurement value. We use the global logarithmic stability, the representability and the distinctiveness because we focus on reducing the size of the lattice using our description and strategies, and it is important to preserve the global stability of the lattice, and to measure how much we can get more information and how much we distinguish objects. Two main experiments are performed, the comparison between strategies, and the impact of using constraints. In this study, we did not compare our methods with studies mentioned earlier, because our description and strategies are very specific and we did not find studies that used FCA to analyse temporal sequences and explore the datasets as we do. We have published a comparison between classical closed sequence mining approaches and our methods [5].

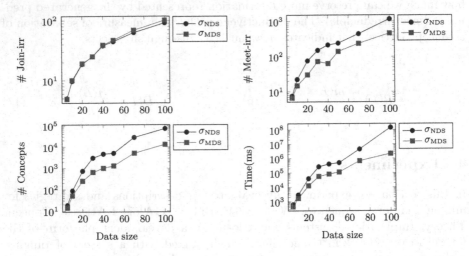

Fig. 3. Execution time and number of concepts and irreducibles generated by the two strategies σ_{NDS} and σ_{MDS} and DISTANTIAL description with the Wine-City dataset.

4.1   Comparison of Strategies

By variating the number of sequences, Fig. 3 shows the execution time, number of concepts and the number of irreducibles generated by the two strategies σ_{NDS} and σ_{MDS} and DISTANTIAL description with the Wine-City dataset. In Fig. 3 and Table 3, we can observe that the MIDDLE strategy reduces the size of the lattice with less meet irreducible. The NAIVE strategy generates more meet irreducible

---

[4]   https://www.kaggle.com/danielkurniadi/catch-me-if-you-can.

because it computes all the possible concepts. The number of join irreducible is the same with the two strategies, meaning that they have the same ability to distinguish between initial sequences. Therefore, the MIDDLE strategy is faster than the NAIVE strategy, as it generated less concepts. Also, one can observe that the logarithmic stability in Table 3 remains stable for the two strategies, even though the MIDDLE strategy generates fewer concepts.

Table 3. # of concepts, execution time, join and meet irreducible generated by the NAIVE and MIDDLE strategies using the `Catch-me` dataset

Data size	Strategy	# concepts	# join	# meet	Time(ms)	Global logarithmic stability
100	σ_{NDS}	172.2	93.8	101.1	5293133	0.8167676425074181
	σ_{MDS}	171	93.9	100.4	5169953	0.8167675958106895
200	σ_{NDS}	368.9	178.6	188.4	26999697	0.8048990577608026
	σ_{MDS}	370.2	180.4	190.6	26360502	0.8048990564763049
300	σ_{NDS}	565.3	261.6	273.6	68418978	0.8173740008873809
	σ_{MDS}	553	263.8	269.9	66631920	0.8173740144837136
400	σ_{NDS}	766.2	339.4	342.8	129194954	0.8164609321862498
	σ_{MDS}	754.5	342.8	340.5	126650950	0.8164609321862498
500	σ_{NDS}	984	416.4	420.8	240743394	0.817745055575167
	σ_{MDS}	964	421.6	416.5	234808014	0.817745055575167

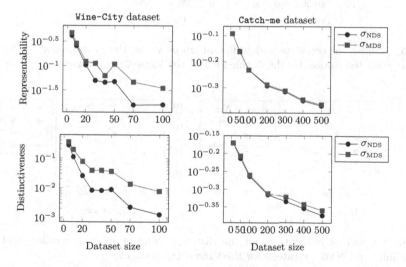

Fig. 4. Representability and distinctiveness using the δ_D description and the two strategies σ_{NDS} and σ_{MDS} for the `Catch-me` and the `Wine-City` datasets

In Fig. 4 we can observe that the representability, and the distinctiveness measures decreases while the size of the data increase. The distinctiveness is higher with the MIDDLE strategy than with the NAIVE strategy. This means that the MIDDLE strategy keeps an higher number of join irreducible as it reduces the size of the lattice. The representability is slightly better using the MIDDLE strategy for the `Catch-me` dataset. For the `Wine-city` dataset, as we have rised the data size, both measurements get higher with MIDDLE strategy comparing to the NAIVE one. This is because the NAIVE strategy generates much more predicates than the MIDDLE strategy.

Figure 5 represents the number of concepts for 3 different steps of the STEP strategy: $step = 1\,\text{s}, 3600\,\text{s}(1\,\text{h})$, and $21600\,\text{s}(6\,\text{h})$. The step precise the size of the reduction in the distances of common subsequences in order to generate candidates for the next iteration.

Therefore, the higher is the step, the smaller is the number of concepts. From 500 sequences of the `Catch-me` dataset, we obtain 1272 concepts with $step = 1\,\text{s}$, and 861 concepts using a step of 1 h and 6 h. From 70 sequences of the `Wine-City` dataset, we get 21916 concepts with $step = 1\,\text{s}$, 1138.5 concepts for $step = 1\,\text{h}$ and only 155.75 concepts for $step = 6\,\text{h}$.

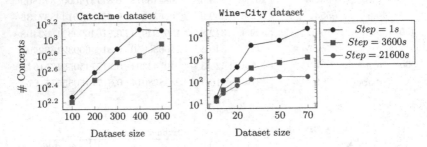

Fig. 5. Number of concepts with different *steps* using the NAIVE strategy and the DISTANTIAL description for the `Catch-me` and the `Wine-City` datasets

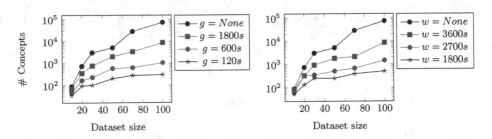

Fig. 6. Number of concepts using the distance description with *window* and *gaps* constraints and NAIVE strategy for the `Wine-City` dataset

4.2   Constraints

Another way to reduce patterns is to limit the description by a window or a gap. Figure 6 shows the size of the generated lattice using the NAIVE strategy and the DISTANTIAL description where window and gap varied. We use 3 values of window: $w = 3600\,\text{s}(1\,\text{h}), w = 2700\,\text{s}(45\,\text{mn})$, and $w = 1800\,\text{s}(30\,\text{mn})$ and 3 values for the gaps : $g = 120\,\text{s}(2\,\text{mn}), g = 600\,\text{s}(10\,\text{mn}), g = 1800\,\text{s}(30\,\text{mn})$. We can see that the number of concepts is significantly reduced. For a dataset of size 100, the number of concepts is reduced from 72427 (without window) to 495 (with 1800 s window). In a similar way, using a gap allows to reduce the size of the lattice to 295.75 with a gap of 120 s minutes.

5 Conclusion

In this paper, we presented a new temporal sequence mining approach using the NEXTPRIORITYCONCEPT algorithm. This algorithm allows a generic pattern computation through specific *descriptions* and *strategies*.

We defined a DISTANTIAL description that describes a set of temporal sequences by their maximal common distantial subsequences, with distances between items. This description is extended with window and gap constraints. We also propose three strategies of exploration. The NAIVE strategy generates all possible patterns, the STEP strategy reduces the distances between items according to a *step* parameter, and the MIDDLE strategy reduces the distance to the middle. We introduced the *logarithmic stability*, the *representability* and the *distinctiveness* to measure the quality of the obtained lattice. We can observe that the MIDDLE and the STEP strategies and the description with constraints allows to reduce the number of concepts while maintaining the ability to distinguish the initial sequences, and the quality of the concepts.

These results were made possible by the use of the NEXTPRIORITYCONCEPT algorithm which allows to focus on the data (descriptions and strategies) for pattern mining and discovery. In future works, we aim at proposing an user-driven approach which would allow the analyst to choose and test several strategies and descriptions with variation of the gap and the window constraints to find the most relevant patterns. Indeed, choosing or testing several strategies at each iteration is possible since strategies are not kept in the final description.

Aknowledgement. We would like to thank the Wine city museum "La Cité du Vin" to let us use their data in our experimentation.

References

1. Barbut, M., Monjardet, B.: Ordres et classifications : Algèbre et combinatoire. Hachette, Paris (1970). 2 tomes
2. Bertet, K., Demko, C., Viaud, J., Guérin, C.: Lattices, closures systems and implication bases: a survey of structural aspects and algorithms. Theor. Comput. Sci. **743**, 93–109 (2018)
3. Bonchi, F., Giannotti, F., Lucchese, C., Orlando, S., Perego, R., Trasarti, R.: Conquest: a constraint-based querying system for exploratory pattern discovery. In: 22nd International Conference on Data Engineering (ICDE 2006), p. 159 (2006)
4. Bordat, J.P.: Calcul pratique du treillis de Galois d'une correspondance. Math. Sci. Hum. **96**, 31–47 (1986)

5. Boukhetta, S.E., Demko, C., Richard, J., Bertet, K.: Sequence mining using FCA and the NextPriorityConcept algorithm. In: Concept Lattices and Their Applications 2020, vol. 2668, pp. 209–222 (2020)
6. Boukhetta, S.E., Richard, J., Demko, C., Bertet, K.: Interval-based sequence mining using FCA and the NextPriorityConcept algorithm. In: FCA4AI: What can FCA do for AI? vol. 2729, pp. 91–102 (2020)
7. Buzmakov, A., Egho, E., Jay, N., Kuznetsov, S.O., Napoli, A., Raïssi, C.: On projections of sequential pattern structures (with an application on care trajectories) (2013)
8. Buzmakov, A., Kuznetsov, S.O., Napoli, A.: Scalable estimates of concept stability. In: International Conference on Formal Concept Analysis, pp. 157–172 (2014)
9. Casas-Garriga, G.: Summarizing sequential data with closed partial orders. In: Proceedings of the SIAM International Conference on Data Mining, pp. 380–391. SIAM (2005)
10. Codocedo, V., Bosc, G., Kaytoue, M., Boulicaut, J.-F., Napoli, A.: A proposition for sequence mining using pattern structures. In: Bertet, K., Borchmann, D., Cellier, P., Ferré, S. (eds.) ICFCA 2017. LNCS (LNAI), vol. 10308, pp. 106–121. Springer, Cham (2017). https://doi.org/10.1007/978-3-319-59271-8_7
11. Cram, D., Mathern, B., Mille, A.: A complete chronicle discovery approach: application to activity analysis. Expert. Syst. **29**(4), 321–346 (2012)
12. Demko, C., Bertet, K., Faucher, C., Viaud, J.F., Kuznetsov, S.O.: NextPriorityConcept: a new and generic algorithm computing concepts from complex and heterogeneous data. Theor. Comput. Sci. **845**, 1–20 (2020)
13. Diop, L., Diop, C.T., Giacometti, A., Li, D., Soulet, A.: Sequential pattern sampling with norm constraints. In: IEEE International Conference on Data Mining (ICDM), pp. 89–98. IEEE (2018)
14. Dousson, C., Duong, T.V.: Discovering chronicles with numerical time constraints from alarm logs for monitoring dynamic systems. In: IJCAI, vol. 99, pp. 620–626. Citeseer (1999)
15. Dousson, C., Gaborit, P., Ghallab, M.: Situation recognition: representation and algorithms. In: IJCAI: International Joint Conference on Artificial Intelligence, vol. 93, pp. 166–172 (1993)
16. Ferré, S.: Systèmes d'information logiques : un paradigme logico-contextuel pour interroger, naviguer et apprendre. Doctorat, Univ. of Rennes 1, France (October 2002)
17. Ganter, B., Kuznetsov, S.O.: Pattern structures and their projections. In: LNCS of International Conference on Conceptual Structures (ICCS 2001), pp. 129–142 (2001)
18. Ganter, B., Wille, R.: Formal Concept Analysis, Mathematical Foundations. Springer Verlag, Berlin (1999)
19. Giannotti, F., Nanni, M., Pedreschi, D., Pinelli, F.: Mining sequences with temporal annotations. In: Proceedings of the ACM Symposium on Applied Computing, pp. 593–597 (2006)
20. Gizdatullin, D., Ignatov, D., Mitrofanova, E., Muratova, A.: Classification of demographic sequences based on pattern structures and emerging patterns. In: Supplementary Proceedings of 14th ICFCA, pp. 49–66 (2017)
21. Guyet, T.: Enhance sequential pattern mining with time and reasoning (2020)
22. Guyet, T., Quiniou, R.: Mining temporal patterns with quantitative intervals. In: IEEE International Conference on Data Mining Workshops, pp. 218–227 (2008)
23. Guyet, T., Quiniou, R.: Negpspan: efficient extraction of negative sequential patterns with embedding constraints. Data Min. Knowl. Disc. **34**(2), 563–609 (2020)

24. Hirate, Y., Yamana, H.: Generalized sequential pattern mining with item intervals. JCP: J. Comput. **1**(3), 51–60 (2006)
25. Jay, N., Kohler, F., Napoli, A.: Analysis of social communities with iceberg and stability-based concept lattices. In: Medina, R., Obiedkov, S. (eds.) ICFCA 2008. LNCS (LNAI), vol. 4933, pp. 258–272. Springer, Heidelberg (2008). https://doi.org/10.1007/978-3-540-78137-0_19
26. Kahn, G., Loiseau, Y., Raynaud, O.: A tool for classification of sequential data. In: European Conference on Artificial Intelligence (FCA4AI) (2016)
27. Kaytoue, M.: Contributions to Pattern Discovery. Habilitation, Univ. of Lyon, France (February 2020)
28. Kaytoue, M., Codocedo, V., Buzmakov, A., Baixeries, J., Kuznetsov, S.O., Napoli, A.: Pattern structures and concept lattices for data mining and knowledge processing. In: ECML-PKDD: European Conference on Machine Learning and Principles and Practice of Knowledge Discovery in Databases (2015)
29. Kuznetsov, S.O.: On stability of a formal concept. Ann. Math. Artif. Intell. **49**(1), 101–115 (2007)
30. Lam, H.T., Mörchen, F., Fradkin, D., Calders, T.: Mining compressing sequential patterns. Stat. Anal. Data Min. ASA Data Sci. J. **7**(1), 34–52 (2014)
31. Linding, C.: Fast concept analysis. In: Working with Conceptual Structures-Contributions to ICC, pp. 235–248 (2002)
32. Nica, C., Braud, A., Le Ber, F.: RCA-SEQ: an original approach for enhancing the analysis of sequential data based on hierarchies of multilevel closed partially-ordered patterns. Discret. Appl. Math. **273**, 232–251 (2020)
33. Pei, J., et al.: Prefixspan: mining sequential patterns efficiently by prefix-projected pattern growth. In: ICCCN, p. 0215. IEEE (2001)
34. Sahuguède, A., Le Corronc, E., Le Lann, M.V.: An ordered chronicle discovery algorithm. In: 3nd ECML/PKDD Workshop on Advanced Analytics and Learning on Temporal Data, AALTD 2018 (2018)
35. Srikant, R., Agrawal, R.: Mining sequential patterns: generalizations and performance improvements. In: Apers, P., Bouzeghoub, M., Gardarin, G. (eds.) EDBT 1996. LNCS, vol. 1057, pp. 1–17. Springer, Heidelberg (1996). https://doi.org/10.1007/BFb0014140
36. Tatti, N., Vreeken, J.: The long and the short of it: summarising event sequences with serial episodes. In: Proceedings of the 18th ACM SIGKDD International Conference on Knowledge Discovery and Data Mining, pp. 462–470 (2012)
37. Ugarte, W., et al.: Skypattern mining: from pattern condensed representations to dynamic constraint satisfaction problems. Artif. Intell. **244**, 48–69 (2017)
38. Wang, J., Han, J.: Bide: efficient mining of frequent closed sequences. In: Proceedings of the 20th International Conference on Data Engineering, pp. 79–90. IEEE (2004)
39. Wille, R.: Restructuring lattice theory: an approach based on hierarchies of concepts. In: Ferré, S., Rudolph, S. (eds.) ICFCA 2009. LNCS (LNAI), vol. 5548, pp. 314–339. Springer, Heidelberg (2009). https://doi.org/10.1007/978-3-642-01815-2_23
40. Yan, X., Han, J., Afshar, R.: CloSpan: mining closed sequential patterns in large datasets. In: Proceedings of the SIAM International Conference on Data Mining, pp. 166–177. SIAM (2003)
41. Yen, S.J., Lee, Y.S.: Mining non-redundant time-gap sequential patterns. Appl. Intell. **39**(4), 727–738 (2013)
42. Zaki, M.J.: Spade: an efficient algorithm for mining frequent sequences. Mach. Learn. **42**(1–2), 31–60 (2001)

Restricted Bi-pattern Mining

Guillaume Santini[2], Henry Soldano[1,2,3]($\boxtimes$), and Stella Zevio[2]

[1] NukkAI, Paris, France
[2] LIPN CNRS UMR 7030, Université Sorbonne Paris Nord, Villetaneuse, France
`Henry.soldano@lipn.univ-paris13.fr`
[3] Muséum d'Histoire Naturelle, ISYEB, Paris, France

Abstract. Bi-pattern mining has been previously introduced to mine attributed networks in which nodes may have two types or two roles. In particular a bi-partite network have two vertex sets and attributes describing node labels depends then on the node type, still some attributes may be relevant to describe both kind of nodes. It is then natural to consider bi-patterns made of two pattern components. In directed networks there is only one vertex set, but we may consider the out and in roles of a node. In both cases it may be interesting to enforce both components of a bi-pattern to share part of their description. We discuss how to impose such a restriction in closed bi-pattern mining.

Keywords: Closed pattern mining · Core subgraph · Attributed network · Bi-pattern mining

1 Introduction

When considering knowledge discovery in attributed graphs, recent work focuses on combining the attribute patterns, which may occur in the label nodes, with connectivity constraints. In particular, the *core closed pattern* methodology has been introduced to enumerate patterns occurring in core subgraphs [1]. As an example, the k-core subgraph is the greatest subgraph in which all vertices have degree at least k [2], and by changing this topological property we obtain various core definitions [3]. In *core closed pattern mining*, the vertex subset in which an attribute pattern occurs is reduced to its core vertex subset to which is associated a *core closed pattern* i.e. the most specific pattern common to the nodes in the core vertex subset.

Now, two-mode networks are made of two vertex sets representing in general two kind of entities, for instance actors and movies, together with edge relating entities of each kind, as for instance "G. Clooney acted in Ocean's Eleven" [4]. In such a network each kind of vertex is described according to a proper attribute set and we have then to consider patterns made of two attribute subsets, called *bi-patterns*. A bi-pattern selects a vertex subset pair that is then reduced to a *bi-core* [5]. When applying bi-pattern mining to expert finding from bibliographical data [6], the authors encountered the following situation: both authors and

© Springer Nature Switzerland AG 2021
T. Braun et al. (Eds.): ICCS 2021, LNAI 12879, pp. 200–207, 2021.
https://doi.org/10.1007/978-3-030-86982-3_15

articles were described using semantic concepts, i.e. scientific domains in which authors may be expert but which also describe the scope of the article. It seems then natural to consider a subclass of bi-patterns in which both pattern components contains the same semantic concepts. There are various studies about enumerating patterns from a subclass of a pattern language. In particular [7] investigates the conditions to apply closed pattern mining to a set system, i.e. a part of the powerset of items, so resulting in a restriction of closed itemset mining. Still, there are still no investigation on restricting bi-pattern mining. We discuss here both informally and formally how to define such a restricted bi-pattern language and how to efficiently enumerate its closed bi-patterns.

2 Single Pattern and Bi-pattern Mining

2.1 Core Closed Single Pattern Mining

In closed pattern mining, a pattern q has an *extension* also called a *support set* $e = \text{ext}(q)$ representing its set occurrences in a set of objects V. This support set defines the equivalence class of all patterns with support set e. The most specific pattern with support set e is unique as far as the pattern language is a lattice and will be considered as the representative of this class and is called a *closed pattern*. We may then enumerate closed patterns that represent a *condensed representation* of all patterns in the object dataset. A closed pattern is obtained by using an intersection operator *int* that applies the lowest upper bound operator $\wedge$ to the set of object descriptions $d[e]$[1]. In our attribute pattern setting objects are described as itemsets i.e. subsets of a set of items I. In this case the intersection operator simply is the set theoretic intersection operator $\cap$. Overall we obtain the closed pattern with same support set as q as follows:

$$f(q) = \text{int} \circ \text{ext}(q) \tag{1}$$

f is then a *closure operator*. When applying an interior operator[2] p to $\text{ext}(q)$, it reduces the support set into a so-called *abstract* support set, and we define then a coarser equivalence relation. The most specific pattern c of the class of pattern with same abstract support set $c = p(\text{ext}(q))$ as pattern q is obtained by defining a new closure operator f:

$$f(q) = \text{int} \circ p \circ \text{ex.t}(q) \tag{2}$$

Such a situation arises when the object set V is the set of vertices of a graph $G = (V, E)$ and that p is a core operator, i.e. an operator that, given a vertex subset e returns the *core* of the subgraph induced by c [1]. There are various core

---

[1] $d[e]$ is the image of e by d, i.e. $d[e] = \{d(v)|v \in e\}$.

[2] Let S be an ordered set and $f : S \to S$ a self map such that for any $x, y \in S$, f is monotone, i.e. $x \leq y$ implies $f(x) \leq f(y)$ and idempotent, i.e. $f(f(x)) = f(x)$, then If $f(x) \geq x$, f is called a closure operator while if $f(x) \leq x$, f is called an interior operator.

definitions and therefore various core operators p. A core definition is associated to a *core property* P which has to be satisfied by each vertex v within a vertex subset w. For instance, the k-core of the subgraph G_w of G induced by some vertex subset w is defined as the largest vertex subset c of w such that all vertices in c have degree at least k in G_c, i.e. $P(v,c)$ holds for all v in c. The subgraph induced by the k-core c is called the k-core subgraph of G_w. To summarize, as long as we have a core property P, we also have an interior operator and abstract closed patterns called *core closed patterns*.

2.2   Core Closed Bi-pattern Mining

Closed bi-pattern mining [5] follows from the remark that we may extend single pattern mining by:

- considering pairs of patterns $q = (q_1, q_2)$ called bi-patterns. The pattern q_1 is a subset of some set of items I_1 while q_2 is a subset of another set of items I_2. I_1 and I_2 may have common items.
- extending support sets to support set pairs $\text{ext}(q) = (\text{ext}_1(q_1), \text{ext}_2(q_2))$ where $\text{ext}_1(q_1)$ is the support set of q_1 within the object set V_1 and $\text{ext}_2(q_2)$ is the support set of q_2 within V_2.
- defining the intersection operator *int* that applies to a pair of object subsets $e = (e_1, e_2)$ with $e_1 \subseteq V_1$ and $e_2 \subseteq V_2$. The intersection operator is defined as $\text{int}(e) = (\text{int}_1(e_1), \text{int}_2(e_2))$ where $\text{int}_i(e_i)$ is the intersection of the descriptions of the objects in e_i.
- considering an interior operator which reduces the pair of object subsets $e = (e_1, e_2)$ to a smaller pair $e' = (e'_1, e'_2)$, i.e. a pair such that $e'_1 \subseteq e1$ and $e'_2 \subseteq e_2$.

We then find back Eq. 2 and define accordingly the core closed bi-pattern $f(q)$ as the most specific bi-pattern (considering both components) whose core support set pair is the same as bi-pattern q [5].

Cores have then to be pairs of vertex subsets, we may also call *bi-cores*. Bi-core definitions rely on pairs of bi-core properties (P_1, P_2). P_1 has now three arguments: two vertex subsets (w_1, w_2) and a vertex v_1 from w_1. P_2 is defined in the same way but applies to a vertex v_2 from w_2. It is required that in the bi-core $C = (c_1, c_2)$ all vertices v_1 from c_1 are such that $P_1(v_1, c_1, c_2)$ hold and all vertices from v_2 are such that $P_2(v_2, c_1, c_2)$ hold. Bi-core definitions may straightforwardly apply to two-mode networks which are made of two sets of nodes V_1 and V_2. Bi-core definitions may also concern undirected or directed networks. We give hereunder the bi-core definition we use for directed networks and in which we consider the subgraph G_{w_1,w_2} induced by w_1, w_2 whose edges relate nodes from w_1 to nodes from w_2:

- Directed networks: The h-a BHA bi-core (H, A) of the subgraph G_{w_1,w_2} is such that in $G_{H,A}$ all nodes from H have outdegree at least h and all nodes from A have indegree at least a.

In this directed bi-core, nodes in H are called *hubs* while nodes from A are called *authorities*. This is a reference to the hubs and authorities notions as introduced by Kleinberg [8]. Note that directed networks are defined from a single vertex set $V = V_1 = V_2$ and that in that case the components c_1 and c_2 of the bi-core may obviously intersect.

Example 1. We consider a directed graph, displayed Fig. 1, with vertex set $V = 012345$ and edge set $E = \{03, 14, 12, 25\}$ and bi-patterns core subgraphs using the 1-1 BHA bi-core definition: within the bi-core (H, A) any node in H as outdegree at least 1 towards nodes in A while any node from A has indegree at least 1 from nodes in H. As a result, the $(\emptyset, \emptyset)$ bi-pattern selects $(H = 012, A = 2345)$ as its 1-1 BHA bi-core. In this example the vertices are described as itemsets from $I = abcxy$ as follows $d(0) = abx$, $d(1) = abx$, $d(2) = abcxy$, $d(3) = acy$, $d(4) = acy$, $d(5) = acxy$. When considering the bi-pattern $(\emptyset, \emptyset)$ we select within each component support set the attributes common to the nodes. This results in $f(\emptyset, \emptyset) = (int(012), int(2345)) = (abx, acy)$ as associated core closed bi-pattern.

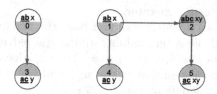

Fig. 1: A 1-1 BHA bi-core subgraph. Nodes from H are in blue while nodes from A are in red and items from F are in bold. (Color figure online)

3   Restricted Bi-pattern

Informal Presentation. In this section we discuss a way to syntactically restrict bi-pattern mining: whenever the two sets of items I_1 and I_2 used to describe nodes intersect we may consider only bi-patterns q_1, q_2 such that q_1 and q_2 have the same items on a part F of this intersection.

We have then two extreme cases:

- $F = \emptyset$ is the unrestricted bi-pattern mining case.
- $F = I_1 = I_2 = I$ comes down to the single pattern mining case. It concerns only networks on which the two pattern languages are identical. Bi-patterns have then the form (q, q) where q is an itemset from I.

The first natural scenario where restricted bi-pattern mining appears is whenever investigating a two-mode network in which there is some common attribute subset $I_1 \cap I_2$ shared by nodes from the two modes. It may be, for example, because both authors and articles they write are labelled by scientific domains.

Though the meaning of the attribute may slightly differ depending on the node mode, is still makes sense to investigate bi-patterns in which the scientific domain has to be shared by all nodes in the bi-core subnetwork. Another obvious case is the lawyers advice network [5] whose directed edges relates a lawyer who asks for advice from another lawyer. It could be then interesting to restrict the investigation to bi-patterns for which lawyers with opposite in and out role have to share their law domain, still allowing age or seniority to vary depending on the role.

Such restricted closed bi-pattern mining requires to change the definition of the closure operator:

Example 2. Consider again Example 1 and suppose that we want to constrain bi-patterns (q_1, q_2) in such a way that q_1 and q_2 should have in common items from $F = abc$. The closed bi-pattern (abx, acy) does not satisfy the constraint as b only belongs to the first component of the bi-pattern while c only belongs to its second component. However by removing b and c we obtain the bi-pattern (ax, ay) which satisfy the constraint: a belongs to both components while x and y are outside F. (ax, ay) is then the unique most specific restricted bi-pattern with same core support set pair as bi-pattern $(\emptyset, \emptyset)$. We obtain it as $f_F(\emptyset, \emptyset)$ where f_F is the new closure operator.

Using this (informal) definition we find back the two extreme cases referred to above: unrestricted bi-pattern mining and single pattern mining: i) $F = \emptyset$: nothing is removed from (abx, acy), ii) $F = abcxy$: b, x have to be removed from abx while c, y have to be removed from (acy) and we obtain $f_F(\emptyset, \emptyset) = (a, a)$ which is equivalent to a single pattern.

Restricted Bi-pattern Mining Definition. We give here a formal definition of restricted bi-pattern mining and associated results.

Let B be the bi-pattern language $B = 2^{I_1} \times 2^{I_2}$, and $B_F \subseteq B$ be the language of restricted bi-patterns associated to $F \subseteq I_1 \cap I_2$. The required membership condition to B_F is that when considering any item i from F the two components q_1 and q_2 either both contains i or neither contains i. To perform closed bi-pattern mining on B_F we need then a closure operator f_F on B_F that given some bi-pattern q from B_F with associated bi-core $p \circ ext(q) = (c_1, c_2)$, returns the most specific bi-pattern in B_F with same bi-core as q. It has been previously shown that when restricting any pattern language L, a closure operator is obtained from the closure operator f on L when applying an operator p_I to the closed pattern $f(q)$ [9]:

$$f_I(q) = p_I \circ int \circ p \circ ext(q) = p_I(f(q)) \tag{3}$$

The condition for f_I to be a closure operator is that p_I is an interior operator on L. This means that we want p_I to be such that $p_I(q)$ is the greater lower bound of q in $L_I = p_I(L_I)$, i.e. the most specific pattern in L_I more general than q. In the restricted bi-pattern mining we define $p_I(q)$ by removing from bi-pattern $q = (q_1, q_2)$ the items of F that are in one component of q and not in the other.

We obtain then the largest $q' = (q'_1, q'_2)$ smaller than or equal to $(q1, q2)$ and that satisfy the membership condition to B_F. Consider p_I defined as follows:

$$p_I((q_1, q_2)) = (q'_1, q'_2) \text{ with} \tag{4}$$
$$q'_1 = (q_1 \cap (I_1 \setminus F)) \cup (q_1 \cap q_2 \cap F) \text{ and} \tag{5}$$
$$q'_2 = (q_2 \cap (I_2 \setminus F)) \cup (q_1 \cap q_2 \cap F) \tag{6}$$

Equation 5 states that elements of q'_1 are those among q_1 that either are not in F or also belong to q_2. In the same way Eq. 6 states that elements of q'_2 are those among q_2 that either are not in F or also belong to q_1. Clearly $p_I(q)$ belongs then to B_F, i.e. its range $p_I(B)$ is B_F, as any item violating the membership condition have been removed. Furthermore, $p_I(q)$ is the greater lower bound of q in B_F. Intuitively this is because any item satisfying the membership condition has been kept. Formally, in order to apply Eq. 3 we have to prove that p_I is an interior operator on B:

Proposition 1. *p_I as defined in Eq. 4 is an interior operator on B*

Proof. We need to check three conditions. p_I has to be intensive, monotone and idempotent:

- $p_I(q) \leq q$? Let us denote $p_I(q)$ by $q' = (q'_1, q'_2)$. q'_1 may then be rewritten as $q_1 \cap ((I_1 \setminus F) \cup (q_2 \cap F))$ implying $q'_1 \subseteq q_1$. In a similar way we obtain $q'_2 \subseteq q_2$ and therefore that $q' \subseteq q$.
- $w \subseteq q$ implies $p_I(w) \subseteq p_I(q)$? We have $w = (w_1, w_2)$ and $q = (q_1, q_2)$ with $w_1 \subseteq q_1$ and $w_2 \subseteq q_2$. Let us denote $p_I(w)$ by w' and $p_I(q)$ by q'. We have then i) $(w_1 \cap (I_1 \setminus F)) \subseteq (q_1 \cap (I_1 \setminus F))$ and ii) $(w_1 \cap w_2 \cap F) \subseteq (q_1 \cap q_2 \cap F)$. This means that we have $w'_1 \subseteq q'_1$. In a similar way we obtain that $w'_2 \subseteq q'_2$ and therefore $w' \subseteq q'$ i.e. $p_I(w) \subseteq p_I(q)$.
- $p_I(p_I(q)) = p_I(q)$? Let us denote $p_I(q)$ by q' and $p_I(q')$ by q''. We note that $q'_1 = (q_1 \cap (I_1 \setminus F)) \cup (q_1 \cap q_2 \cap F)$ is made of two disjoint parts q'^a_1 and q'^b_1, the first resulting from an intersection with $(I_1 \setminus F)$ and the second with an intersection with F. In the same way q''_1 is made of two disjoint parts q''^a_1 and q''^b_1 using the same partition $\{I_1 \setminus F, F\}$. We consider the first component of the latter: $(q'_1 \cap (I_1 \setminus F))$ rewrites as $(q_1 \cap (I_1 \setminus F)) \cup (q_1 \cap q_2 \cap F) \cap (I_1 \setminus F)$ which in turn reduces to $(q_1 \cap (I_1 \setminus F)) \cap (I_1 \setminus F)) = (q_1 \cap (I_1 \setminus F))$. As a consequence we have $q'^a_1 = q''^a_1$. In the same way we obtain $q'^a_2 = q''^a_2$. Turning to the second component, we have $q''^b_1 = (q'_1 \cap q'_2 \cap F) = q''^b_2$. It rewrites as $(q'^a_1 \cup q'^b_1) \cap (q'^a_2 \cup q'^b_2) \cap F = q'^b_1 \cap q'^b_2 \cap F)$ i.e. $(q_1 \cap q_2 \cap F) \cap (q_1 \cap q_2 \cap F) \cap F = (q_1 \cap q_2 \cap F)$. It follows that $q''^b_1 = q''^b_2 = q'^b_1 = q'^b_2$. Overall we have shown that $(q''^a_1 \cup q''^b_1) = (q'^a_1 \cup q'^b_1)$ and $(q''^a_2 \cup q''^b_2) = (q'^a_2 \cup q'^b_2)$, i.e. $q'' = q'$.

This is a general guide to define restricted patterns language such that existence of a closure operator is preserved: find an interior operator to apply to the unrestricted pattern language.

Restricted Bi-pattern Enumeration. Bi-pattern mining relies on an enumeration algorithm, following the divide and conquer pattern enumeration algorithm from [7]. The latter algorithm have first been adapted to core closed pattern mining by turning the closure operator definition from Eq. (1) to Eq. (2) [1]. Then it has been adapted to bi-pattern mining by simply adding at each specialisation step starting from some bi-pattern (q_1, q_2) one item to either q_1 or q_2 [5]. We propose to again extend the algorithm to restricted bi-pattern mining as defined here by changing the specialisation steps. For that purpose, first note that the current algorithm may use as a pattern language any *atomistic* pattern language. More precisely, first recall that an *atom* a of a (finite) ordered set A with a minimum $\perp$ is an element greater than $\perp$ and such that there is no other element between $\perp$ and a. A is said *atomistic* if any element q is the least upper bound of the set of atoms $a(q)$ smaller than or equal to q [10]. Regarding unrestricted bi-pattern mining, B atoms are of the form $(x, \emptyset)$ where x belongs to I_1 or $(\emptyset, x_2)$ where x_2 belongs to I_2. Any B subset S has a least upper bound which is its join $\vee S$ and therefore B is atomistic. For instance, (a, c) rewrites as $(a, \emptyset) \vee (\emptyset, c)$ $= (a \cup \emptyset, \emptyset \cup c)$. Regarding restricted bi-pattern mining, we note that B_F is also atomistic:

Proposition 2. *Let B_F be a restricted bi-pattern language with sets of items I_1 and I_2 and $F \subseteq I_1 \cap I_2$, B_F is atomistic and atoms are of the form:*

- *$(x, \emptyset)$ where x belongs to $I_1 \setminus F$,*
- *$(\emptyset, x)$ where x belongs to $I_2 \setminus F$ and*
- *(x, x) where x belongs to F.*

The algorithm may then access any element q' greater than q by adding successively atoms from $a(q') \setminus a(q)$. The availability of such a path from any ordered pair q, q' is known (in the itemset case) as the *strong accessibility* property and is required to ensure completeness of the enumeration algorithm [7].

Example 3. Let $I_1 = abc$, $I_2 = bcd$ and $F = c$. The atoms are then $(a, \emptyset), (b, \emptyset)$, $(\emptyset, b), (\emptyset, d)$, (c, c). We may then specialise restricted bi-pattern (a, d) by adding either $(b, \emptyset)$, resulting in (ab, d), or $(\emptyset, b)$, resulting in (a, bd), or adding (c, c) resulting in (ac, cd).

4   Conclusion

We have adapted a current implementation of closed bi-pattern mining[3] to the general restricted closed bi-pattern mining setting as defined in this manuscript. Results on a bibliographic two-mode network whose nodes all share the same set of semantic concepts appear in [6]. Note that as there are less ways to specialize a bi-pattern in the restricted case than in the unrestricted case, there are fewer restricted bi-patterns to enumerate and the enumeration is faster. Restricted bi-pattern mining allows then to focus on interesting bi-pattern subclassses without

---

[3] available at https://lipn.univ-paris13.fr/MinerLC/.

enumerating all bi-patterns. We are currently performing restricted bi-pattern mining experiments on the lawyers advice network explored in [5] and that resulted in 930 4-4 HA core closed patterns to be compared to 293 490 4-4 BHA core closed (unrestricted) bi-patterns. The number of restricted bi-patterns is somewhere between these two numbers. Restricted bi-pattern mining allows then to focus on interesting bi-pattern subclassses without enumerating all closed bi-patterns.

References

1. Soldano, H., Santini, G.: Graph abstraction for closed pattern mining in attributed networks. In: Schaub, T., Friedrich, G., O'Sullivan, B. (eds.), European Conference in Artificial Intelligence (ECAI), volume 263 of Frontiers in Artificial Intelligence and Applications, pp. 849–854. IOS Press (2014)
2. Seidman, S.B.: Network structure and minimum degree. Soc. Netw. **5**, 269–287 (1983)
3. Batagelj, V., Zaversnik, M.: Fast algorithms for determining (generalized) core groups in social networks. Adv. Data Anal. Classif. **5**(2), 129–145 (2011)
4. Borgatti, S.P., Everett, M.G.: Network analysis of 2-mode data. Soc. Netw. **19**(3), 243–269 (1997)
5. Soldano, H., Santini, G., Bouthinon, D., Bary, S., Lazega, E.: Bi-pattern mining of attributed networks. Appl. Netw. Sci. **4**(1), 37 (2019)
6. Zevio, S., Santini, G., Soldano, H., Zargayouna, H., Charnois, T.: A combination of semantic annotation and graph mining for expert finding in scholarly data. In: Proceedings of the Graph Embedding and Mining (GEM) Workshop at ECML PKDD (2020)
7. Boley, M., Horváth, T., Poigné, A., Wrobel, S.: Listing closed sets of strongly accessible set systems with applications to data mining. Theor. Comput. Sci. **411**(3), 691–700 (2010)
8. Kleinberg, J.M.: Authoritative sources in a hyperlinked environment. J. ACM (JACM) **46**(5), 604–632 (1999)
9. Pernelle, N., Rousset, M. C., Soldano, H., Ventos, V.: Zoom: a nested Galois lattices-based system for conceptual clustering. J. Exp. Theor. Artif. Intell. **2**/3(14), 157–187 (2002)
10. Davey, B., Priestley, H.: Introduction to Lattices and Order, second cdn. Cambridge University Press, Cambridge (2002)

A Semantic-Based Approach for Assessing the Impact of Cyber-Physical Attacks: A Healthcare Infrastructure Use Case

Mohamad Rihany[1], Fatma-Zohra Hannou[1(✉)], Nada Mimouni[1],
Fayçal Hamdi[1], Philippe Tourron[2], and Pierre-Alain Julien[2]

[1] CEDRIC Lab, CNAM - Conservatoire National des Arts et Métiers Paris,
Paris, France
{mohamad.rihany,fatma-zohra.hannou}@lecnam.net,
{nada.mimouni,faycal.hamdi}@cnam.fr
[2] Hôpitaux universitaires de Marseille (APHM), Marseille, France
{philippe.tourron,pierre-alain.jullien}@ap-hm.fr

Abstract. This paper proposes an integrated approach to study impact propagation of cyber and physical incidents within critical healthcare infrastructures. This approach is based on a semantic modeling and reasoning engine which takes into account assets and input/output incident types while running propagation through a network graph. Besides, it calculates impact scores based on the protection degree value of each asset. We illustrate our contribution through an attack scenario on the "Covid vaccine theft". The evaluation of the approach shows promising results.

Keywords: Semantic modeling · Critical infrastructures ·
Cyber-physical attacks · Impact propagation

1 Introduction

Hospitals are cyber-physical systems that are inherently vulnerable to a multitude of attacks that can occur at their communications, networks, and physical entry points. The sources of these threats are heterogeneous, either cyber or physical and could happen simultaneously. These cyber-physical attacks can have detrimental effects on their operations and the safety of their patients. Thus threats should not be analyzed solely as cyber or physical and it is essential to develop an integrated approach to fight against a combination of both types of threats. To that aim and to properly secure these systems, it is of utmost importance to: (i) understand their underlying assets with associated vulnerabilities and threats, (ii) quantify their effects, and (iii) prevent the potential impacts of these attacks. In the context of the EU Horizon 2020 SAFECARE project[1], we propose a solution to better understand the tight relationships

---

[1] https://www.safecare-project.eu.

T. Braun et al. (Eds.): ICCS 2021, LNAI 12879, pp. 208–215, 2021.
https://doi.org/10.1007/978-3-030-86982-3_16

between the assets' characteristics of a hospital's infrastructure and the propagation of attacks' effects to better prevent the impacts and consequences of incidents. Since these infrastructures host a variety of medical and IT assets with very different characteristics, an effective reaction to attacks needs to capture the detailed knowledge of intrinsic and contextual assets properties. To meet this challenge, we propose a model able to capture the essential characteristics related to incidents understanding and propagation and that takes into account the possible evolution of this knowledge. The impact propagation mechanism that we conceive considers the assets, their vulnerabilities, their interdependencies, their contextual knowledge, and the incidents that occurred in their environment. In the following, Sect. 2 describes our approach, Sect. 3 presents the model implementation, an attack scenario use case, and provides evaluation results, Sects. 4 and 5 give related work and conclusions with future research directions.

2   Semantic-Based Impact Propagation Approach

The approach we proposed is three folds: (i) semantic modeling of the critical infrastructure (assets and their relationships), (ii) capturing of the expert's knowledge by generating generic rules that describe the propagation of cyber-physical attacks, (iii) assessing the impact a threat could have on different assets.

2.1   Semantic Modeling

We designed within the Safecare project a modular ontology, "SafecareOnto", based on the knowledge acquisition process outcome, completed with project security experts. The ontology comprises three sub-ontologies: "asset", "impact", and "protection". For lack of space, we give a brief description of the asset sub-ontology. "Impact" and "Protection" concepts are formulated by referring to existing security ontologies and risk management standards (NIST [4], ISO 27001, EBIOS [1]). The full ontology definition can be found in [5]. Figure 2 depicts key concepts in SafecareOnto.

- $Asset \sqsubseteq \top$: any valuable resource for an organization.
- $AccessPoint \sqsubseteq \top$: gateways that enable the use of the resource, and the occurrence of incidents.
- $Controller \sqsubseteq \top$: physical equipment or virtual protocols implementing the restriction of access to assets.
- $Device \sqsubseteq Asset$: any tangible equipment, possibly associated to software.
- $Software \sqsubseteq Asset$: Virtual program with data processing capabilities.
- $Network \sqsubseteq Asset$: Data exchange channel linking at least two devices.

Relations. The relationships capture asset dependencies and represent potential vectors of incident propagation. They have been organized into patterns that reflect both cyber and physical propagation channels: **'Leads to' pattern** characterizes access mechanism. It relies on "leads to asset" and "leads to control

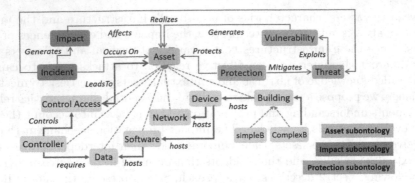

Fig. 1. SafecareOnto concepts and relations

point "relations. **'Hosts-Content' pattern** comprises different hosting possibilities connecting assets. If an incident occurs on the hosting asset, it may strongly impact its content. **'Controls' pattern** corresponds to the control system that usually restricts access to assets. **'Whole-part' pattern** covers complex assets that can be decomposed into smaller entities (Fig. 1).

2.2   Impacts Propagation

In order to model experts' knowledge about common and probable incidents on healthcare infrastructures, a set of detailed threat scenarios was defined in the Safecare project. We use these scenarios as a base model to extract a set of generic logical rules aiming at characterising how impacts could propagate between different assets within such infrastructures. The idea is to study all cyber and physical incidents and assets that belong to the same or close categories and identify the relationships that may convey the impacts. Actually, the complexity lies in identifying in which case a cyber incident could propagate to physical assets and a physical incident to cyber assets and when to stop propagating an impact through a path connecting different assets.

Hereafter a Jena rule example that addresses the physical incident "Suspicious Interaction" that occurs on a device such as wall socket plug internet. This incident is propagated as a cyber incident "Network Service Scanning" to the hospital's internal network.

```
(?incident sco:occurs ?asset1), (?incident sco:realizes ?threat1),
(?threat1 rdf:type sco:suspicious_interaction), (?asset1 rdf:type sco:Device),
(?asset1 sco:HostsNetwork ?asset2), (?asset2 rdf:type sco:Network),
  -> (?new_incident rdf:type sco:Incident), (?new_incident sco:realizes ?threat2),
    (?threat2 rdf:type sco:Network_Service_Scanning),
    (?new_incident sco:occurs ?asset2)
```

2.3   Estimating Impact Score

The objective here is to assess the impact a threat could have on different assets within the end users' systems. Indeed, an asset could have different possible threats depending on the considered scenario and kill chain. For each threat, different possible protections are deployed by end users' systems. A value of protection, we call "protection degree", is calculated by experts for each asset per threat per protection. This value is presented as a global numerical value (a percentage) that encompasses different security assessment indicators (availability, intrusion, vulnerability and compliance).

In common cases, multiple protections are added to an asset to make it more robust against a given threat. In this case, the impact score is calculated by aggregating the respective protection degrees as follows:

$$impactScore_{th}(a) = 1 - \sum_{j=1}^{p} protectionDegree_{th}^{j}(a) \qquad (1)$$

where, p is the number of protections for an asset per threat th and the sum value is set to 1 if the sum of the protection degrees is greater than 100%. More generally, while propagating impacts, we are considering the system architecture as a graph linking all available assets. An asset is a node of the graph, and the interface with other assets are the edges. The protection degree at a given node depends on the precedent nodes in the propagation path of the incident. As a result, the impact score is calculated as follows:

$$impactScore_{th1}(a_t) = \begin{cases} 0, \text{ if } \exists a_i \in Path(a_s, a_t) \text{ s.t. } impactScore_{th2}(a_i) = 0 \\ 1 - \sum_{j=1}^{p} protectionDegree_{th1}^{j}(a_t), \text{ otherwise} \end{cases}$$

$$(2)$$

where $Path(a_s, a_t)$ is the set of all the assets in the path connecting the asset a_s to the asset a_t.

3   Experiments and Results

The presented impact propagation model (IPM) was developed within the European project Safecare. Beyond the technical implementation of the semantic model and inference rules, several interfaces were required to ensure data exchange with the project partner's modules. This work is detailed in Sect. 3.1.

3.1   Implementation

The impact propagation solution requires interacting with other project modules to acquire the necessary inputs to its functioning, such as Central DataBase (CDB) to gather the information needed, the physical and cyber detection systems to get notified of incidents' occurrences. The IPM communicates with the other modules by exchanging JSON messages via the MQTT (Message Queuing Telemetry Transport) broker.

The model is organized into two parts, the online part, and the offline part. In the offline sub-module, the knowledge base is created by retrieving information from CDB. When the IPM receives an incident, the online sub-module will be triggered to generate the impact propagation message containing the impacted assets with their impact score. Concretely, when an incident message is received, the CDB is queried to update the protection degree value for all the assets in the knowledge base. After that, the list of impacted assets is generated by running the inference rules. The impact score is calculated for each impacted asset based on the last updated value of the protection degree in the CDB. The final step is to publish the impact propagation message by using the MQTT broker.

The visualization of the propagation is made in a graphical way, where the nodes represent the assets, and the edges represent the relationship between them. The impact score on impacted assets is expressed by changing the color of the corresponding node. Red color represents a strong impact and orange represents a moderate impact. The experiments have been performed on Intel Core i7 with 32GB RAM. We have used Java 8 and Apache Jena to implement the model and NodeJs with the library vis.js for the visualization.

3.2 Use Case

The following use case details a cyber-physical attack scenario used to illustrate the experiments since real project data can not be revealed (confidentiality reasons). During the COVID health crisis, the hospital dedicates part of its infrastructure to the vaccination campaign, which mobilizes medical staff to carry out vaccines and requires particular logistics. With malicious purpose, An attacker contacts a hospital staff member to identify his email address. He then sends a spearphishing email to break into the hospital's information system. Then, the attacker accesses the appointment scheduling system to modify the appointment planning and set them at one date DD and hour. Many patients gather in the hospital on the chosen day DD, claiming their vaccination, with the received phone confirmation. The attacker joins the crowd. Taking advantage of the situation, the attacker steps near the pharmacy to spy on the nurse when she types the security access code. The attacker enters the pharmacy, accesses the freezer, and steals the vaccines carrying them out in an isothermal backpack.

This attack's direct consequence is the theft of the hospital's vaccine stock, leading to a significant financial loss and the patient vaccination campaign's stopping. This seriously harms the hospital's reputation. It contributes to delaying the health crisis's release, with significant challenges, such as hospital resources unavailability, the scheduling of operations, etc. Besides, the attacker's actions lead to a series of indirect impacts, such as the non-availability of the hospital's information system following the cyberattack, the stopping of the care process, or the potential theft of drugs from the pharmacy.

3.3 Evaluation

The evaluation phase aims at assessing the efficiency of the IPM proposed solution on attack scenarios. We present in this section two evaluation results parts.

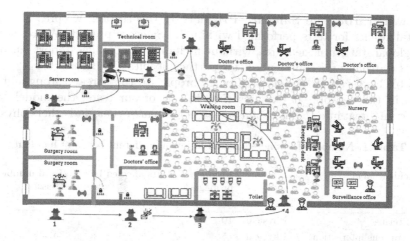

Fig. 2. Steal Covid vaccine: the attacker path

First, the COVID attack scenario has been simulated. The second part provides some metrics related to the evaluation of our module during the tests carried out in SAFECARE (some results have been omitted for confidentiality reasons).

Evaluation of the Scenario. In this step, we study the different impacts generated by the scenario incidents on the architecture (instantiation of the ontology) described in Fig. 2. The first incident we receive is "malicious file" on "mailing system". This incident will generate an impact on the "appointment data", defined as "data manipulation", which means that the attacker can manipulate the data and change all the appointments for a specific date DD and specific hour HH. The propagation of the impact is shown in Fig. 3 where the initial incident is colored in orange, and the appointment data is colored in yellow. In addition to the "appointment data", other important assets suffer from this incident impacts, such as the "hospital information system" as it appears in Fig. 3. Changing the "appointment planning" and setting all of them at one date DD and hour HH will lead to "crowding" in "the waiting room". This incident potentially generates an impact on "vaccines" stored in the pharmacy room.

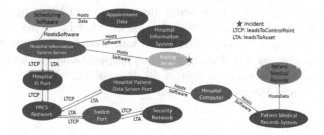

Fig. 3. Graphical representation for the incident (malicious file in mailing system)

Evaluation from the Safecare Project. In this section, we present experimental results for tests performed within the Safecare project. We restrict to only global statistical measures, without including the detailed report since the project outcomes are confidential (for partner hospitals' security).

Table 1 shows our model's ability to propagate the threat throughout the assets in the network. It explains that in one of our tests, the model could propagate threat into 15 different assets, 5 of them are cyber, and others physical.

Table 1. Number of impacted assets following different types of incidents

Incident label	Incident type	Number of assets affected by propagation		Total number of assets
		Cyber assets	Physical assets	
Loitering	Physical	10	5	35
Suspicious interaction	Physical	5	12	35
Network service scanning	Cyber	11	0	21
Malicious File	Cyber	9	0	16

4   Related Work

We organize the related works in two categories: The semantic-based contributions for risk management and the studies providing solutions for risk assessment and propagation analysis with various base models.

Most ontologies covering the semantic modeling of security and risk management are exclusively dedicated to cyber or physical security management [3,6]. Only a few cover assets cyber-physical interdependencies. Some of the studies focus on specific security task such as attack detection [8] or security requirements [12]. To the best of our knowledge, there is no ontology covering integrated cyber-physical security dealing with the incident propagation.

The incident propagation analysis task has been investigated in many research works discussing attack cascading effect mitigation. These studies can be grouped into two different sets. The first category focuses on physical infrastructure as in [7], where authors study the inter-dependency relationship among physical elements to detect indirect propagation of critical assets. In another hand, cyber incident propagation has been studied in [2] for example. Several approaches can be applied to deal with the risk assessment in cybersecurity, such as Bayesian networks [11]. These works do not cover incident propagation The work of [10] addresses the impact propagation of cyber incidents using the Petri Nets model, to identify impacted elements and assess their impacts. In recent work, one of the only papers dealing with the propagation of incidents in an integrated cyber-physical context is that of [9]. It considers asset interdependencies for the estimation of the cascading effects of threats.

5   Conclusion

This paper presents a semantic-based approach that assesses the impact propagation of complex cyber-physical attacks against critical infrastructure. It is based on semantic modeling and reasoning engine considering assets categories, relationships and input/output incident types to propagate received threat incidents. It allows anticipating impact propagation and helps mitigating potential harming effects while distinguishing highly and moderately impacted assets. The approach effectiveness and efficiency were evaluated against a simulation scenario and is currently being tested in real hospitals. Current results from both cases are promising and encourage us to extend the semantic model and generate more generic rules to cover new infrastructures.

References

1. ANSSI: Ebios risk manager - the method (2019). https://www.ssi.gouv.fr/en/guide/ebios-risk-manager-the-method/
2. Ben-Asher, N., Oltramari, A., Erbacher, R.F., Gonzalez, C.: Ontology-based adaptive systems of cyber defense. In: STIDS, pp. 34–41 (2015)
3. Fenz, S., Ekelhart, A.: Formalizing information security knowledge. In: Proceedings of the 4th International Symposium on Information, Computer, and Communications Security, pp. 183–194 (2009)
4. Guttman, B., Roback, E.A.: An Introduction to Computer Security: The NIST Handbook. Diane Publishing, Collingdale (1995)
5. Hannou, F.Z., Atigui, F., Lammari, N., Cherfi, S.S.: An ontology-based model for cyber-physical security management in healthcare context. In: Strauss, C., Kotsis, G., Tjoa, A.M., Khalil, I. (eds.) Expert Systems Applications. LNCS, vol. 12924, pp. 22–34. Springer, Heidelberg (2021). https://doi.org/10.1007/978-3-030-86475-0_3
6. Kim, M., Dey, S., Lee, S.: Ontology-driven security requirements recommendation for apt attack, pp. 150–156 (2019). https://doi.org/10.1109/REW.2019.00032
7. Liu, C.Y., Jeng, A.P., Chang, C.H., Wang, R.G., Chou, C.C.: Combining building information modeling and ontology to analyze emergency events in buildings. In: ISARC. Proceedings of the International Symposium on Automation and Robotics in Construction, vol. 35, pp. 1–6. IAARC Publications (2018)
8. Luh, R., Marschalek, S., Kaiser, M., Janicke, H., Schrittwieser, S.: Semantics-aware detection of targeted attacks: a survey. J. Comput. Virol. Hack. Tech. **13**(1), 47–85 (2016). https://doi.org/10.1007/s11416-016-0273-3
9. Schauer, S., Grafenauer, T., König, S., Warum, M., Rass, S.: Estimating cascading effects in cyber-physical critical infrastructures. In: Nadjm-Tehrani, S. (ed.) CRITIS 2019. LNCS, vol. 11777, pp. 43–56. Springer, Cham (2020). https://doi.org/10.1007/978-3-030-37670-3_4
10. Szpyrka, M., Jasiul, B.: Evaluation of cyber security and modelling of risk propagation with petri nets. Symmetry **9**(3), 32 (2017)
11. Szpyrka, M., Jasiul, B., Wrona, K., Dziedzic, F.: Telecommunications networks risk assessment with Bayesian networks. In: Saeed, K., Chaki, R., Cortesi, A., Wierzchoń, S. (eds.) CISIM 2013. LNCS, vol. 8104, pp. 277–288. Springer, Heidelberg (2013). https://doi.org/10.1007/978-3-642-40925-7_26
12. Velasco, J.L., Valencia-García, R., Fernández-Breis, J.T., Toval, A.: Modelling reusable security requirements based on an ontology framework. J. Res. Pract. Inf. Technol. **41**(2), 119–133 (2009)

Author Index

Printed in the United States
by Baker & Taylor Publisher Services